# THE JULIAN ALPS OF SLOVENIA

# THE JULIAN ALPS OF SLOVENIA

## MOUNTAIN WALKS AND SHORT TREKS

by Justi Carey and Roy Clark

JUNIPER HOUSE, MURLEY MOSS,
OXENHOLME ROAD, KENDAL, CUMBRIA LA9 7RL
www.cicerone.co.uk

Second edition 2015
ISBN: 978 1 85284 7098
Reprinted 2017, 2019 and 2024 (with updates)
First edition 2005

MIX
Paper from responsible sources
FSC® C004791
FSC www.fsc.org

Printed in Singapore by KHL printing on responsibly sourced paper.
A catalogue record for this book is available from the British Library.

## Dedication

*Dovje-Mojstrana: Zelena prihodnost*, and all the other Transition towns across the world working to make positive environmental change
www.transitionnetwork.org

## Acknowledgements

Stanko Klinar, Gregor and Anita Kofler, the lovely staff of Pogačnikov dom, particularly Urška, Claus Fischer, Michael Christopher, Andrew and Cheryl Blaikie, Dorothy Heffernan, Donal O'Herlihy, and as always the patient and dedicated staff at Cicerone.

## Updates to this Guide

While every effort is made by our authors to ensure the accuracy of guidebooks as they go to print, changes can occur during the lifetime of an edition. Any updates that we know of for this guide will be on the Cicerone website (www.cicerone.co.uk/709/updates), so please check before planning your trip. We also advise that you check information about such things as transport, accommodation and shops locally. Even rights of way can be altered over time. We are always grateful for information about any discrepancies between a guidebook and the facts on the ground, sent by email to info@cicerone.co.uk or by post to Cicerone, Juniper House, Murley Moss, Oxenholme Road, Kendal LA9 7RL, United Kingdom.

**Register your book:** To sign up to receive free updates, special offers and GPX files where available, register your book at www.cicerone.co.uk.

*Front cover:* The spectacular group of mountains above Gozd Martuljek with the striking pyramid form of Špik seen from Srednji Vrh (Walk 3)

# CONTENTS

**Warning**

Mountain walking can be a dangerous activity carrying a risk of personal injury or death. It should be undertaken only by those with a full understanding of the risks and with the training and experience to evaluate them. While every care and effort has been taken in the preparation of this guide, the user should be aware that conditions can be highly variable and can change quickly, materially affecting the seriousness of a mountain walk. Therefore, except for any liability that cannot be excluded by law, neither Cicerone nor the author accept liability for damage of any nature (including damage to property, personal injury or death) arising directly or indirectly from the information in this book.

To call out the Mountain Rescue, ring the international emergency number 112: this will connect you via any available network. Once connected to the emergency operator, ask for the police.

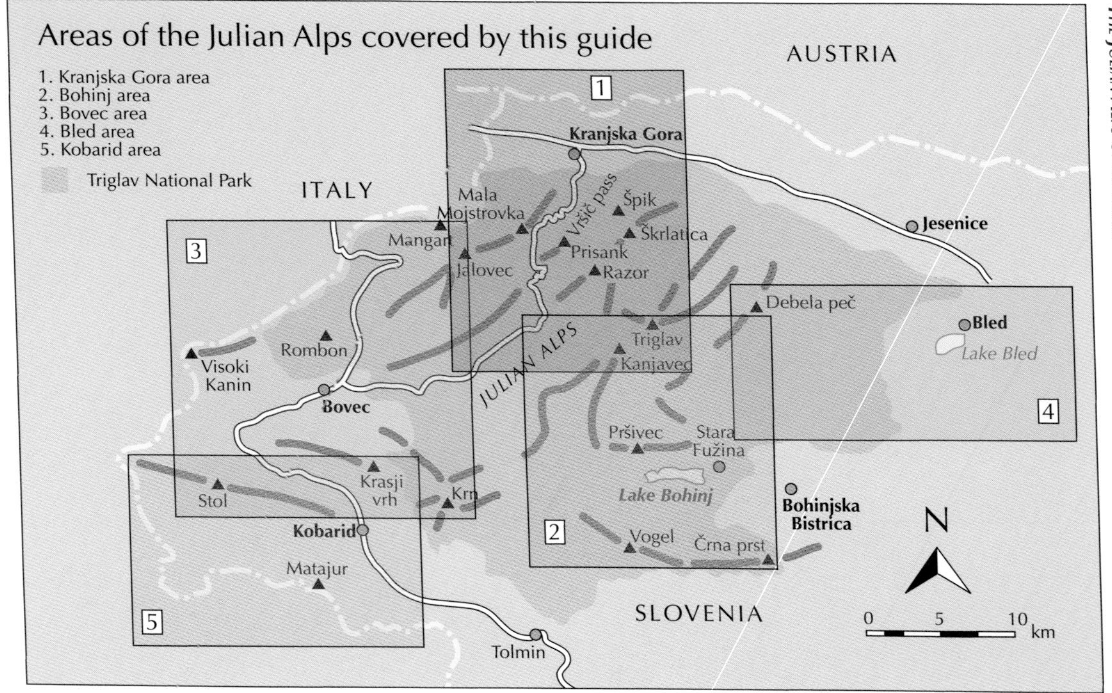

Areas of the Julian Alps covered by this guide
1. Kranjska Gora area
2. Bohinj area
3. Bovec area
4. Bled area
5. Kobarid area
Triglav National Park
AUSTRIA
ITALY
SLOVENIA
JULIAN ALPS
Kranjska Gora
Mala Mojstrovka
Vršič pass
Špik
Škrlatica
Prisank
Razor
Mangart
Jalovec
Jesenice
Debela peč
Bled
Lake Bled
Triglav
Kanjavec
Rombon
Visoki Kanin
Bovec
Pršivec
Stara Fužina
Lake Bohinj
Krasji vrh
Krn
Stol
Kobarid
Bohinjska Bistrica
Vogel
Črna prst
Matajur
Tolmin
N
0
5
10
km

The Zelenci pools (Walk 1) never freeze even in the coldest winter

## Map Key

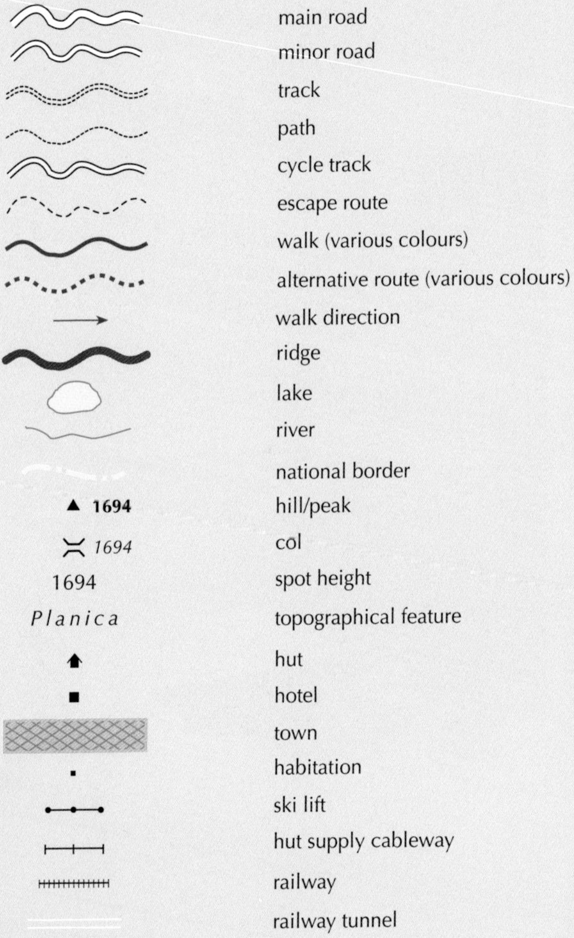

main road
minor road
track
path
cycle track
escape route
walk (various colours)
alternative route (various colours)
walk direction
ridge
lake
river
national border
▲ **1694** hill/peak
*1694* col
1694 spot height
*Planica* topographical feature
hut
hotel
town
habitation
ski lift
hut supply cableway
railway
railway tunnel

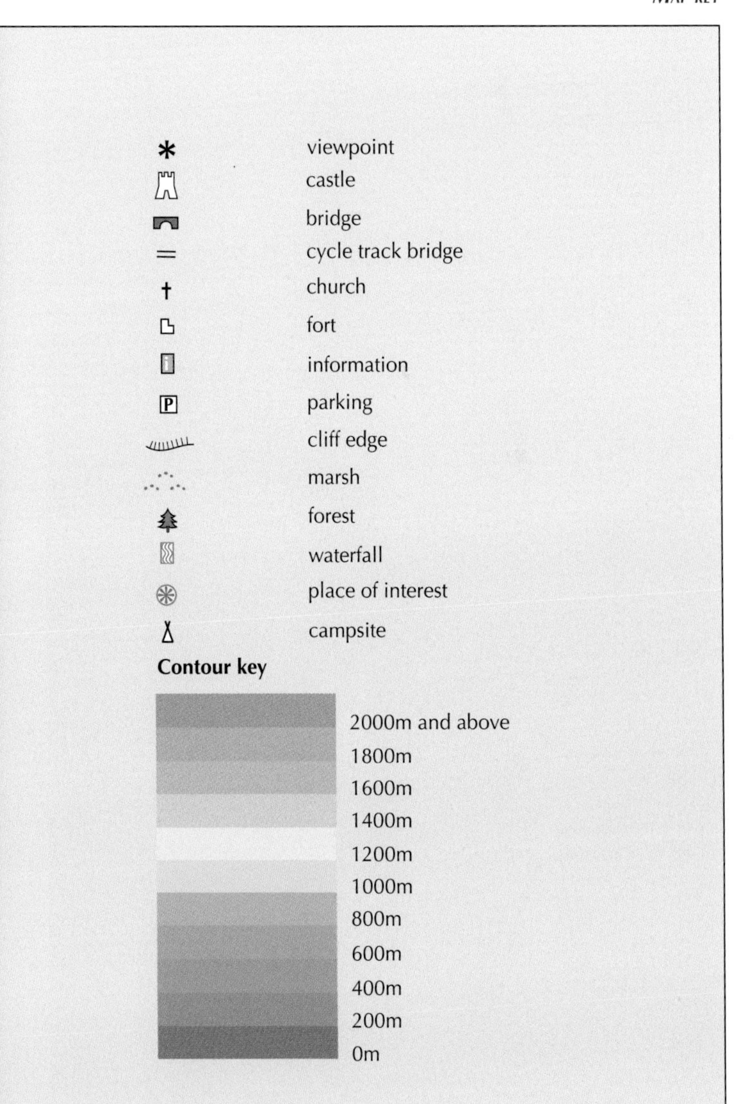
viewpoint
castle
bridge
cycle track bridge
church
fort
information
parking
cliff edge
marsh
forest
waterfall
place of interest
campsite
Contour key
2000m and above
1800m
1600m
1400m
1200m
1000m
800m
600m
400m
200m
0m

Mangart (climbed on Walk 44) towers above a Napoleonic fort, seen from the Predel pass

# INTRODUCTION

*Podkoren in the upper Sava valley (Walk 1)*

> [The Julian Alps] have become for me, after forty years' devotion to mountain scenery, the most desirable of all mountains...I believe this feeling is greatly due to their surprising quality of mystery...Triglav reigns over a dreamworld, sundered from time, full of unbelievable hidden nooks, of unsuspected passages, of sudden visions of cliffs which cannot be real. Surely there is no other mountain land like this.
>
> *T Longstaff, in a letter to Julius Kugy*

Thus wrote Tom Longstaff, former president of the Alpine Club, of this mountain range at the south-eastern end of the Alpine chain that stretches across Europe. The Julian Alps are not as high as their western relations – the highest peak, Triglav, is 2864m – but they are no less imposing. The limestone scenery here is outstanding – steep rock faces plunge into forests and flower meadows, while waterfalls and rivers cascade from the cliffs only to mysteriously disappear into the bedrock and re-emerge elsewhere. Beautiful open pastures nestle beneath crags and are scattered through the forests that abound as far as the eye can see. The flowers, painted an amazing rainbow of colours, change with height and situation but always retain the same great variety of hue. The mountain walker can return here again and again, but always find a new delight in the changing landscape and seasons.

The main bulk of the Julian Alps lies within the borders of Slovenia, in the north-west corner of the country, with a small part of the range extending into Italy. The name was known in Roman times, and is thought to be linked to the imperial Roman family of Julian. Slovenia has been called 'Europe in miniature' because this tiny country, only about half the size of Switzerland, really does have a bit of everything – coast, caves, plains and rivers – as well as some truly magnificent mountain scenery, which is the focus of this book. Although only 11% of the land area is covered by high mountains, 90% is higher than 300m above sea level, and Slovenia still proudly considers itself an Alpine country. It is hard to overestimate the place of Triglav in Slovenes' hearts; it is considered the soul of the nation, and essential for all true Slovenes to climb the mountain at least once in their lives.

The Triglav National Park, which contains most of the Julian Alps range, is Slovenia's only national park. Development is kept to an absolute minimum – this is an area where the walker, not the motorist, reigns supreme. The footpaths and protected routes on the mountains are well maintained and signed, and the many mountain huts are strategically placed for refreshment and overnight accommodation – so it is possible to wander for days or even weeks without descending to the valley at all. The abundant wildlife – chamois, ibex, marmots, choughs and even eagles – seem comfortable with the walkers who share their landscape, making for excellent animal and bird watching, and plenty of photo opportunities.

In spite of its modern cities and excellent transport networks Slovenia still has an air of the past, when the pace of life was slower. Slovenes keep close contact with their families and their land; in many cases the same family has worked the land for hundreds of years. Much of the population still lives in villages, where almost every house has its vegetable patch; even in the cities allotments are common. The country, independent since 1991, has a total population of only about 2 million centred on Ljubljana, the capital city. There are only a handful of other large towns, the most important being Maribor, Celje and Kranj. Mountains have shaped the country and its culture, and it is common to see whole families out walking together, such is the Slovenes' enthusiasm for the outdoors.

However, the mountains provide more than enough room for all walkers – even in the summer season of July, August and September – to find places where they can be alone on the hill, where there is a surprise in the form of a new vista around every corner, and where the limestone scenery is as unspoilt as it was when the glaciers first receded. This is a country to enjoy and return to over and over again.

Looking down through the great window on Prisank on Walk 14

## GEOLOGY AND LANDSCAPE

At the heart of the Julian Alps stands Triglav, which at 2864m is over 100m higher than its nearest contender, Škrlatica. The area around Triglav is an upland of peaks and ridges, bounded to the north by the upper Sava valley and to the south by Bohinj. Komna and the Lower Bohinj mountains form the southern boundary of the National Park, and to the north-west, close to the Italian border, lie the Kanin range and the peaks of Mangart and Jalovec.

The Julian Alps are mostly composed of limestone, primarily from the Triassic geological period. Its main characteristic, which has a dramatic effect on the topography of the range, is its porous nature, which means that water sinks directly into the rock. The term 'karst', derived from the Slovene word *kras*, is used all over the world to describe the characteristic landscape of areas like the Julian Alps where the rock is readily dissolved by water. Karst features include deep, steep-sided gorges and dry valleys, sink-holes, springs, water-dissolved caves and tunnels underground, and water-eroded surface rocks that result in the formation of limestone pavements.

The porosity of the rock in the Julian Alps means that, compared to other European Alpine ranges, there is little surface water. Many river beds in the National Park are dry for most of the year. Those streams and lakes that exist on the surface are linked below ground level by complex systems of caves and channels, many of which are still not fully explored. Several cave systems are known to be well over 1000m deep.

As throughout the Alps, glaciation has played a major part in forming the landscape. There are many textbook examples of features such as U-shaped valleys, glacial moraines and erratic boulders. Fast-flowing rivers like the Soča, with their great erosive power, have carved steep-sided valleys in the surrounding mountains.

The Julian Alps also contain areas of high mountain karst, typified by the Kaninski podi in the Kanin range. High mountain karst is formed from limestone plateaus situated above the treeline, with little vegetation cover, in areas of high precipitation. Here, snow and water remain at the surface for more than half the year, so water erosion is greatly increased and results in diverse rock formations that are of great interest to geologists and cavers.

## THE TRIGLAV NATIONAL PARK

The idea to protect the area around Triglav was first conceived in 1908, though it was not until 1961 that the Triglav National Park (Triglavski Narodni Park) was established. The borders of the park were finalised in 1981, and it covers over 84,000 hectares – around 3% of the territory of Slovenia.

The park includes most of the Julian Alps within Slovenia and is divided into two areas. The highland area, including all the main mountain

## NATIONAL PARK CODE OF CONDUCT

- Respect the customs and traditions of the people who live in the park.
- Avoid noise and disturbing wildlife.
- Take all your waste away with you.
- Do not pick the plants.
- Dogs should be kept on a lead.
- Park trails are intended for walkers; cycling is not permitted.
- Follow the signs on information posts along the trails.
- Leave vehicles in designated places.
- Spend the night in accommodation facilities (campsites, rooms, huts); wild camping is illegal.

ranges, has the strictest protection, while the valley areas have slightly more relaxed regulations in order to accommodate the communities that live and work there, and to acknowledge the fact that the lowland landscape has, to some extent, been shaped by humans.

The park has a number of regulations which aim to protect, and encourage respectful treatment of, this fragile environment. The most important and relevant for the visitor are listed in the Code of Conduct box.

## LONG-DISTANCE ROUTES

Three long-distance routes weave their way across the Julian Alps:

### The Via Alpina

The Via Alpina (www.via-alpina.org) is a series of trails which link across the whole of the Alps. The Red trail starts in Trieste and heads north to eventually reach the Dolič hut below Triglav – here it goes down to Trenta and on to Kranjska Gora before heading into Austria. Another branch, the Purple trail, heads north-east from Dolič and down the Vrata valley to Mojstrana, then goes through the Karavanke mountains. You will often see the distinctive logo on routes in this guide.

### The Alpe Adrija Trail

This is a new long-distance path leading from the Grossglockner in Austria to the Adriatic Sea, and again you will see the signs on many of our routes. The website, www.alpe-adria-trail.com, is in German, Italian, Slovene and English (look under Sprache in the top right-hand corner of the web page).

### Pot miru, the Walk of Peace

This walk links outdoor museums and other monuments along the line of the Soča (Isonzo) Front of the First World War, which resulted in over a million casualties in the greatest mountain battle in history. Three routes in this book specifically visit places on the Pot miru – Walk 33, Kluže, Walk

*Steep walking high on the Prag Route (Walk 18)*

35, Čelo and Walk 54, the Historical Walk. For more information visit www.potmiru.si.

## WHAT THE WALKING'S LIKE

The Julian Alps are everything a mountain walker could wish for, but they can be a bit daunting for first-time visitors. The nature of limestone means that the Julian Alps are very steep and the rock is generally loose. Once out of the valleys, the going can be rough over rocks and tree roots even at a relatively low level, and higher up there is loose rock, scree, stone fall, steep cliffs and exposure. The many protected sections, which give a sense of security when via ferrata equipment is used appropriately, are interspersed with steep loose paths which give no security at all.

Make sure that you are fit, have a good head for heights and the right equipment, and are a competent scrambler, before attempting any of the higher, longer routes. Also be aware of the weather forecast and the time it is likely to take you to get to safe ground if you need to.

Limestone mountains are generally dry, and there are not many springs in the high mountains; this means almost every drop of water must be carried from the valley, or bought in the huts at premium prices. Food is not a problem – there are mountain huts on most of the walks which provide food as well as accommodation.

### A fragile environment

The Alps are a fragile and endangered environment, under pressure from climate change, noise, traffic and pollution, and not least by the erosion caused by the walking boots of those who love them. As a visitor to the area, it is your responsibility to keep your environmental impact to the minimum by sticking to the footpaths and taking all your litter away with you. Remember, too, that this is a working landscape – leave gates as you found them, keep dogs on a lead, and avoid disturbing livestock.

## CLIMATE AND WEATHER

Slovenia's position in Central Europe means that, in spite of its small size, it has three distinct climatic zones: a Mediterranean climate by the coast, with warm sunny weather throughout much of the year along with mild winters; a Continental climate in eastern Slovenia, with hot summers and cold winters; and an alpine climate in the north-west with warm summers, cold winters and abundant precipitation. Most of the area covered by this guide is in the alpine climate area, although as you go further south the Julian Alps are increasingly influenced by the Mediterranean.

Trends over the past 20 years or so suggest that the effects of global warming are now being felt. Temperatures are rising, resulting in less snow in winter (the Triglav glacier marked on older maps is now reduced to a large snow patch), and summers are hotter. Wind patterns are also changing, and long periods of drought have been followed by extensive flooding, which can be devastating in an area of steep-sided valleys and mountains.

In any mountain area weather is notoriously difficult to forecast. Snow can occur at any time of year and can render a summer walking trip a disaster for those not adequately prepared. In summer the snow does not tend to lie for long, but the peaks and high-altitude paths can be snowbound from October to May in some years. April and November are times of maximum rainfall. Thunderstorms are common in July and August, and can obviously be particularly dangerous on ridges and high-altitude routes; they can spring up out of clear air within half an hour, perhaps not leaving enough time to get to safer ground. Thunderstorms are most common in the afternoon and evening, so it's often advisable to make an early start so you have a chance of achieving your objective before a storm occurs.

Weather forecasts can be obtained from the local people where you are staying. There are forecasts on television (Slovenia 1) daily at 6.55pm, which cover the whole country and give a long-range forecast for about four days ahead (although it is of course in Slovene, the map symbols are universal). The Tourist Information Office will also have a forecast. The internet site www.arso.gov.si is in Slovene only, but click

*Ponca reflected in the Zelenci pools visited in Walk 1 – lower-level walks can be spectacular in winter*

on the words *vremenska napoved* (weather forecast) to find *vremenska napoved v sliki* (weather forecast in pictures); this gives the next day's forecast with symbols. Another useful site is www.windguru.cz – it specialises in detailed forecasts for paragliders and windsurfers, and offers the full week ahead, although of course it decreases in accuracy after a couple of days. Look in the Slovenia section for Julijske Alpe, Vogar (paragliding).

Floods are common after heavy rainfall, and these have greatest effect on lower valleys as the water can bring down tons of boulders and rubble from the loose limestone. They can have profound effects on paths, completely re-routing them in some cases, and bridges may be washed away.

Limestone is usually pale and can be extremely bright when the sun shines on it. Sunglasses are therefore recommended, even on a day that appears cloudy.

## WILDLIFE AND FLOWERS

Over 5500 species of plants and wildlife have been identified in the Triglav National Park, some of which are unique to the area. This section describes only some of the key

*Butterflies abound in the Julian Alps, while edelweiss and Zois' bellflower brighten cracks among the rocks*

species that can be observed; books giving more detailed information are suggested in Appendix D.

Partly because they are lower than other Alpine ranges, the Julian Alps, from lush valley to rocky summit, are a botanist's delight. The thin soil does not allow any one species to become dominant, with the result that an astonishing variety of plant life flourishes here, even among the rocks of the highest peaks. Some of the best places to see the high-alpine plants are the Lower Bohinj mountains (Walks 26, 27 and 28), the Triglav Lakes valley (Walk 30) and Debela peč (Walk 52), but all the routes described in this book are studded with flowers. The white stars of edelweiss are common, along with the deep blue of various gentians, but two flowers in particular the Slovenes have made their own. The pink cushions of the Triglav rose (*Potentilla nitida*) are supposed to have sprung from drops of the blood of Zlatorog, the golden-horned ibex. Zois' bellflower (*Campanula zoysii*) is related to the harebell; it has grown in the rock crevices of this area since last the Ice Age.

About half of Slovenia is covered with trees, and almost all the walks pass through sections of beautiful woodland. Spruce, beech, pine and larch are interspersed with other species in true mixed forest which gradually changes its nature with height. The highest of all is the dwarf pine, before the trees give out altogether, leaving only short grass studded with flowers among the rocks. If you visit in late June, notice the pendulous yellow flowers of Alpine laburnum, which can be seen as splashes of yellow in a band across the hillsides at an altitude of roughly 800–1200m. Particularly good forest walks are Pršivec (Walk 25) and Debela peč (Walk 52), as well as most of the valley walks.

The wonderful lush growth of alpine hay meadows needs no introduction here. Regular cutting of the plants, two or three times a year, means that hardier species do not get the chance to dominate more delicate ones. Yellow, blue, purple and white are the predominant colours, and they are reflected in the many species of butterflies. The valley walks around Kranjska Gora (Walks 1, 3 and 9) provide many excellent examples of hay meadows.

The chamois (*Rupicapra rupicapra*) is perhaps the most typical of the alpine mammals and a common sight on the high-level walks. They are smaller and have shorter horns

*Female ibex*

Hay-drying in the upper Sava valley

*The fire salamander – sometimes seen in the lower forests, usually during rain*

than the ibex (*Capra hircus ibex*), which was made extinct in Slovenia in the 17th century, but successfully reintroduced in the 1960s and is now thriving. Marmots (*Marmota marmota*) were also introduced here in the 1960s and have multiplied across large areas of the Triglav National Park.

Alpine choughs, ravens and golden eagles can all be seen in the high mountains; choughs in particular are more than happy to eat your sandwiches on the summits! In the forests listen out for capercaillie (*Tetrao urogallus*), a large game bird whose call when disturbed is reminiscent of the gobbling sound of a turkey – you are more likely to hear them than see them. A common amphibian which can often be seen in the beech forests, especially on damp days, is the strange black and yellow fire salamander (*Salamandra salamandra*). The rarer black Alpine salamander (*Salamandra atra*) can sometimes be seen even on the ridges in rainy weather; interestingly, they do not spawn in water but give birth to two live young.

Most wildlife is protected within the boundaries of the National Park. Identifying animals and plants is a pleasure for all – take care to disturb them as little as possible.

## WHEN TO GO

The main walking season is from mid-June to the end of September, when most of the routes are snow-free and the weather is generally stable. Most of the high-mountain huts are open from July to September, but each has its own opening times; see the Slovene Alpine Club website www.pzs.si.

The spring flowers are wonderful during May on the lower-level routes, and the autumn colours are fabulous; however, the weather can be unsettled at this time of year and there is less choice of accommodation. In winter it is skiing, and the resorts, that draw the crowds, but many high-level huts have an unmanned 'winter room' supplied with blankets for ski-tourers and winter mountaineers.

One of the appeals of the Julian Alps for walkers is that there are no glaciers and therefore no crevasses to worry about, but snow and ice can still be a factor throughout the summer if the previous winter has seen heavy snowfall. Snow patches can lie all year in the high gullies and on

Nearing the summit of Mali Triglav (Walk 18)

north faces, and an ice axe is sometimes (though rarely) necessary on high routes even in July.

## GETTING THERE

Travel information goes out of date very quickly, particularly in these days of online bookings, so only a rough guide is given here. Shop around and check for up-to-date information through tourist agencies or on the internet before you go.

### Red tape

Citizens of most European countries, Australia, Canada, New Zealand and the USA do not require a visa to visit Slovenia for up to 90 days. Slovenia has had open borders with the 26 countries of the Schengen Agreement since 2007.

### By air

Slovenia's main international airport is at Brnik, 23km north of Ljubljana and 1 or 2hrs from the walking centres around which this guide is based. Adrija Airways is the national carrier (www.adria-airways.com), but the budget airlines Easyjet (www.easyjet.com) and Wizzair (wizzair.com) also fly to Ljubljana from London. Flights from the USA require a change somewhere in Europe. Other possibilities for air connections are Klagenfurt in Austria, with easy access to Bled, Bohinj and Kranjska Gora; and Trieste in Italy, which is nearer to the southern centres of Kobarid and Bovec. Both Klagenfurt and Trieste are served by Ryanair (www.ryanair.com).

It is also worth searching online for holiday packages; some companies will provide transport to the main centres while allowing you to make your own accommodation arrangements. Numerous companies offer walking holidays.

### By train

Bled and Bohinj (Bohinjska Bistrica) lie on the main rail link between north and south Europe, between Munich and Trieste, and so are easy to get to by rail. Kranjska Gora can be reached from the international rail link at Jesenice by a regular bus connection. The nearest railway station to Kobarid and Bovec is at Most na Soči, on the Jesenice–Bled–Bohinj–Nova Gorica line; the link is then by bus.

## GETTING AROUND

### By car

Slovenia has a good road transport network, with motorways linking all the major centres. Some of the routes are difficult to access by public transport and a car makes life a lot easier in the rural areas described here; cars can be hired at the airports and in reasonably sized towns.

### Public transport

Slovenia has a modern and efficient system of public transport by train and bus, which serves most, but not all, of

A walker just below Pogačnikov dom, with Planja and Razor in the background (Walk 40)

the rural villages adequately or even well. For bus timetables the website www.ap-ljubljana.si will help you, although its English translation is a little shaky at times. Enter the start point and the destination to get the timetable, but remember that it would be as well to check the times with the local Tourist Information Office or on the timetable displayed at all bus stops. For trains use www.slo-zeleznice.si, which has an English version, but again, check before you travel. Generally, in Slovenia it's cheaper to take the train than go by bus.

Buses run every hour from Brnik International Airport (Letališče Brnik) to the main bus and train station in Ljubljana. If you are taking an onward train from Ljubljana, note that it is a good five minute walk from the ticket office to most of the platforms. Buses leave from outside the train station.

### Addresses

In towns, the streets have names (*ulica* and *cesta* for street and road), with the number following the street name (eg Prešernova ulica 23), but in small villages the houses tend to be identified simply with the name of the village and a number.

## AREAS AND BASES

This guide is divided into five regional sections each centred around a base: Kranjska Gora, Bohinj, Bovec, Bled and Kobarid. The bases make a rough circle around the main Julian Alps massif. They were chosen for ease of access by public transport, tourist infrastructure (accommodation, eating houses and so on) and for the variety and appeal of the walks in the area. Due to the compact nature of the range many of the mountains can be reached by several different approaches; where this is the case, routes that are most practical for people without their own transport have been selected. However, as many visitors to Slovenia hire a car, car parking and alternative starts for those with their own transport are also mentioned.

**Kranjska Gora** is a winter ski resort and a superb base from which to explore the full range of alpine walking in the summer. The area includes beautiful easy valley treks as well as some of the most demanding peaks in the Julian Alps.

**Lake Bohinj** and its surrounding area is one of the gems of Slovenia, and several villages near the lake (there is no town called Bohinj) provide access to a variety of walks, from valley waterfalls to long mountain ridges.

The upbeat, sporty town of **Bovec** is close to the river Soča, a mecca for canoeists. Within easy reach of the town are several interesting walks which investigate some of the history of the area, particularly from the First World War era, and the Kanin ski gondola gives easy access to the high mountains.

**Bled**, with its lake island, is probably Slovenia's most visited resort, and its unique setting provides the

*Dom v Tamarju, one of Slovenia's many mountain huts, is passed on Walks 9 and 15*

backdrop for some lovely village walks with excellent viewpoints.

The little Italianesque town of **Kobarid**, to the south of the main peaks of the Julian Alps, has some fascinating First World War sites, as well as long mountain ridges with views all the way to the Adriatic Sea.

Note that the bases are relatively close together; Kranjska Gora and Bohinj are about an hour's drive from each other, with Bled in between, and Kobarid is only 20 minutes from Bovec. It's about an hour's drive from Kranjska Gora to Bovec (via Italy and the Predel pass; going via the Vršič pass takes longer, especially in the busy times of the summer). This means that staying in one base does not limit you to only the walks in that area, especially if you have your own transport.

## ACCOMMODATION

Slovenia offers a full range of accommodation, from five-star hotels to campsites and bivouac huts. Generally prices are reasonable compared to other European countries. A small tourist tax is payable for each night, and proprietors of all types of accommodation will need to see your passport. Information and booking can be found in the local Tourist Information Office or on the town's website.

All the towns used as bases in this guide have a range of hotels and pensions, with varying facilities and prices. Private rooms offer a bed for the night and some offer breakfast as well. There is usually a surcharge of up to 30 per cent for staying fewer than three nights. Bookings can be made through a

Tourist Office or direct with the owner; these days most have websites, or when you are there look out for signs for 'sobe' or the German 'Zimmer'. Apartments (*apartma*) are also common. Youth hostels and backpackers' hostels have become more popular in recent years: there is one in Bled, Kranjska Gora and also in Mojstrana. Membership of a hostelling organisation is not required. Tourist farms (*turistična kmetija*) offer comfortable rooms and excellent home cooked and produced food.

Slovene campsites are clean and the facilities are of a high standard. Most are equipped for tents, caravans and motorhomes, and some offer cabin-type accommodation. All the bases used in this guide have campsites within a kilometre or so. Camping gaz and other screw-type gas cartridges can be bought in sports shops. Wild camping is illegal throughout Slovenia.

**Mountain huts**

Mountain huts are called *dom* or *koča* in Slovene – a dom is usually larger but otherwise there is no difference in the type of facilities available. Mountain huts are ubiquitous in Slovenia and are part of the country's culture. They are divided into categories depending on their ease of access, and the prices of both meals and accommodation are fixed by this. Sleeping accommodation is in dormitories (*skupna ležišča*) or rooms (*soba*), with rooms being more expensive. Bedding, including blankets, sheets and pillowcases, is provided, so there is no need to carry a sleeping bag. Prices (for accommodation but not food) are cheaper if you are a member of the Slovene Alpine Association (Planinska Zveza Slovenije – PZS) and there are reciprocal agreements with the Alpine Clubs of some other countries.

The lower huts usually have running water and often showers, but the higher huts have no water except rainwater, which means limited washing facilities. You will need to buy drinking water too; make use of any springs for drinking that you find en route – they are mentioned in the text and marked on the local maps as drinking water (*pitna voda*). *Voda ni pitni* means it is not potable. The high huts will be busy in good weather in July and August, and you should book beforehand. However, you will never be turned away in bad weather, even if you have to sleep on the floor.

Staying in Slovene mountain huts can be a delight or a necessary evil, depending on when you go, where you are, and luck. Also one person's delight can be another's nightmare; whether you are a party animal and it's very quiet, or you are shattered and wanting a peaceful early night and a large group arrive wanting to party. On a sunny evening, after a good day on the hill, it's a joy to sit outside with a beer and watch the sun set.

Hut opening times can be checked on the PZS (Slovene Alpine Club) website: www.pzs.si – this is

*You can often find fresh local produce for sale at planina farmsteads*

in Slovene only, but from the homepage click the tab *planinske koče* and then *Julijske Alpe*; this leads to a full and up-to-date list of all the huts and their phone numbers. Take care to look for the full name of the hut, as written on the map. The *Delovni čas* column shows whether or not the hut is open at the moment; thus, the high-level huts are shown as being closed in the winter-time. *Odprt(a/o)* is open, *zaprt(a/o)* is closed, OS means it's permanently open, and OPSNP means it is open on Fridays, Saturdays, Sundays and holidays. *Razen* means except. Most have a 'winter room' with open access to basic facilities outside the times when the hut is manned.

Huts serve basic, reasonably priced meals even if you are not staying the night there. There is no problem with eating food you have brought with you in the huts (eg sandwiches), but there are no facilities for self-catering. The food in the huts is filling and nutritious, but somewhat repetitive. Vegetarians will manage (but with even more repetition), but vegans will struggle.

## FOOD AND DRINK

Slovenes love to eat, and food is generally fresh and well prepared. Prices are reasonable and portions large – there seems to be an almost pathological fear that you might go home hungry! It is difficult to define typical Slovene food, as it is heavily influenced by the different countries and culinary traditions that surround it. From Italy come pastas and pizzas, from Austria sausages and schnitzel, from Hungary goulash and from ex-Yugoslavia treats like *burek*, a puff-pastry roll filled with meat or cheese. Generally Slovenes dislike spicy food. Ethnic restaurants such as Chinese and Indian are rare; however, this is not to imply that there is a lack of culinary choice. Large towns and villages will have a variety of eating places, called *gostilna*, which provide excellent home-cooked food. Many hotels and pensions also have restaurants which are open to non-residents. An *okrepčevalnica* is a snack bar.

Food is freshly prepared and served (look out for signs saying *domača kuhinja*, meaning 'home made'). In some cases the ingredients are even freshly collected, as there is a great tradition in Slovenia of eating food from the land. For example, dandelion leaves are made into delicious salads with eggs and potatoes in the early spring, and in many areas wild herbs are collected for teas and medicines. Slovenes are enthusiastic mushroom collectors in the late summer and autumn.

Particular specialities include trout from the Soča river, Adriatic fish, dishes made with buckwheat, and sweet or savoury *štruklji* (dumplings). Slovene cakes and pastries are delicious, for example *gibanica*, a layered cake with fruit and poppy seeds, or *potica*, a nut-filled sponge roll traditionally made for special occasions – every Slovene family seems to have its own recipe!

The Slovene diet is generally a meaty one, and vegetarianism is not very common. However, most restaurants will have meat-free options. The word for meat is *meso*.

**Where to eat**

All the bases mentioned in this book offer a range of places to eat, with Bled and Kranjska Gora being particularly well endowed. Many hotels and pensions also have restaurants which are open to non-residents.

Slovenes take their main meal in the middle of the day, although they will eat out in the evenings for special occasions. This means that a full meal can be obtained easily at almost any time of day, but it may be difficult to find lunchtime snacks (some supermarkets sell ready-made sandwiches or will make them up for you). Slovene soups (*juha*) are excellent. Try mushroom soup for a hearty snack – you will often find it made with several different sorts of locally gathered mushroom. Soups sometimes arrive in a 'bowl' made of bread, which you can eat as well.

Mountain hut food is filling and cheap, so sausages (*klobasa*) and thick soups and stews with hunks of bread prevail. You can eat in a mountain hut even if you are not staying there;

The cross on the summit of Mangart (Walk 44)

many of the walks in this book pass by a hut for just that purpose! Typical dishes include:

- *jota* – stew with sauerkraut, served with or without meat (*meso*)
- *ričet* – barley stew, again served with or without meat
- *golaž* – goulash, not normally spicy in Slovenia
- *vampi* – tripe
- *žganci* – hard boiled corn mush (much tastier than it sounds!)
- *špageti, njoki* – pasta (spaghetti and gnocci)

Some huts, especially lower ones which are frequented by locals, will serve local specialities.

Sweets include *palačinke* (pancakes), *štruklji* (a kind of dumpling, often with cream cheese) and *zavitek* (strudel).

### Drinks

Slovenia produces several beers, of which the most popular are Union and Laško. Laško's Zlatorog is a lager-type beer, which holds up its head, as it were, with the best beers in Europe. Slovenia's climate also provides the raw materials for some excellent wines – the white wines are particularly good.

All bars and mountain huts serve not only alcoholic drinks but also tea, coffee and hot chocolate. If you ask for *čaj* (tea) you will get a fruit tea without milk; for English-style tea ask for *angleški čaj* or *črni čaj z mlekom* (black tea with milk), although not all places stock it, and mountain huts usually don't – there, you can ask for hot water (*vroča voda*) and bring your own teabags. Coffee (*kava*) is usually served black unless you ask for milk (*z mlekom*) – *bela kava* is coffee made with milk. Hot chocolate is *kakov;* note also that *vroča čokolada* is served in some places, literally meaning hot chocolate, but turning out to be more like hot chocolate dessert.

## MONEY AND SHOPPING

The currency in Slovenia is the euro. All five base towns in this guide have banks and ATMs are common. Banks are usually open 8am–12noon and 2–5pm on weekdays only. Most village shops and B&Bs will only accept cash, but in larger hotels you will probably be able to pay by card.

Mountain huts take cash only, so take plenty of cash with you. Allow around €50 per person per day for accommodation, food and drink in the huts (more if you like a few beers).

### Opening hours

Shop opening hours are long in Slovenia, from early in the morning until 6 or 7pm, with no break for lunch. At weekends, some shops close a bit earlier, although they may be open for longer during the main tourist seasons. Some supermarkets are open on Sunday mornings. Post offices usually keep shop hours during the week and Saturday mornings.

*The peaks of Razor and Prisank form an impressive backdrop to Kranjska Gora*

**Public holidays**

Most shops and banks will be closed on the following days:

- 1 January (New Year)
- 8 February (France Prešeren Day – commemorating a 19th-century Romantic poet from Slovenia)
- Easter Monday
- 27 April (Insurrection Day)
- 1 and 2 May (Labour Days)
- 25 June (National Day)
- 15 August (Assumption Day)
- 31 October (Reformation Day)
- 1 November (All Saints' Day)
- 25 December (Christmas Day)
- 26 December (Independence Day)

## COMMUNICATIONS

Slovenia has one of the highest mobile phone ownerships in Europe. Network coverage is high even in mountain areas, but you may lose the signal in dense forest or in certain locations. The international prefix for Slovenia is 386. The emergency services number is 112 and 113 is for the police.

Internet access is generally available in hotels and cafés.

Slovenia is in the CET zone (Central European Time), which is 1hr ahead of GMT.

## HEALTH AND HAZARDS

Slovenia is generally a healthy place to be. No specific vaccinations are required for the short-term visitor, although, as anywhere, it's as well to make sure routine vaccinations such as polio and tetanus are up to date. Tap water is safe and good to drink throughout the country – help reduce environmental impact by bringing a water bottle and filling it from the tap, rather than buying water in plastic bottles.

Make sure you carry a European Health Insurance Card (EHIC) at all times, and then medical care should be free at source. Travel insurance is a sensible precaution for anyone travelling outside their own country. Visitors from outside Europe will need medical insurance; wherever you are from, you should check to see if your travel insurance covers you for mountain activities.

**Medical services**

Small towns have a medical centre where GPs and dentists are based, while larger centres have a hospital; specialists are based in Ljubljana. A pharmacy – *lekarna* – is identified by a green cross. You will need to ask for what you require, rather than helping yourself from the shelf, but pharmacists usually speak at least some English and are very helpful. Basic medical supplies, like painkillers and plasters, are not normally available in supermarkets.

**Hazards**

There are few hazards in Slovenia, but one to mention here is the tick. In Slovenia they can carry not only Lyme's disease, a nasty infectious illness, but also encephalitis, an inflammation of the brain which can be very serious indeed. Ticks thrive in grassy areas and meadows on the edge of forests – fortunately they are less common the higher you go. If you find one attached, use tweezers to pull it out from as close to the skin as possible to make sure you remove the head as well as the body. Pulling from the rear of the tick carries a risk of leaving the head in situ, increasing the possibility of infection. If a rash develops around the site of the bite, consult a doctor. Wearing long trousers reduces the chances of picking up ticks.

There are few other biting creatures; mosquitoes are easily kept at bay with insect repellent. Snakes are common in mountain areas of Slovenia, particularly the adder, but there are no deadly ones and they pose little threat to walkers as they usually seek cover immediately they sense danger.

**Fitness**

As with any mountaineering holiday, it pays to get fit before you go. There is no better way to get fit for walking than to walk, but there are many other possibilities including cycling, gym workouts and jogging.

## LANGUAGE

Slovene (or Slovenian) is spoken throughout the country; it is a Slavic language related to Croatian, Polish and Russian. An introduction to pronunciation, translation of common words used on Slovenian maps and signs, and a glossary of useful Slovene words and phrases are given in Appendix C.

*The north face of Mala Mojstrovka – the Hanzova pot (Walk 11) starts by following the obvious ramp line leading from the left of the crag*

The Slovenes are the first to admit that their language is complex and difficult to learn, but they are always pleased when a visitor makes an attempt! However, foreign language learning is considered a high priority in Slovenia – it is impossible to get into any university course without passing 'Matura' in a foreign language – and most Slovenes will speak at least one foreign language, and many speak four or five. English is the most commonly spoken foreign language, especially among the young, followed by German, Italian and Croatian.

## MAPS

Maps have improved since the first edition of this guide, and almost the entire area is now covered by 1:25,000 or 1:30,000 scale maps. Six maps cover every route in the book except two:

- Kranjska Gora (Geodetski inštitut Slovenije) 1:30,000 – Walks 1–18
- Triglav (Sidarta) 1:25,000 – Walks 1–9, 10–11, 14–25, 29–31, 39, 40–42, 53
- Bohinj (Sidarta) 1:25,000 – Walks 20–31, 52–53
- Bovec–Trenta (Sidarta) 1:25,000 – Walks 5, 10–11, 14–15, 29–30, 32–44, 56
- Bled (Geodetski inštitut Slovenije) 1:30,000 – Walks 18, 24, 45–53
- Krn (Planinske zveze Slovenije) 1:25,000 – Walks 43, 54–55, 56

Specific maps required are listed in the information boxes for each route.

Only Walks 57 (Stol) and 58 (Matajur) are not on a large-scale map. The access to both is on the Krn map which may help with orientation – otherwise the full route is on the Julijske Alpe 1:50,000 map (Planinske zveze Slovenije).

## WAYMARKING AND NAVIGATION

Generally routes in the Julian Alps are very well marked and signposted. Signs often give times to the next destination. The usual waymark is a 'target' – a red circle with a white centre painted on trees, rocks, buildings and so on, and there are occasional red direction arrows.

Lower-level routes are marked by yellow signs and numbers which correlate to routes on the local sheet map, and yellow target waymarks and direction arrows. These local routes don't necessarily follow exactly the same paths as the routes in this book, and our routes may overlap several local routes with different numbers. In order to reduce confusion, where local routes are mentioned in the text they are prefixed with the word 'local' in brackets before the route number.

Much of Slovenia is covered with forests, which contain a plethora of tracks and paths. One of the charms of many of the valley paths and tracks in this country is that they are as likely to be used by the locals on their way to the shops as by a fully togged-up hillwalker! However, this can mean, especially on forest or lower valley walks, that there are numerous potentially misleading paths.

When in doubt about the way forward, consult the route description and the sketch map and compare this to the sheet map. Significant landmarks along the route are shown in bold in the text to help with navigation. However, most of the walks offer no navigational difficulties and are liberally scattered with waymarks and signposts.

## WHAT TO TAKE

Weather conditions in the mountains are notoriously changeable, and while you may spend your entire holiday in T-shirts and shorts, it's important to carry appropriate equipment and clothing in case of need. This equipment list is by no means comprehensive and is offered as a guide only; obviously you will need to be selective depending on weather conditions and route choice.

### Clothing

- Walking boots that are comfortable, support the ankle and have good mid-soles
- Windproof and waterproof jacket and overtrousers
- Warm hat and sunhat or cap
- Light gloves
- Fleece or warm sweater
- Thermal wicking shirts and T-shirts
- Long trousers (not jeans) – those with zip-off legs to convert them to shorts are particularly useful
- Loop-stitched socks

### Miscellaneous

- Comfortable, roomy rucksack
- Bivvy bag for emergencies
- Trekking poles
- Self-belaying equipment – there are many different brands of via ferrata equipment form which to choose
- Helmet if you are planning to do any routes with via ferrata
- Ice axe – may be useful on high-level routes in the early part of the walking season – check the snow situation before you go
- Headtorch and batteries
- Water bottle
- Sunglasses, suncream and lip salve (essential – limestone reflects like snow)
- First-aid kit
- Map and compass (GPS if you have it)
- Whistle
- Guidebook
- Camera
- Binoculars
- Passport or identity card (if staying in a hut, though a good idea at any time)

*The Bear's Crag on the Prag Route on Triglav (Walk 18)*

**MOUNTAIN SAFETY**

- Check the weather forecast before you go (see 'Climate and weather' above)
- Study the route details beforehand, and make sure you have enough time to safely complete the route
- Carry enough food and liquid
- Leave details of your planned route and expected time of return with a responsible person
- Carry first-aid equipment
- Carry a map and compass and know how to use them – don't just rely on GPS, which can lose power or malfunction
- Avoid knocking rocks and stones downhill – people may be below you
- If in doubt, don't be afraid to turn back – but don't forget to inform people who may be expecting you
- Know the International Distress Signal – six blasts on a whistle (or torch flashes at night); the answer is three signals

### Mountain rescue

Unusually for the Alps, mountain rescue is free in Slovenia unless you are shown to have been ill-prepared or unduly negligent, in which case charges can be fearsome. Mountain rescue teams are extremely well organised. There is a network of 17 bases around Slovenia, and a helicopter with an experienced team on board is on duty at Brnik airport every weekend from June to September.

In case of an accident call the 112 emergency number; much of the area is covered by mobile phone

*Koča pri Savici visited on Walk 22*

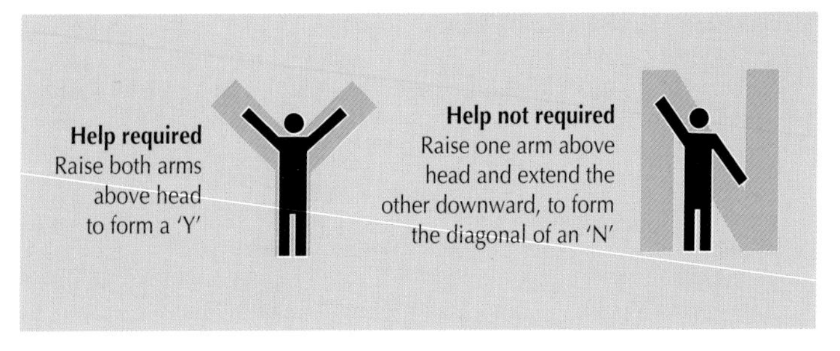


networks. If the injured person is not unconscious and does not have possible back injuries, move them to an accessible place. If possible, find a flat area where the helicopter can land and indicate your position using brightly coloured items.

Secure all equipment, because the helicopter will create a lot of wind when it arrives. Signal to it by raising both arms above your head in a 'Y' shape to indicate that you are the people who need help. When it lands, stand well back and do not approach until the crew indicate you to do so.

## USING THIS GUIDE

The guide aims to appeal not only to experienced hill walkers but also to more casual walkers who wish to explore some of Slovenia's fine pathways. Each section contains routes for walkers of all abilities – from short, easy orientation walks and visits to viewpoints, waterfalls and alpine villages, through to full mountain days. Also included among the routes are longer, more difficult peaks which demand all the skills of a mountaineer; some of these may require two or more days to complete.

### Arrangement of routes

Kranjska Gora, Bohinj and Bovec are the main bases for the high mountain routes, while Bled and Kobarid are situated in the foothills of the main range, and therefore have somewhat easier routes.

Within each section easier walks can be used as an orientation to the area before tackling harder and lengthier routes. Routes in the same area have been grouped together, for example, Walks 26, 27 and 28 are all in the Lower Bohinj mountains, to the south of Lake Bohinj.

Walks follow a circular route wherever possible, to heighten the interest and to cover more of the area, but in some cases, for example, Walk 57 (Stol), the only practical return is by the same way. For some of the longer routes an overnight stay in one of the mountain huts is recommended in the text.

*Routes are generally very well signed and waymarked*

Walkers on the lower section of the Prag Route with the Luknja pass in the background (Walk 18)

*Mangart from the Predel pass*

**Walk information**

Each section of the guide begins with a short introduction to the area, giving details of its location, access, the range of tourist facilities available, and a brief summary of the routes.

Each route begins with an information box showing the start and finish points, distance, grade and approximate ascent; and a short introduction, giving the highlights and 'feel' of the route.

Some walks follow an easy path with little height gain while others require alpine experience, a good level of fitness and a head for heights.

Distances are given in kilometres – if the route is out-and-back, the distance includes both directions. Distance is less useful for higher routes; on steep or difficult ground it could take many hours to cover a small number of kilometres. When planning your walk, consider the distances in conjunction with the time given in the box.

The time given for each walk is offered as a guide only, and takes no account of rest stops or taking photographs and so on. Usually the timings coincide with those suggested by signposts; in the few instances where this is not the case it is noted in the text.

Each walk has been given a grade from 1 to 4, to indicate its length and difficulty. Of course, this is subjective and is intended as a guide only – it does not correspond directly to international grading systems. Some walks are easier or more difficult than others even within the same grade; any particular points are mentioned in individual walks.

The start point is also the finish point, unless stated otherwise. Where the start point is not situated in the main base for the section, details on how to access the route are given in the information box. If the route involves an overnight stop, accommodation information is provided.

All the routes in the book are illustrated by a sketch map, which shows the outline of the route and key landmarks. **The sketch maps are not intended to be used alone**, but in conjunction with the relevant sheet map. Note that forests are not shown on the sketch maps; forests are almost everywhere in the Julian Alps and you can expect to be walking in trees for most of the time below about 1800m.

**Grades**

1 An easy walk, without much height gain, usually of short duration (not more than 3–4hrs). These routes are ideal as an introduction to the area around each base.

2 A longer route over rougher ground, with some height gain. There are no scrambling sections, but some parts of the path may be steep and/or rocky.

3 A full mountain day, with significant height gain, rough ground and possibly a short section or two of easy scrambling.

4 A serious, high route, long and strenuous, often exposed and usually with sections of fixed protection such as steel pegs and cables. Self-belaying equipment and a helmet are strongly recommended. A high level of fitness and competence in general mountaineering skills are required.

**EXTREME WEATHER**

Slovenia is being particularly affected by climate change. Recent years have brought an increase in extreme weather events, such as the terrible floods of 2023, and these can have catastrophic effects on paths, roads, bridges and other infrastructure, which can take time to repair. We recommend that you check routes with the local tourist office if in any doubt.

# 1 KRANJSKA GORA

*Walkers on the steep scree slopes that lead to Rdeča škrbina, with Dovški Gamsovec and Razor in the background (Walk 17)*

# INTRODUCTION

*The Planica valley seen from the path to Jalovec*

The resort village of Kranjska Gora (810m) lies near the head of the Zgornjesavska dolina, the upper Sava valley, and is an excellent centre for walking and mountaineering. It is only a few kilometres from both the Italian and Austrian borders, in the far north-west corner of Slovenia. The village has a wonderful setting, surrounded by the northern mountains of the Julian Alps and the Karavanke range, and it has managed to retain its attractiveness in spite of a well-developed tourist infra-structure. Kranjska Gora is one of the best known of Slovenia's mountain resorts, particularly in relation to ski-ing, which is plentiful in a good year.

Visitors can explore the local area by a series of numbered and waymarked walks, several of which feature in the 20 routes described in this section. The proximity of the Vršič pass (1611m) means that several mountain routes can be shortened by taking a bus or car to the top of the pass and making the most of the height gain. A number of mountain huts offering accommodation are within comfortable walking distance of Kranjska Gora.

Access to the resort is by the main 201 road running from Jesenice, which continues into Italy, or from Austria via the Karavanke tunnel, south of Klagenfurt, which joins this road. Alternatively, the Korensko sedlo (Wurzenpass, 1077m) is a steep road pass over the Karavanke range from Villach. Slovenia's highest road pass, the Vršič, links Kranjska Gora with Bovec and ultimately with Nova Gorica to the south, and boasts 50 impressive hairpin bends built by Russian prisoners of war during the First World War. In July and August there are several buses a day over the Vršič pass to Bovec, but the pass is usually closed from December to April. There is no train station in Kranjska Gora (the railway closed in 1966 and is now a cycle track), but hourly buses link the resort to the international railway station at Jesenice. A local taxi service can provide transport to the start of some of the walks if required.

The whole range of tourist accommodation can be found in Kranjska Gora and its immediate surroundings. There are several large hotels and a number of smaller hotels and *penzions*. Private rooms are plentiful both within Kranjska Gora and nearby villages, and there is also hostel-style accommodation. There are two campsites in the upper Sava valley – an eco camp in the woods just opposite Kranjska Gora and one at Dovje-Mojstrana, about 13km away. Likewise there are many eating places in Kranjska Gora and the surrounding villages, where anything from a quick pizza to a traditional Slovenian meal can be obtained at the usual relatively cheap prices.

The village is centred on the church and has a full range of tourist services, including a health centre and pharmacy. The Tourist Information Centre is in the large Vitranc Sports hall.

Kranjska Gora is busy in the season, and a quieter, village atmosphere can be found in Mojstrana, 13km down the valley. Mojstrana has a range of accommodation, along with a supermarket, post office and ATM. It is on the bus route between Kranjska Gora and Jesenice, and is used to access Walks 12 and 13, 18 and 19.

## THE ROUTES

There are 20 routes described in this section – all within easy reach of Kranjska Gora.

- Walks 1, 3, 4, 9 and 12 are delightful walks in the upper Sava valley, with an abundance of flower meadows, old villages and views of the surrounding mountains.
- Walks 2, 5–8 and 13 are walks to lower peaks in the area – excellent for orientation and views.
- Walks 10, 11 and 14–20 are high mountain routes to some of the most well-known summits of the Julian Alps, including Prisank (Walk 14), Jalovec (Walk 15) and Triglav (Walks 18 and 19).

## MAPS REQUIRED

The 1:30,000 Kranjska Gora map, which also shows the numbered walks referred to above, and Triglav 1:25,000.

# WALK 1

*Zelenci*

| | |
|---|---|
| **Start/finish** | Church in Kranjska Gora |
| **Distance** | 14km |
| **Total ascent/descent** | 100m |
| **Grade** | 1 |
| **Time** | 3–3½hrs |
| **Maps** | 1:30,000 Kranjska Gora, 1:25,000 Triglav |
| **Refreshments** | Plenty of bars and gostilnas along the way |

This easy walk visits the main sites of interest between Kranjska Gora and the village of Rateče, in particular the wonderful emerald-green pools of Zelenci, with its mountain reflections and cathedral-like air of peace. This is a place not to be missed during your visit to Kranjska Gora; if you don't have time to do the walk, then drive or take a taxi to the car park on the road between Podkoren and Rateče and stroll the 250m to see the pools.

But a far nicer way to visit is to follow the marked paths and trails described here, which pass through beautiful flower meadows as well as the unspoilt historic villages of Podkoren and Rateče, with stunning mountain vistas all around.

From the church in Kranjska Gora, walk east through the pedestrian area to another square with the Hotel Kotnik on the right. Turn left (north) here, and walk on past the sports hall and culture centre Dvorana Vitranc. Reach a T-junction and turn right then immediately left past the entrance of the Penzion Lipa at the bus stop.

Take the narrow walkway between the restaurant and houses for a short distance to come out opposite the excellent cake shop, Slaščičana Kala. Turn right and take a track across the fields for about 200m. Cross the main road that bypasses Kranjska Gora, and then cross the fledgling Sava river. Take the track directly opposite, past some hayracks, signed (local) routes 4 and 10. A sign advertising the Natura Eco campsite points the same way.

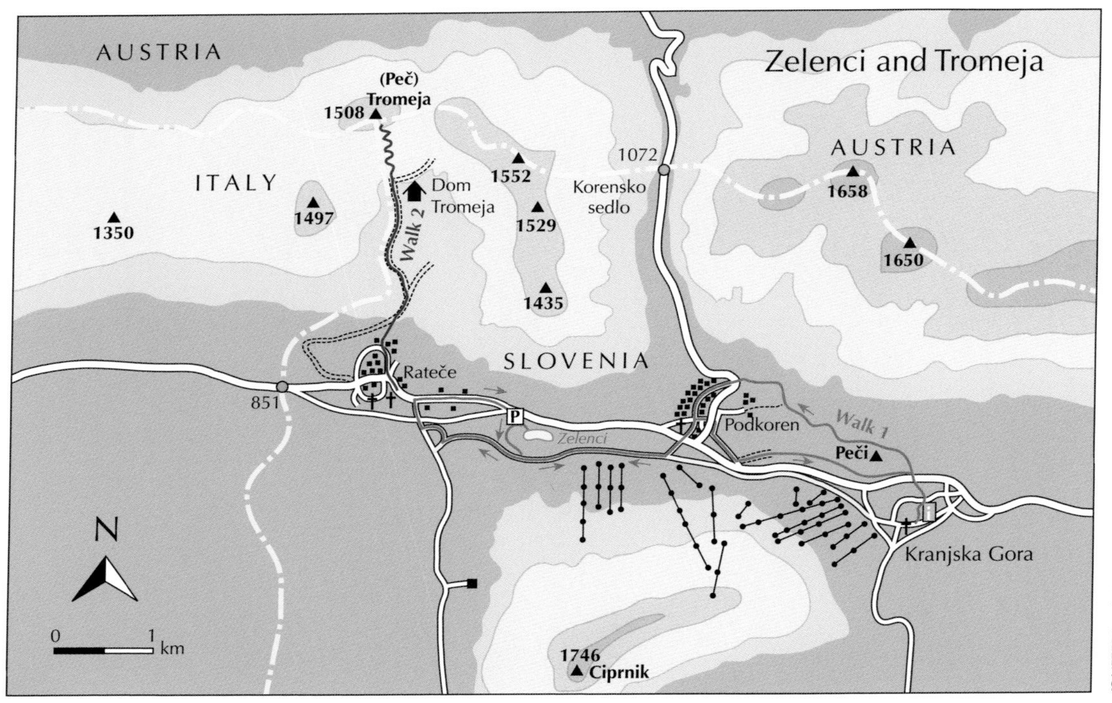
Zelenci and Tromeja
AUSTRIA
(Peč)
Tromeja
1508
ITALY
1350
1497
Dom
Tromeja
Walk 2
1552
1529
1435
1072
Korensko
sedlo
AUSTRIA
1658
1650
SLOVENIA
Rateče
851
P
Zelenci
Podkoren
Walk 1
Peči
Kranjska Gora
N
0
1
km
1746
Ciprnik

Continue into woods with a field to the right, skirting the crags of the little hill **Peči**. A narrow path, (local) route 10, heads up left here, but carry on along the broad track past the campsite and a row of horse stables. Arrive at a large hayfield where the track forks to the right, but continue straight on to cross the meadow on a grassy track. At the very far end, as the meadow narrows, the track passes through a line of trees and continues into another much smaller meadow, with a tiny wooden chalet about 50m to the right.

For a more **direct route to Podkoren** from here, take the main track going straight on, soon passing houses and the Penzion Sportel to reach the Korensko sedlo road on the edge of Podkoren. From there, do not cross the road but turn left and walk down the track parallel to the road for 100m, then turn right, through an underpass, and follow the road into the village.

The steep ski slopes opposite, on Vitranc, host World Cup slalom competitions each year in February.

A signpost for (local) route 4 directs you to the right on a narrow tree-lined path; leave the broad track and walk up here, past the chalet, for about 150m, and then turn left onto a broad track once more. After 500m carefully cross the Korensko sedlo (Wurzenpass) road at a hairpin bend and begin to walk down what was once the old road into **Podkoren**. ◂

The village of **Podkoren** dates back to medieval times, and its wealth was built around trade, which flourished because of the proximity of the pass into Austria. Heavy horses could be hired here to haul laden goods carts over the pass. There are new buildings here, but among them you can still recognise the old wooden houses and barns. At Podkoren 63, a house on the right as you walk down the road, there is a plaque indicating that Sir Humphrey Davy, the English inventor of the miner's safety lamp, lived here.

Carry on to a small square with an ancient linden tree, and the Hotel Vitranc if you are ready for some refreshment. Alternatively, the 400 year old Gostilna Pr' Serc can be found 50m to the left. Cross the square and walk down the narrow lane straight ahead, which continues on the other side of the main road to reach the young Sava river at a small bridge. Turn right after the bridge and continue on the cycle track, which was originally the railway line (closed in 1966) and is now tarmacked for the use of pedestrians, cyclists and rollerbladers.

It is well worth a detour to the left to explore the pretty village of Rateče with its two churches and attractive square; there are several gostilnas in the village as well.

Continue along here for about 2km, passing the Podkoren ski slopes and the small bar called Pehta, and ignoring two signed paths to Zelenci on the right. Further on a wonderful view of the Planica valley opens out on the left. Finally reach houses and turn right at a junction, signed for the cycle track. In about 300m meet the main road again; cross over and soon reach a T-junction. ▶

*Zelenci, where underground springs bubble up into the emerald green pools*

Follow the road to the right and walk down this quiet lane past attractive houses. By the last house on the left there is an example of painted beehives, a Slovene tradition. Continue along the old road, with good views up the Planica valley, and join the main road once more. Turn left and walk about 250m along the main road before crossing it to the Zelenci car park, where there is also a snack bar. The pools are signed along an easy track through beautiful woodland.

## THE ZELENCI POOLS

The pools are generally regarded as the source of the Sava, Slovenia's longest river, which crosses the country into Croatia, eventually flowing into the Danube at Belgrade. The true source is at Nadiža, a waterfall near **Dom v Tamarju** (see Walk 9), whose waters disappear underground almost immediately to emerge again at the Zelenci pools. The springs can be seen on the bottom of the pools, stirring up the silt like miniature volcanoes. The temperature of the water is 5–6°C all year round; the water never freezes no matter how cold the air temperature.

The position of the pools is spectacular, against the backdrop of the mountains of Ponca and Jalovec. In spite of the proximity of the road, the area has a wonderful sense of peace and calm, and it is a place to linger for a few minutes to watch the wildlife. The whole area around Zelenci is a nature reserve. Orientation boards at the top of the viewing tower explain the geology and identify flowers and wildlife in four languages, including English.

After visiting the pools return along the path towards the car park, but take the first left, signed with a wooden post. Cross a small wooden footbridge, and after about 100m reach a fork – the right-hand path goes back up to the car park, but take the left, crossing another bridge and continuing on a good path through the woods of the nature reserve to eventually rejoin the cycle track. Turn left and walk for 1km or so to reach the little bridge over the Sava by the turn-off to Podkoren.

The cycle track continues back to Kranjska Gora from here; to walk it would take 30mins. However, it is more interesting to return to the square in Podkoren by turning left, crossing the main road and retracing your steps up the lane. This time turn right in the square and walk past the Gostilna Pr' Šerc, then, as the road bends round to the right, continue straight ahead. Go through an underpass under the Korensko sedlo road to a track on the other side. Turn right and continue down the track, parallel to the main road, then turn left as the track joins a minor road by two houses.

After 200m or so take the left fork, past some more houses, and cross a stream on a little wooden bridge. The track becomes unmade and crosses some meadows. Where the track turns right, continue straight ahead on a grassy path, and at the edge of the trees turn right, following a sign for Kranjska Gora, and follow the line of a stream for about 100m before turning left and crossing it on a plank bridge. The path bears slightly right and crosses a small meadow. After 100m re-enter the wood and bear left uphill, ignoring a track to the right which leads past a house.

Continue through the wood for 200m to a wooden signpost, turn right and continue to a T-junction where you turn right again. The path descends a little, curving round to the left, then crosses a stream and enters a meadow. Cross the meadow and join a track running parallel to the main road for a few hundred metres before reaching the hayracks where you crossed the road earlier; retrace your steps from there into **Kranjska Gora**.

# WALK 2

*Peč (Tromeja)*

| | |
|---|---|
| **Start/finish** | Bus stop in Rateče |
| **Distance** | 7km |
| **Total ascent/descent** | 640m |
| **Grade** | 2 |
| **Time** | 3½–4hrs |
| **Maps** | 1:30,000 Kranjska Gora, 1:25,000 Triglav |
| **Access** | Rateče, 5.5km west of Kranjska Gora, can be reached by an hourly bus from Kranjska Gora; alternatively, walk along the cycle track (about 1hr 15mins). |
| **Note** | This walk could be combined with the Zelenci walk (Walk 1) for a longer day out. |

This summit is marked as 'Peč' on the sheet map, but it is known locally and on all the signposts as Tromeja (literally 'three border point'). It is not in the Julian Alps, being the first peak of the 120km-long Karavanke chain which marks the border between Slovenia and Austria, but it is included in this book for three good reasons. Firstly, it is a fine walk; secondly, it offers terrific views of both the northern Julian Alps and the mountains of southern Austria; and, thirdly, it is just about as symbolic a summit as any one mountain can be. On its top meet not only the borders of Slovenia, Italy and Austria, but also the three great linguistic traditions and cultures of Europe – the Germanic, Romance and Slavic. It was here that representatives of the three governments of Italy, Austria and Slovenia met to welcome Slovenia into the European Union in 2004.

See the route map in Walk 1.

◂ From the bus stop in Rateče, turn left and walk along the main road through the village, past a small store and a church. Continue on to the attractive square, and then turn right, seeing ahead of you a building with a sign on it saying Tromeja, 2hrs. Walk up this lane and cross a little river, before arriving at a track heading off right between two houses, signed Tromeja. Walk between

farm outbuildings to a fork where you take the right-hand path, again signed Tromeja. Continue through woodland and pasture for about 10mins to emerge on a forest road opposite a field. Turn right and follow the forest road gently uphill. Ignore several side tracks; the correct way is well signed or waymarked.

*Haflinger ponies near the summit of Tromeja with Dobratsch in the background*

In 2017 Dom Tromeja had been closed for some time, and although the Tourist Office was hoping it would reopen, no date had been set..

After about 2km there is a sign for **Dom Tromeja** to the right. ◂ It is only a short diversion to the hut for refreshments, if required. The route continues up the forest road, and soon reaches a sharp right-hand bend. A sign directs you onto a path climbing into the forest – this is the Krajša (short) pot. It is also possible to continue up the road on the Daljša (long) pot; this way is less steep but also less interesting.

The final section is quite steep, zigzagging up through the forest following the line of a swathe of open land about 30m across which marks the border between Slovenia and Italy. The path weaves in and out of the forest, so at each alternate hairpin you see more and more of the stupendous view of the Julian Alps opening out behind you.

Emerge onto the summit of **Peč** (1508m), with the flags of the three countries blowing in the breeze, to find

## MONUMENT TO PEACE

There is a monument, built in 1994, just below the summit of Peč on the Slovenian side, with text in Italian, Slovene and German. It says:

TROMEJA
The Mountain of Peace by Šri Činmoj
Mountains are a symbol of peace, tranquillity and inner depth. Mankind needs all these virtues on its way to growing worldwide harmony.
'FINDING ONE'S INNER PEACE IS MAN'S GREATEST NEED.'
May this monument to understanding and friendship among nations be erected at this important meeting point of three great language groups and cultures.
Tromeja has become a link in the chain of several hundred different monuments dedicated to peace. There are buildings, mountains, bridges, cities, parks and natural phenomena which should encourage harmonious coexistence of people and nations, improve harmony and help to overcome both inner and outer borders.
PEACE DOES NOT ONLY MEAN NO WAR. PEACE MEANS THE RULE OF HARMONY, LOVE, SATISFACTION AND UNITY.

*(translated by Rosvita Veselič)*

that the forest which covers the Slovenian side has given way to a small ski resort on the Austrian side.

**Peč** is the westernmost peak of the 120km-long Karavanke mountain chain, and there is a good view along the ridge. The view into Austria is extensive. Directly opposite is Dobratsch (2166m) with its large aerial, while the Wörthersee lake near Klagenfurt is visible in the distance about 30km away, along with other hills and mountains near and far. There is a very marked difference between the comparatively rounded hills of this part of Austria and the steep limestone peaks of the Julian Alps.

The return route takes the same path back to **Rateče**.

## WALK 3

*Srednji Vrh*

| | |
|---|---|
| **Start/finish** | Church in Kranjska Gora |
| **Distance** | 11km |
| **Total ascent/descent** | 300m |
| **Grade** | 2 |
| **Time** | 3½–4hrs |
| **Maps** | 1:30,000 Kranjska Gora, 1:25,000 Triglav |
| **Refreshments** | Gostišče Srnjak at Galerše |

This is a very fine walk, with stunning views of the high-mountain scenery of the Julian Alps and the valley pastures below. The route climbs up to Gostišče Srnjak at Galerše and then meanders along a balcony path about 200m above the valley floor, through meadows full of flowers and butterflies. It continues through forest of mixed trees to reach the alpine village of Srednji Vrh. The return to Kranjska Gora is alongside the Sava river. This is not a particularly long walk in terms of distance, but you should allow plenty of time because the enchanting surroundings and views will entice you to linger.

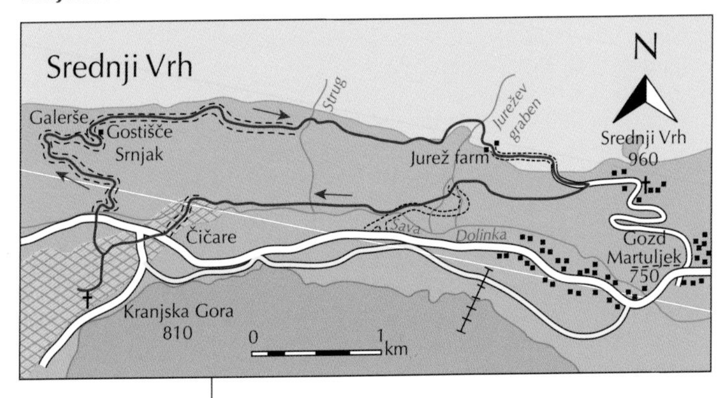


From the church in Kranjska Gora, walk east through the pedestrian area to another square, with the Hotel Kotnik on the right. Turn left (north) here, and walk on past the sports hall and culture centre Dvorana Vitranc. Reach a T-junction, turn right and walk past the Penzion Lipa then turn immediately left at to a bus stop, turn left again and walk between houses for a short distance to come out opposite the excellent cake shop, Slaščičana Kala. Turn right and take a track across the fields for about 200m. Cross the road and the little **river Sava** and then turn right on a vehicle track which heads east for about 200m before swinging round to the left.

Continue past some houses to begin a gentle ascent, and in another 100m or so the track turns sharply left. It continues up for just over 1km, with hairpin bends to ease the ascent. ◂ After about 1.5km, reach a small clearing at **Galerše**, where the outside tables of **Gostišče Srnjak** invite you to stay for a drink in the sunshine.

An alternative path ascends steeply through the forest – it starts on the right about 50m after the sharp left turn and rejoins the vehicle track about 50m before a bench at a hairpin bend.

After the gostišče continue on the track as it heads off to the right into the trees. After about 300m come to a fence and gate which mark the end of the woods. The path leads out onto the open hillside, providing wonderful views up the Velika Pišnica valley behind Kranjska Gora towards Vršič, Razor and Prisank. Continue very pleasantly on this balcony path through open flower meadows with shepherd's buildings scattered about. The air is full of the sound of cowbells and the scent of wild flowers.

After about 1.5km, at the second of two metal gates, a sign marked (local) route 2 directs you left onto a much narrower path disappearing into the forest. The path climbs steeply up through the wood before levelling out to cross a stream (**Strug**) which can be just a dry stony bed in summer. It then wanders on through beautiful mixed forest of beech, pine and spruce, crossing a number of small streams.

At the first of two junctions in the path, take the left fork signed (local) route 2 – the right fork is taped off. In less than 200m reach the second junction, but this time the left fork is taped off, so continue in the same direction of travel, soon confirmed by another route 2 sign. Shortly after, cross a larger stream, called the **Jureževgraben**, by a wooden footbridge. After 100m the path merges with a broader track, and you continue along this track for about 60m, now slightly downhill, to pass through a wooden gate at the small Jurež farm, which is marked on the map.

Walk between the farm buildings, making a sharp dog-leg turn right then left, before continuing on an

*Walkers enjoying the view of the Julian Alps from the balcony path*

unmade vehicle track. This now runs through open pastures once more, with fine views down to Kranjska Gora and across to the massive cirque of rock walls above Gozd Martuljek. Soon afterwards the track becomes a tarmac road, then makes a sharp right turn and leads down towards the hamlet of **Srednji Vrh**.

Turn sharp right, leaving the road at a wooden signpost (local route 19) and pass directly in front of a farm building; the route doubles back on itself just below the road. Pass a bench and painted shrine, and continue through a gate into a beautiful open flower meadow with views of Špik and the mountains behind Kranjska Gora. Reach a left-hand hairpin, and here continue straight ahead on a path that enters the woods, signed (local) route 19. The path descends through the trees, passing another religious shrine and bench, where a gap in the trees gives a good view of Kranjska Gora with Vitranc behind. After that the path descends a little more steeply, before passing two attractive chalets and a small millwheel over a stream.

About 50m past the chalets the path divides – take the right fork towards Kranjska Gora. Cross a stream on a wooden bridge with a small hydro-electric power station just below. Level out at a T-junction by another stream at a bench with a signpost, and then turn right onto a broad open track. Continue through the forest and after 200m or so pass a beautiful small open glade studded with flowers, and stay on this side of the river, ignoring a bridge. The path continues on through more open land with occasional wooded sections, staying close to the river bank, to reach another bridge – cross here, and walk through the residential area of **Čičare** before reaching a zebra crossing over the main road and returning to **Kranjska Gora**.

## WALK 4

*Slap Martuljek (Martuljek waterfall)*

| | |
|---|---|
| **Start/finish** | Bus stop in Gozd Martuljek, 4km east of Kranjska Gora |
| **Distance** | 8km |
| **Total ascent/descent** | 400m |
| **Grade** | 2 |
| **Time** | 2½–3hrs |
| **Maps** | 1:30,000 Kranjska Gora, 1:25,000 Triglav |
| **Refreshments** | Brunarica pri Ingotu at Jasenje |
| **Access** | Hourly buses run from Kranjska Gora to Gozd Martuljek. Or walk along the cycle track from Kranjska Gora for about 3km, to reach the meadow with the pylon by a side track to the right. |
| **Parking** | Driving east from Kranjska Gora, park on the outside of a left-hand bend just before a bridge crossing the river Sava, by a big old pension. Turn right along the cycle track from the car park; after 150m turn left at a junction onto a gravel track and in 50m turn right, following signs for Slap Martuljek, (local) route 6. After about 300m reach an open pasture, to join the route at the charcoal burning site. |

This walk passes through natural forest to reach two waterfalls beneath the massive rock walls of the Martuljek peaks. The lower fall (spodnji slap) is at the head of a gorge, where it cascades 29m down the cliff, observed from a well-maintained path and viewpoint. The higher fall (zgornji slap) drops a total of 130m in three stages; the last part of the route to its foot involves a steep scramble. Be sure to make the short detour to Jasenje, a stunningly beautiful planina surrounded by forest, with views up to the sheer rock spires of the mountains, where Brunarica pri Ingotu offers delicious home-made drinks and food.

From the bus stop in Gozd Martuljek you can already admire the fabulous scenery of the Martuljek cirque. Walk back, towards Kranjska Gora, for about 50m, and take a track on the left, signed (local) route 6. Leave the houses

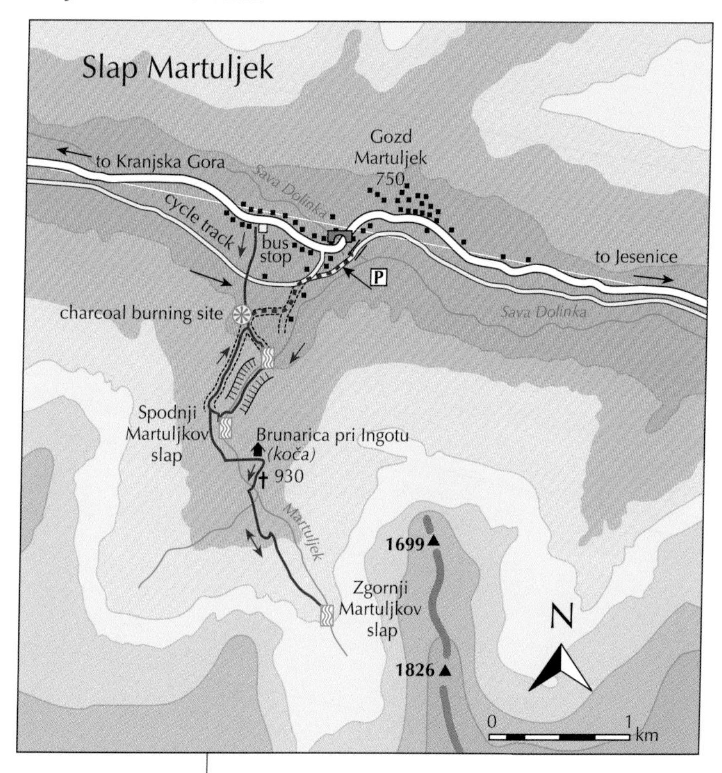


behind and walk across the open meadows for about 300m, before walking under the **cycle track** through an old stone railway bridge. Skirt the edge of another pasture, with the view unfortunately marred by a big pylon, to reach the forest by a **charcoal burning site** used for demonstrations, with information boards and a small hut.

There is an excellent explanatory leaflet about **charcoal burning** in several languages including English. Charcoal burning was a critical industry in the past, when the iron found in the Karavanke hills was first being developed.

Just after the charcoal burners' area the tracks divide at a sign – the right-hand track is the descent route, while the left-hand track leads in 5mins to a bridge at the lower end of the gorge, where there is a man-made waterfall built to control the flow. There is an orientation board, but it is unfortunately in Slovene only – another sign in English warns that you enter the gorge at 'your own risk'. ▶

In 2014 the bridges in the upper section of the gorge were in a poor state of repair. Repairs should be finished by the time this guide is published.

The path continues on the left-hand side of the gorge, with the impressively steep walls closing in on either side. After about 200m one or two simple wooden footbridges are crossed over the now narrow river. This is followed by a steep ascent up wooden steps to cross another bridge above the river and the path continues up to a good viewpoint for the lower falls (**spodnji slap**) from another wooden bridge.

Carry on along the waymarked path quite steeply for about 15mins to the top of the gorge, and reach a T-junction with the broad gravel track. Turn left along it, signed Brunarica pri Ingotu 15mins. After 100m ignore a waymarked path on the right, signed Pod Špik 1hr, and

*Brunarica pri Ingotu at Jasenje provides home-produced food and drink*

*The impressive lower falls of Martuljek*

continue on the main track, signed Drugi slap 45mins. In another 5mins or so cross a stream bed, and just beyond ignore a path to the right, signed Drugi slap 40min, and continue on towards **Brunarica pri Ingotu**. In another 20m cross a wooden bridge and walk up to reach the planina in about 100m. ▸

Family-run Brunarica pri Ingotu offers a wonderful place to sit and take in stunning mountain scenery while enjoying their delicious home-made food and drinks.

From the gate of the hut, follow the grassy track straight ahead on the right-hand side of the planina, and at the end of the field keep right and take a broad track. In 20m reach an amazing tree – Mama Lipa (lime) and her seven daughters. Another 100m brings you to a small wooden chapel and a memorial listing those who have died in these mountains. Now walk down into the stream bed, crossing it on a small wooden plank, and continue through the wood for about 50m and turn left to join the waymarked path to the second waterfall passed just before the bridge.

Soon afterwards the path bears right, away from the river, and begins to ascend with a small stream to the left. In another 5mins the path turns left and crosses the stream, then continues to climb steadily through the woods.

After a further 10mins the path begins to rise more steeply, ascending a small rocky bluff, and then continues climbing through the woods for another 10mins to reach a path junction by a bench. Ignore the path heading right to Za Ak 30mins (which leads to a bivouac hut), and continue bearing left, following a (local) route 6 Slap 2 sign, along the now narrow path, traversing the steep wooded hillside with the sound of the river down below. After 300m the path descends quite steeply with the aid of a cable handrail to reach the fast-flowing water which it crosses on a small footbridge. Then ascend carefully over steep, eroded ground to a good viewpoint for the impressive upper falls (**zgornji**). The protected ascent to the foot of the main cascade climbs a steep cleft to the left of the falls for about 25m – it's an awkward scramble, and remember that you may find it even more difficult coming down!

Return by the same route, and when you reach the river crossing to the chapel, continue on down the waymarked path if you don't wish to revisit the hut. Retrace your steps down to the junction where you joined the gravel track and continue straight on steeply down for about 15mins. The track levels out at the charcoal burning area, where from you can choose your return route depending on how you came.

## WALK 5

*Vršič pass*

| | |
|---|---|
| **Start/finish** | Tourist Information Office, Kranjska Gora |
| **Distance** | 19km |
| **Total ascent/descent** | 800m |
| **Grade** | 2 |
| **Time** | 5½–6hrs |
| **Maps** | 1:30,000 Kranjska Gora, 1:25,000 Triglav |
| **Refreshments** | Plenty of huts passed on or near the route |
| **Parking** | There are possibilities for parking at the several doms along the way, as well as at various laybys. |
| **Note** | The 50 hairpin bends of the Vršič pass are numbered on the Kranjska Gora map (but not on the Triglav one) and on the ground, and are useful reference points. The river crossing early in the walk presents no problems under normal water conditions; if the river is in flood, you can still complete the route either by walking up the road or by taking the bus up to Mihov dom just below bend 5. |

This fine walk climbs to the top of Slovenia's only true alpine road pass, the 1611m Vršič pass. The paved road was built by Russian POWs in the First World War, when a good supply route south to the Isonzo front was vital. Today it is popular with tourists who drive or cycle up the 24 bends to the top (and 26 down the other side). This walking route avoids the busy road for the most part and meanders through attractive forests to reach the top of the pass, returning down the old pass road with terrific views of the north face of Prisank.

This is quite a long walk if tackled both ways from Kranjska Gora, but regular buses that cross the pass in summer mean you can shorten the walk by as much as you wish (check times at the Tourist Information Office). If you want to visit the top of the pass but don't have time for a long walk, park at Tonkina koča at bend 16, then walk up the road to bend 17 to begin the walk there. The old road taken on the descent ends at the pretty Tonkina koča, making a really pleasant round trip of 2½–3hrs.

## ACCESS TO OTHER WALKS

This walk can be used for access to Walks 8 (Sleme), 10 and 11 (Mala and Velika Mojstrovka) and 14 (Prisank); there are two huts at the top of the pass if you need to stay overnight. Link this with Walk 39, the Soča Trail, for a wonderful long day out – from Trenta you can return to Kranjska Gora or go on to Bovec by bus.

To reach the first point on the route, Jezero Jasna (Lake Jasna, meaning 'clear') from Kranjska Gora, follow the

*Lake Jasna at the foot of the Vršič pass*

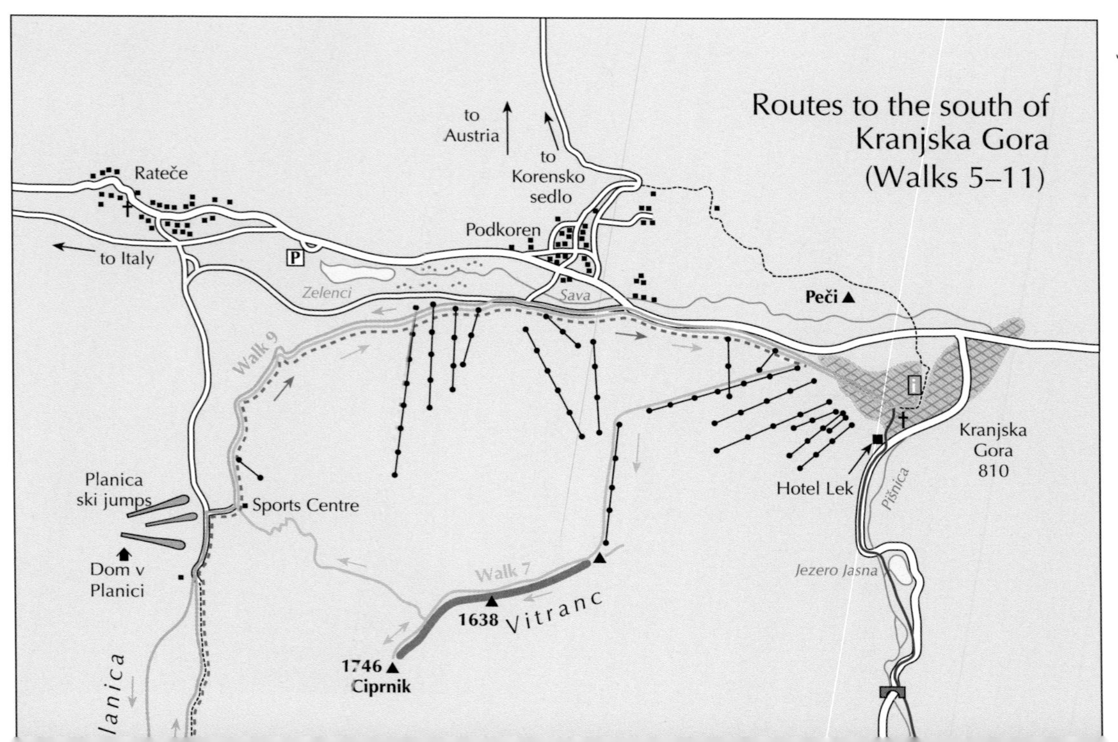
Routes to the south of Kranjska Gora (Walks 5–11)
to Austria
to Korensko sedlo
Rateče
Podkoren
to Italy
P
Zelenci
Sava
Peči
Walk 9
Kranjska Gora 810
Hotel Lek
Pišnica
Planica ski jumps
Sports Centre
Dom v Planici
Jezero Jasna
Walk 7
1638
Vitranc
1746 Ciprnik

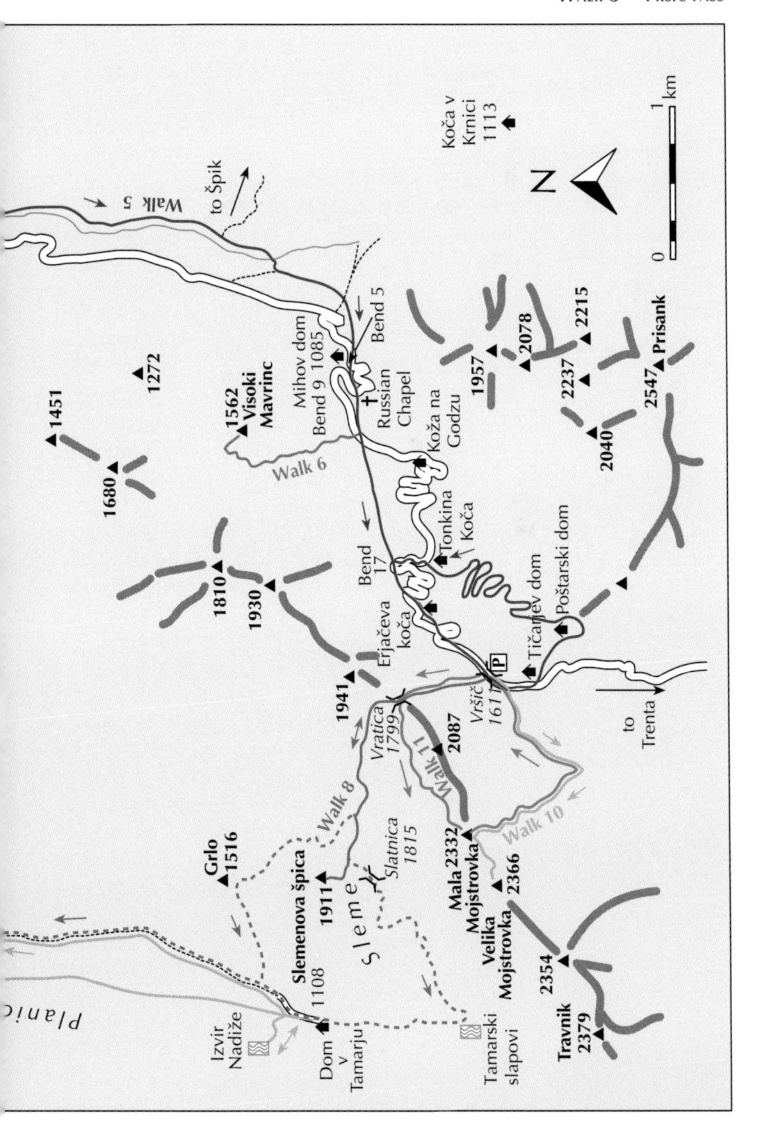
Walk 5
to Špik
Koča v Krnici 1113
N
0
1 km
1451
1272
1680
1562 Visoki Mavrinc
Mihov dom Bend 9 1085
Bend 5
Russian Chapel
Koča na Godzu
Walk 6
1957
2078
2215
2237
2040
2547 Prisank
1810
1930
Bend 17
Tonkina Koča
Erjačeva koča
Tičarjev dom
Poštarski dom
P
1941
Vratica 1799
2087
Vršič 1611
to Trenta
Walk 8
Walk 11
Walk 10
Grlo 1516
Slemenova špica 1911
Slatnica 1815
Sleme
Mala Mojstrovka 2332
Velika Mojstrovka 2366
2354
Travnik 2379
Slemenova 1108
Izvir Nadiže
Dom v Tamarju
Tamarski slapovi

sign to the Vršič pass (heading south), which winds through the village to join the main pass road at the Hotel Lek, and continues along the pavement to the lake.

The beautiful lake lives up to its name, with the mountain backdrop reflected in its clear waters.

Reach a wooden signpost just past a road bridge, and follow signs for (local) route 8 to Krnica. Cross the small car park to reach **Jezero Jasna**, where a statue of Zlatorog, the golden-horned ibex (in this version!), stands at the shore. ◂

Follow the walking track that goes past the lake on the right until it rejoins the road, and then continue along the road to a second bridge across the Pišnica river. Don't cross it, but take the broad track to the left, heading south on the east bank of the river and signed Koča v Krnici. After about 2km on the easy track, notice a sign on a large boulder indicating a path heading left to Špik. About 300m past this, an open planina comes into view on the other side of the river bed, which marks the start of the track up to Vršič. There is no bridge, but under normal conditions the river is easily forded without wet feet at this point – just pick your way carefully across the mostly dry bed to reach the planina. ◂

Here the Krnica valley opens out before you; Škrlatica is to the left with its red rock walls, then Razor and Prisank further to the right.

On the far side of the river a track leads up over the grassy planina. Take the left fork at the top, and continue for 100m or so to another fork, where you bear right. Another 2–3mins brings you to a crossroads with a track coming down from bend 3, just by a wooden bridge on the right. Keep straight on up the comfortable track, which gradually narrows to a path, climbing steadily through the woods for about 5mins to pass a sign to Mihov dom. In another 2–3mins join the road, just below bend 5 (1102m).

At the bend, just to the left of a stream, take a side path to cut off the next hairpin. Meet the road again at bend 7, but continue on the woodland path, a little steeper this time. In 2–3mins emerge at the road again just above a car park; turn left, and after about 30m take a path on the opposite side of the road which takes you up to the **Russian Chapel**.

In the years 1915–16 more than 10,000 **Russian POWs** were involved in building this road. In March 1916 over 100 Russian prisoners and some Austrian guards were buried by an avalanche. The Russian chapel was built in 1917 by the surviving Russian prisoners to commemorate the disaster.

Just to the right of the chapel, on the other side of the bridge, walk up between two benches and up a rough path for a short distance to meet a waymarked track – turn left and continue through the attractive woodland. The track comes back to the road again after about 5mins and continues opposite, signed 7 Vršič, Erjavčeva koča 40mins and Tonkina koča. ▶ The path climbs steadily but not steeply through the woods, which are scattered with the tall arching stems of purple willow-leaved gentian, gorgeous in early autumn.

Koča na Gozdu is also 5mins up the road for refreshment.

After about 25mins reach a junction to the left signed Tonkina koča – if you need refreshment you can take this way to the koča at bend 16, then walk back up the road to bend 17 to rejoin the route. Otherwise continue up; soon reach a scree slope and look left for a fine view of the 'window' on Prisank. Cross the stony slope and continue into the forest again, and in another 2–3mins reach the road at **bend 17** (1418m). On the outside of the bend is a small parking area with an excellent view, from left to right, of Špik, Škrlatica and the north face of Prisank.

About 30m past the bend, just before a wooden crash barrier, take a path heading right into the trees, marked by a faded arrow on a rock. Cross the road again at bend 21 and continue on the obvious but unmarked path, which brings you to an open grassy area by the road, just below **Erjavčeva koča**. A sign points left to a small graveyard of Russian POWs about 40m away. After the short detour return to the road where a sign points to the koča.

From the koča, walk across the car park and turn left up the road for a short distance to a path on the right which cuts off bend 23. Continue across the road to another path, rather overgrown by dwarf pine at first,

*The natural rock sculpture of the Ajdovska deklica, the pagan maiden*

which runs close to the road on the left-hand side to reach the top of the **Vršič pass** in around 10mins.

If you are going on to the **Vratica pass** for the walk to Sleme (Walk 8) or the Hanzova pot (Walk 11), there is no need to go to the top of Vršič. Instead take a rocky path just opposite the Erjavčeva koča car park, signed Slemenova špica.

From the top of the pass, turn left just opposite the souvenir kiosk and walk 100m or so to **Tičarjev dom**. Continue past the dom following a sign for Poštarski dom. In less than 10mins reach a junction and turn left, signed Poštarski dom. Pass some First World War buildings and continue round a corner to a terrific view of the north face of Prisank. ▶ Continue round the corner to **Poštarski dom**, looking very attractive against the backdrop of Mala Mojstrovka, at the highest point of the ancient route over the pass.

Notice particularly the sad 'face' in the rock of Ajdovska deklica, a natural rock sculpture on the crags straight ahead.

The giant face in the rock is explained by a local legend. Long ago a giant maiden, **Ajdovska Deklica** (the pagan girl) lived high on Prisank and guided people over the pass in mist or snow. One day she made a prophecy that a small boy would grow up to hunt Zlatorog, the beloved golden-horned ibex of Triglav. The idea was so appalling that the girl's sisters turned her into stone, so she is doomed for ever to look sadly down on the pass.

The route continues below the dom, bearing right. The grassy, well-built cart track weaves gently down the hillside in sharp hairpins, offering delightful walking and tremendous views of Prisank, Škrlatica and Špik through the thin larch forest. After 15mins or so reach a right-hand hairpin, with Erjavčeva koča a short distance below; a way-marked path leads back to the koča from here if you wish. Otherwise continue down the hairpins for another 15mins or so to reach **Tonkina koča** at bend 16. You could simply walk down the road from here, but it is not recommended because there are few side paths and the road is very busy in the height of the summer season. Instead turn left up the road for a short distance to bend 17, and retrace the much pleasanter ascent route back to **Kranjska Gora**.

## WALK 6

*Visoki Mavrinc*

| | |
|---|---|
| **Start/finish** | Vršič pass road, about 400m up from bend 9 |
| **Distance** | 3km |
| **Total ascent/descent** | 360m (from Vršič road) |
| **Grade** | 2 |
| **Time** | 2hrs |
| **Maps** | 1:30,000 Kranjska Gora, 1:25,000 Triglav |
| **Access** | Drive (there is a small parking area just after the bend) or take a bus to Koča na godzu, and walk back down the road for 5mins to the start of the route (on the left looking down). |

This is a pleasant walk through forest to Visoki Mavrinc (1562m), a magnificent airy viewpoint high above Velika Pišnica, the valley leading up to the Vršič pass. The position of the small peak of Visoki Mavrinc gives an impression of being suspended high above the main valley floor, with wonderful views of the mountains all around. This is a short walk if you have your own transport, otherwise add a further 3½hrs to walk to the start of the route and back to Kranjska Gora.

See the route map in Walk 5.

◀ The walk starts about 400m past **bend 9** on the Vršič pass road, where the Vršič path leaves the road on the right-hand side, signed 7 Vršič. Almost immediately, after only 20m, take an unmarked path leading to the right. After about 15m turn left at a fork and follow the path heading steeply up through the forest (the right-hand path rejoins the route after a hairpin).

Although it is not waymarked the path follows an obvious route to reach some large boulders after about

*Enjoying early winter sunshine and spectacular views from the summit of Visoki Mavrinc*

10mins. Wind between these and continue, keeping to the left of more boulders which litter the steep slope of the hillside, for another 10mins to reach a T-junction at a mossy rock with a tree growing on it. Turn right here and almost immediately cross a narrow rocky stream bed. The path then continues zigzagging up through the woods, bearing to the right before it eventually steepens to reach a narrow saddle, still forested, which drops steeply away on the other side.

The path turns right and follows the ridge. Although it is not difficult it is somewhat narrow and a little eroded in places, but you soon emerge from the trees to a truly magnificent view from **Visoki Mavrinc** summit.

> Although not a high peak (its summit is about 100m lower than the top of the Vršič pass), there is a lovely feeling of airiness at the top of **Visoki Mavrinc** as the ground drops steeply away on all sides, as if you are suspended on a platform in the middle of the pass with the mountains all around. A wooden cross and a visitors' book adorn the summit and there is even a bench.
>
> The view is dominated to the south by Razor and the massive north wall of Prisank, while below to the right the road can be seen snaking up through the trees to the top of the Vršič pass. Further to the right is what is arguably the best view of Mala Mojstrovka, showing the popular walking route up the large gully and the skyline ridge (Walk 10). To the north you can see Lake Jasna and Kranjska Gora, and behind them the Karavanke ridge, and beyond are the rounded mountains of southern Austria. To the east lie Špik and Škrlatica.

The return route retraces your steps back down to the **Vršič pass** road.

# WALK 7

*Vitranc/Ciprnik*

| | |
|---|---|
| **Start/finish** | Church, Kranjska Gora |
| **Distance** | 15km |
| **Total ascent** | 640m (from top of 1st chairlift) |
| **Total descent** | 930m |
| **Grade** | 2/3 |
| **Time** | 4½–5hrs (from top of 1st chairlift) |
| **Maps** | 1:30,000 Kranjska Gora, 1:25,000 Triglav |
| **Refreshments** | Dom v Planici (detour) |
| **Note** | The chairlift to Vitranc is not open every day even in the high season, so check with the Tourist Information Office or nearby notices. In 2014 the second chairlift was no longer in use, and it is unlikely it will ever be reopened. Instead, it's about a 45–60min walk from the top of the first chairlift, climbing steeply up the line of the old second chairlift to the ridge. |

This is a beautiful walk to an excellent viewpoint, and is a good route for orienting yourself within the area. The walk follows the ridge of the obvious hill to the west of Kranjska Gora; ski slopes are ranged along its lower slopes. On the ascent the described route makes use of a chairlift, so the walk can be shortened or lengthened according to whether the chairlift is used. The main walk along the ridge from the top of the second chairlift to the viewpoint at Ciprnik (1746m) takes about 50mins one way; to follow the descent from Ciprnik to Kranjska Gora described here allow 2½–3hrs.

▸ From the church walk west along the main street of shops for about 500m to the ski slopes. The chairlift to Vitranc is the furthest west of the string of ski lifts. From the top of the first lift it is only a short walk across to the bottom station of the second one. If the second chairlift is not operating, take the path which follows its line, climbing up steeply to reach the wooded ridge in about 45mins, and turn right to start the walk along it.

See the route map in Walk 5.

The path is very obvious throughout, so the absence of waymarks is not a problem. It passes through a beautiful forest of pine, larch and beech, and between the still and silent trees you get occasional glimpses of the views to come. ◂

Notice the large ant-hills made of pine needles to the side of the path.

The summit of **Vitranc** (1638m) passes unremarked among the undulations of the ridge. The last steep section to **Ciprnik** (1746m) seems almost out of character with the level shady forest path; the route suddenly emerges from the forest and onto more open land with rocky steps and dwarf pine. There is a little viewpoint on a shelf of the path, not far below the summit, which looks directly down on the emerald pools of Zelenci, and in another 20m the waters of Jasna Jezero come into view below to the left. Continue up the last short rocky section, which is steep but with no real difficulties.

**Ciprnik** is a justifiably popular hill and the view is spectacular. In the Planica valley far below you can see the ski jumps and the Tamar dom. Jalovec, looking like a magnificent single crystal, bars the

*Ciprnik summit gives fine panoramic views of the Planica valley with Jalovec (Walk 15) at its head*

head of the valley, with Ponca to its right. The ridge joining them forms the border with Italy. East from Jalovec are Velika and Mala Mojstrovka. Razor and Stenar make a foreground to Triglav, which appears somewhat subdued by the nearer peaks. Down below is Kranjska Gora and the whole sweep of the Zgornjesavska dolina. To the north are the Karavanke and the lower hills of eastern Austria beyond. Below lies the village of Podkoren, with the Korensko sedlo (Wurzenpass) snaking up behind.

▸ To continue the walk reverse the route from the summit for about 10–15mins until you see a path dropping down to the left, with a sign to Planica painted on a tree. The path descends, at times steeply, through the wood, following the edge of crags falling to the Planica valley. There are good views through the trees of amazingly complex limestone rock scenery, with Ponca behind and the sentinel of Jalovec standing guard. After about 15mins the path veers away from the edge back into the woods where it continues to descend, following waymarks.

If you wish you can return the same way from the summit and take the chairlift back down.

At around 1350m, just above the height of the topmost ski jump, the path divides at a small cairn and an arrow painted on a large white rock. Either path will take you down to Planica, the left one zigzagging down to the valley floor to a point about 10mins walk from the sports centre. The recommended route takes the right-hand path, which traverses the hillside for about 5mins before beginning to zigzag down on the far (north) side of another, smaller, side valley full of strange rock scenery, with clefts, gullies, arêtes and needles. A short detour from the path brings you to a viewpoint looking directly across to the ski jumps overlooking the floor of the valley that in winter is a wonderful complex of cross-country skiing routes.

The path comes out directly behind the **sports centre** (about 1hr 15mins from Ciprnik summit). ▸ From here follow Walk 9 (Tamar) back to Kranjska Gora.

A short detour following the track east from the sports centre takes you to the ski jumps, and to Dom v Planici for refreshments.

# WALK 8

*Sleme*

| | |
|---|---|
| **Start/finish** | Top of Vršič pass |
| **Distance** | 5.5km; 13km via Slatnica saddle; 11.5km via Grlo |
| **Total ascent/descent** | 300m; 1100m via Slatnica saddle or Grlo |
| **Grade** | 2 (both extensions are grade 3) |
| **Time** | 2½–3hrs; 4½–5hrs via Slatnica saddle or Grlo |
| **Maps** | 1:30,000 Kranjska Gora, 1:25,000 Triglav |
| **Access** | From Kranjska Gora by bus, car (parking charge) or on foot (follow Walk 5) |

Without doubt this is one of the most beautiful walks in this book. The height gain from the top of the Vršič pass is relatively modest, but it is still enough to give a sense of going into the high mountains. The route is delightful in every way, with a new vista around each corner, and a lovely sense of secrecy as you turn away from the bustle of the day-trippers in the Vršič area. The path crosses high-alpine meadows among the white limestone rock before rising to the summit of Slemenova špica (1911m).

Just below the summit is a high pasture which gives stunning views of Jalovec reflected in three or four tiny pools. It is a lovely place to sit for a while and soak up the sun and the scenery. The only disadvantage is that if you go at a weekend or at peak holiday time you may find that most of Slovenia is there with you!

There are two possibilities for extending the walk and returning to Kranjska Gora via Tamar and the Planica valley. The first option over the Slatnica saddle offers alpine scenery below the north walls of Mojstrovka and Travnik that is unsurpassed, and the going is generally easier compared with the second option – the less well-maintained Grlo path. Both take about 4hrs back to Kranjska Gora.

See the route map in Walk 5.

◂ At the top of the Vršič pass, look for a metal sign on the right saying Sleme 1hr 30mins, with an arrow to the right and a waymark on a rock. The route soon enters the dwarf pine, climbing steadily up to the right. Cross several quite steep scree gullies on the stable path to reach the saddle of **Vratica** (1799m) after about 30mins. At the saddle the path divides; left leads to the Hanzova pot, a difficult protected route on the north face of Mala Mojstrovka (Walk 10), and right leads to Sleme. ▶

It is worth lingering here for a few moments; it is a very attractive area with dwarf pine and larch trees beneath the crags of Mojstrovka.

Take the Sleme path, which descends slightly at first and then bears left to reach a very pleasant balcony section after about 10mins, with wonderful views to the Mala Pišnica valley, Ciprnik, the Karavanke and the mountains of Austria beyond. After about 500m the path crosses the top of a large scree gully which falls steeply down to the right. The summit of Slemenova špica is now visible ahead. Just before you start to climb again, a path heads down to Tamar on the right, signed Grlo – this is the route for extending the walk and returning to Kranjska Gora on the Grlo path).

Continue straight ahead on the waymarked path which becomes rockier and begins to ascend. At a junction (the extension via the Slatnica saddle starts here) bear right and climb steeply for a short distance to reach the open pasture with its tiny pools about 10mins below the summit. The beauty of the surrounding mountain scenery makes this a lovely place to relax for a while, and

*The beautiful high pastures of Sleme*

while it can often be busy, there are views enough for everyone. Continue easily to the summit of **Slemenova špica** where the slopes fall away on all sides to give views of Tamar, almost vertically below, and the mountains of the north-west Julian Alps.

The walk back to the **Vršič pass** takes about 1hr.

### Extension via the Slatnica saddle

Retrace your steps to the junction where the last steep pull of the path heads up to the pools, and turn right. After about 100m reach a large boulder with two memorial plaques on it, and continue a short distance past it to reach the **Slatnica saddle** (1815m). At the col a path goes left that skirts the scree at the foot of Mala Mojstrovka's steep north face. Follow a sign for Tamar Črnez 2hr from the saddle and begin to descend the other side, with excellent views of the north wall of the ridge extending from Mala Mojstrovka and Travnik all the way to Jalovec.

The path descends pleasant grassy slopes through small open glades and stands of old larch. After 15–20mins arrive at a group of boulders. ◄ The path passes the boulders to the right and continues down, the beautiful flowers combining with the mountains in a backdrop of classic alpine scenery. Pass a waymark on a tree and cross a scree-filled watercourse, shortly followed by a second one. Another 10mins of descent through the woods brings you to the top of the steep ravine of the **Tamarski slapovi** (Tamar waterfalls), known locally as Črna voda (black water).

A scramble up the largest makes for an impressive picnic stop below the north face of Travnik, with the crystal-shaped rock spire of Jalovec forming a beautiful backdrop.

Descend steeply into this ravine, skirting the foot of the cliffs, with a view of the waterfall in the corner. Despite the low altitude, snow often lies in this gully until late in the summer. The path turns right and continues straight down, keeping to the right-hand side of the gully; the loose rock requires care. Towards the bottom the path bears to the right as it skirts below crags and another waterfall (this is a popular ice-climbing area in the winter) before it heads down once more alongside a man-made dyke, built to help prevent flood damage when Črna voda is in spate. Continue following cairns and waymarks across stony ground for about 100m and then join a more obvious broad path heading towards **Dom v Tamarju**. Follow Walk 9 (Tamar) to return to Kranjska Gora.

**Extension via Grlo**

Retrace your steps to where the Grlo path (signed to Tamar) leaves the main route to the left. The path descends easily at first, through ancient larch trees with crags to the left. After about 30mins reach a gully filled with loose scree to your left. The path steepens as it descends the wall of the gully, protected with steel cables. The cable section is about 25m and is not too difficult, with the main danger being loose rock. Ignore a path going straight down the right-hand side, and follow a waymarked trail which leads across the gully and loose scree before reaching easier ground again and descending through woods to the tree-clad col at the top of the Grlo gully. A signpost on a tree says 'Tamar 45mins' and the path now bears west.

About 100m below the Grlo col on the Mala Pišnica side, in a stand of larch, is one of the biggest **larch trees** in Slovenia, still alive in spite of losing its top. Its girth is 422cm and it is around 1030 years old.

After about 5mins in the forest the route drops down into a big wide gully – the **Grlo** ('throat' or 'gullet') – with impressive crags on both sides and good views down to the Tamar dom on the valley floor. The descent keeps mostly to the right-hand side of the gully for about two-thirds of the way before criss-crossing a couple of times near the bottom. Great care should be taken as there is a lot of loose rock, particularly in the lower section, where water erosion has added to the difficult terrain. The route continues down the scree and boulders that fan out from the base of the gully, and meets the forest track about 10mins beyond Dom v Tamarju. Turn right to follow Walk 9 (Tamar) back to **Kranjska Gora**.

# WALK 9

*Tamar and Planica*

| | |
|---|---|
| **Start/finish** | Church in Kranjska Gora |
| **Distance** | 20km |
| **Total ascent/descent** | 300m |
| **Grade** | 1 |
| **Time** | 4–5hrs |
| **Maps** | 1:30,000 Kranjska Gora, 1:25,000 Triglav |
| **Refreshments** | Dom v Planici, Dom v Tamarju |

This pleasant walk takes you on easy tracks through beautiful alpine scenery of mountains and flower meadows to Planica, where the biggest natural ski jumps in the world (built to follow the slope of the mountainside) rise high above the valley floor. The route continues through mixed forest to Dom v Tamarju, a picturesque mountain hut with a superb view of Jalovec, and then visits Izvir Nadiže, the source of the short Nadiža river, which soon disappears underground to resurface at Zelenci (Walk 1).

See the route map in Walk 5.

◀ Walk west from the church, past the shops towards the ski lifts. Where the main road bends sharply right, continue straight ahead past the chairlifts and parking places. The road soon narrows to become a cycle track which was once the railway, and cars are allowed for access only. After about 2km, at a house which was once the railway station at **Podkoren**, a right turn goes to the village which can be seen a few hundred metres away beyond the main road. Continue west along the cycle track for about another 100m to a wooden signpost, and then take a rough track bearing left, gradually rising away from the cycle track.

At a fork bear left, signed (local) route 9, and continue across the Podkoren ski slopes, masquerading as flower meadows in the summer. Where the track turns left and follows the chairlift up the slope, continue straight ahead on a slightly rougher track across the fields, with Ponca (2228m) dominating the view ahead.

Idyllic pastures in the lower Planica valley

As the track begins to approach the forest, it passes through a second belt of trees and bushes and meets a track curving up and down. Cross this track and continue straight ahead on a narrow path, just to the left of a hazel hedgerow, marked by a wooden post. A dry river bed comes into view on the right. Continue past a small wooden building and begin to ascend slightly, heading into the forest. Emerge from the trees and turn right down a grassy slope; after a short distance arrive at the river bank and bear left, following a marker for (local) route 9.

Continue on this rougher path, ignoring side paths and keeping the river bed on your right, for about 5mins to reach another open pasture by an old stone building. The path skirts the edge of the meadow and re-enters the trees. After about 30m reach a junction, where you turn left onto a broad track and continue south through woods before crossing another open meadow with a ski lift to reach a large **sports centre**. Bear right past the buildings and reach a road where you turn right and soon reach a T-junction opposite the winter sports complex at **Planica**, with its massive ski jumps (1hr 20mins from Kranjska Gora).

The **Planica ski jumps** are a national icon in Slovenia; the World Cup ski-flying competition held every year is a four-day festival that draws enormous crowds. Planica saw the first 100m jump in 1936, and in 1994 the first skier passed 200m; records continue to be broken here. The area continues to be developed with more facilities for winter sports.

Turn left up the road past the ski jumps and the **Dom v Planici** to reach the end of the vehicular valley road just before a wide dry torrent bed. Two forest trails can be seen on the other side of the watercourse; both of these go through the forest to reach Tamar in about 45mins. Take the right hand trail. (The left-hand track is used as the supply route to the hut.)

As you approach the attractive **Dom v Tamarju**, with a small chapel just in front of it, you can see Izvir Nadiže (the true source of the river Sava) up to the right, and the mighty crystal-like profile of Jalovec at the head of the valley. ▶ A track crosses the planina to the foot of **Izvir Nadiže**, where a path leads up steeply to the source with the help of a steel handrail. It is well worth the 30min detour from the hut to see the crystal-clear waters gushing wildly from the dark rock.

The ascent of Jalovec via Walk 15 starts from here.

Return to **Kranjska Gora** down the service road for the hut (not open to private vehicles).

## WALK 10

*Mala and Velika Mojstrovka*

| | |
|---|---|
| **Start/finish** | Top of Vršič pass |
| **Distance** | 5km |
| **Total ascent/descent** | 720m |
| **Grade** | 3 |
| **Time** | 3½–4hrs |
| **Maps** | 1:30,000 Kranjska Gora, 1:25,000 Triglav, 1:25,000 Bovec-Trenta |
| **Access** | By car: park at the top of the pass (parking charge); by bus to the top of the pass from Kranjska Gora; on foot from Kranjska Gora (see Walk 5) |

Mala Mojstrovka (2332m) is a wonderful introduction to the high mountains in the Kranjska Gora area. Velika Mojstrovka (2366m) lies close by, and while it appears an attractive easy extension to the day, in reality its ascent is not so straightforward or pleasant; it is included for the sake of completeness, and to give some guidance for those who can't resist its lure.

The bulk of the height gain can be achieved by car or bus to the top of the Vršič pass, so this is an ideal mountain walk for the beginning of a holiday, allowing both body and head to acclimatise to the area. The views are quite extensive and give a measure of the complexity of the Julian Alps range and an opportunity for orientation. There is a striking contrast between the lush valley and the bare rock, which at first glance looks as though there's nothing living on it – yet during the summer there is a surprising number of flowers.

See the route map in Walk 5.

◀ The route starts from the top of the Vršič pass, at the kiosk on the right-hand side as you approach from Kranjska Gora. Bear right behind the kiosk to a red sign: Mala Mojstrovka 2hrs to the right, and Jalovec 5hrs to the left. Follow the path to the right as it meanders enjoyably up through dwarf pine, quickly gaining height and turning left after about 10mins. Continue for 20mins or so over the dwarf pine roots entangled in the path, before crossing loose rock and scree and arriving at the bottom of a wide gully.

Climb steeply over the loose ground before reaching the final section, which can be somewhat slippery due to erosion, and therefore has a cable and a few steel pegs for protection. From the small grassy saddle (1983m, named Vratca on the 1:25,000 Triglav map) at the top of the gully there are good views of the Vršič pass and the mountains stretching into the distance both north and south.

The path turns right at the top of the gully and follows waymarks over some steepish rocky steps intermingled with easier-angled sections to regain the edge – more an escarpment than a ridge – after about 20mins at a little group of five or six cairns. From here a track bears left, but keep to the right and ascend quite close to the escarpment edge as countless boots have caused many deviations from the left-hand route.

The summit is now about 40mins away, over broken and slabby, though not very steep, ground. There are waymarks painted on the rocks, and you should follow them as much as possible to avoid causing more erosion. Continue up past the group of large boulders which lie just below the summit of **Mala Mojstrovka** on the right, with the craggier top of Velika Mojstrovka to the left.

From the top there are extensive **views** in all directions, showing the great expanse and complexity of the Julian Alps massif, as well as the nearby mountains of Austria and Italy. To the west is Velika Mojstrovka, with Mangart beyond, and then Ponca, with the peaks of north-east Italy behind. To the north are Peč and the Karavanke ridge, with the

*The limestone escarpment with Velika Mojstrovka on the left and Mala Mojstrovka on the right*

view extending into Austria. To the north-east the view is straight down Mala Pišnica to Jezero Jasna, marking the edge of Kranjska Gora. On the opposite side of the Vršič pass are Prisank, Špik and Škrlatica. To the south lies the Trenta valley and the huge pyramid of Bavški Grintavec. Only Jalovec is missing to the west, hidden behind the bulk of Velika Mojstrovka.

The climb to Velika Mojstrovka takes about 25–30mins. However, the route is not as easy as it may appear; small changes over recent years caused by minor rock slides and freeze-thaw action have made it a little more difficult. Although occasionally there are some small cairns, there are no waymarks on this section so it is essential to retrace your steps very carefully to avoid a slip or becoming cragfast. The route crosses the saddle and takes a line up the obvious broken gully which bears somewhat left to the skyline, then turns right over easy-angled broken slabs to the summit of **Velika Mojstrovka**, which also has extensive views, now including Jalovec.

Very carefully retrace your steps to the bottom of the broken gully where you will notice a path that continues down across bouldery ground before reaching rock and scree; from here look for waymarks on the numerous eroded path lines mentioned earlier, that lead back to the top of the broad gully and on down to the **Vršič pass**.

## WALK 11

*Mala Mojstrovka via the Hanzova pot*

| | |
|---|---|
| **Start/finish** | Top of Vršič pass |
| **Distance** | 4.5km |
| **Total ascent/descent** | 720m |
| **Grade** | 4 |
| **Time** | 4–5hrs |
| **Maps** | 1:30,000 Kranjska Gora, 1:25,000 Triglav, 1:25,000 Bovec-Trenta |
| **Access** | By car: park at the top of the pass (parking charge); by bus to the top of the pass from Kranjska Gora; on foot from Kranjska Gora (see Walk 5) |

This is an enjoyable, though difficult, alternative to the normal route (Walk 10) up Mala Mojstrovka. The Hanzova pot (*pot* means 'path') was put in place between the wars, when the state border ran across the Vršič, thus making the southern approach inaccessible for Slovene mountaineers. It ascends the north face via a well-equipped route that offers an excellent short day from the summit of the Vršič. It is a difficult and exposed ascent, and a helmet and self-belaying equipment are strongly recommended if you want to tackle this walk.

See the route map in Walk 5.

◂ At the top of the Vršič pass, look for a metal sign on the right saying Sleme 1hr30, with an arrow to the right and a waymark on a rock. The route soon enters the dwarf pine, climbing steadily up to the right. Cross several quite steep scree gullies on the stable path to reach the saddle of **Vratica** (1799m) after about 30mins. At Vratica turn left, signed Mojstrovka, and follow the gently rising stony path for about 15mins before heading up to the left, following waymarks, towards some large boulders at the foot of the crag. There is a metal plate with the route name (Hanzova pot) on one of the boulders.

The line of the route is obvious; the rocks form a broad rightward-sloping ramp up the crag. The first 100m or so is on good rock, quite steep and well equipped with pegs and cables. The route then continues on slightly easier ground, albeit still exposed and needing care because of loose rock and stones. Reach a narrow ledge which traverses steep rock before arriving at another ramp. This is followed by more exposed scrambling and an ascent of a short, narrow chimney bristling with pegs.

Continue up more sloping rock leading right, and then bear left up a mixture of steep scrambling and easier ground to reach an exposed ledge heading diagonally up and left. Follow this and then continue ascending the steep rocks in a series of short zigzags. Eventually reach a very exposed narrow ledge, which makes a long rightward traverse across the face. The route then heads up again, with more enjoyable scrambling, until finally the angle eases and you bear right and continue over broken rocky ground,

*Stratified ledges high on the Hanzova pot*

still quite steeply, for another 20–25mins before it levels out and turns towards the summit rocks. Waymarks lead you to a narrow cleft in the rock which you ascend, followed by more enjoyable scrambling with occasional steel pegs to arrive directly on the summit of **Mala Mojstrovka**.

From the summit, follow waymarks that direct you south before bearing slightly left (east) to gain the sloping escarpment that eventually leads to the obvious little col or saddle marked as Vratca on some maps. From here, turn left and descend the steep eroded path to gain easier ground on a good path that leads through the dwarf pine to reach the road on the Vršič pass.

## WALK 12

*The Vrata valley*

| | |
|---|---|
| **Start/finish** | Supermarket in Mojstrana, 13km east of Kranjska Gora |
| **Distance** | 20km |
| **Total ascent/descent** | 350m |
| **Grade** | 2 |
| **Time** | 6hrs |
| **Maps** | 1:30,000 Kranjska Gora, 1:25,000 Triglav |
| **Refreshments** | Koča pri Peričniku and Aljažev dom |
| **Access** | Buses run hourly from the bus station in Kranjska Gora to Mojstrana; check the times in the Tourist Information Office or at the bus stop. |

The route up to the Aljažev dom is a delightful walk up the Vrata valley, gateway to the northern Julian Alps, with something of interest around every corner. Don't be tempted to simply walk up the road, which is relatively dull apart from the Peričnik waterfall; the Triglavska Bistrica Pot was developed in 2006 to take advantage of local tracks and is well supplied with information boards in Slovene and English, explaining the fascinating geology and wildlife of the area.

If you have time, make sure you visit the Alpine Museum in Mojstrana, which covers the history of mountaineering in Slovenia's Alps.

Walk along the road for about 10min, passing a Triglav National Park (TNP) sign, to reach a couple of attractive houses at **Pri Rosu**, and just beyond them a small weir with sluices. To the right is an information board about the TNP and the Triglavska Bistrica Pot (TBP), with parking room for a few cars. Cross the pretty green **river Bistrica** on a footbridge, and turn right along the river bank on a narrow path which enters the woods. The path becomes narrower as it traverses a steep section a few metres above the river, but soon after this it joins a broader track by a bridge, and you continue straight ahead.

Soon pass the first information boards and continue up the track, through extremely attractive forest, carpeted with pink cyclamen and full of birdsong. After about 20mins reach a TBP sign directing you right across a footbridge to Slap Peričnik (Peričnik waterfall). On the other side of the river rejoin the valley road, turning left, and walk up here for just over 5mins to reach **Koča pri Peričniku** and a small car park at the base of the waterfall.

Although you can see the **waterfall** from the road, it's well worth the detour to go and have a proper look. The upper fall is 16m and the lower one 52m, and you can actually walk behind the lower one. In winter it forms a vast curtain of icicles across the cliff.

After the waterfall the route continues along the road for about 250m before starting to climb steeply, and in another 100m leave the road following an unmarked path left into the wood. The path begins to descend towards the river and then continues along the bank, joining a wider track coming in from the left. This area contains many springs which flow down to join the river.

After about 15mins the path begins to climb up a little from the river and continues to traverse the hillside before passing another group of information boards. In another 200m the path merges with another track

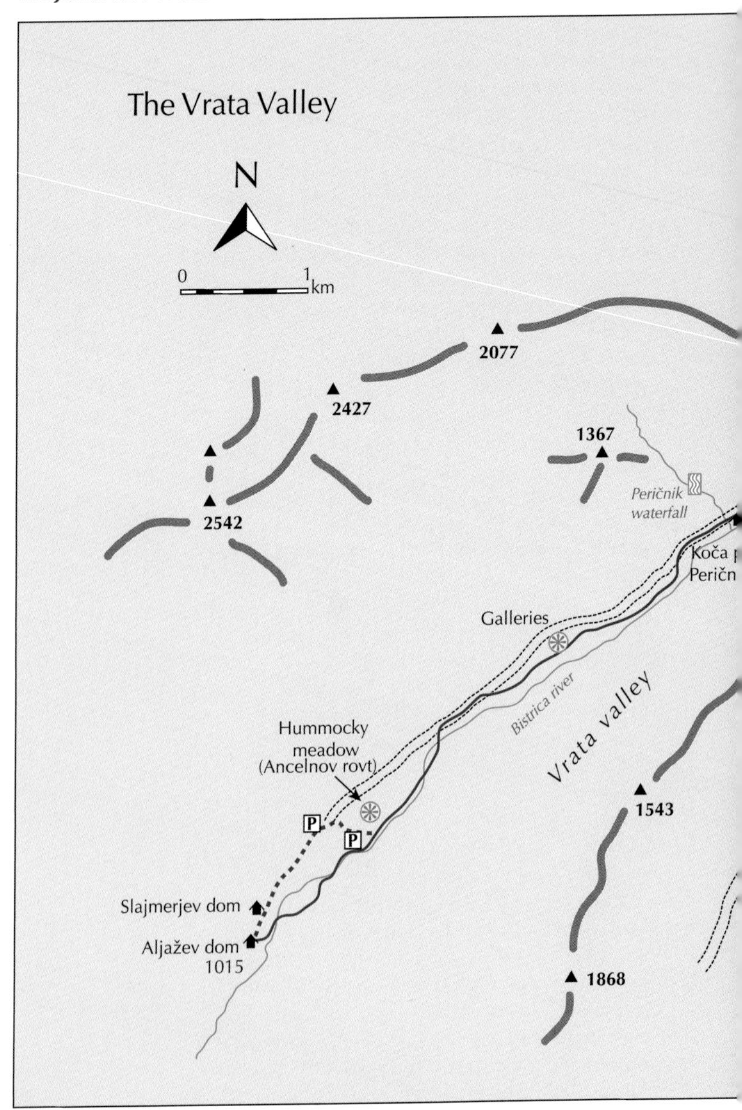
The Vrata Valley
N
0
1
km
2077
2427
1367
2542
Peričnik waterfall
Koča p
Peričn
Galleries
Bistrica river
Vrata valley
Hummocky meadow (Ancelnov rovt)
P
P
1543
Slajmerjev dom
Aljažev dom
1015
1868

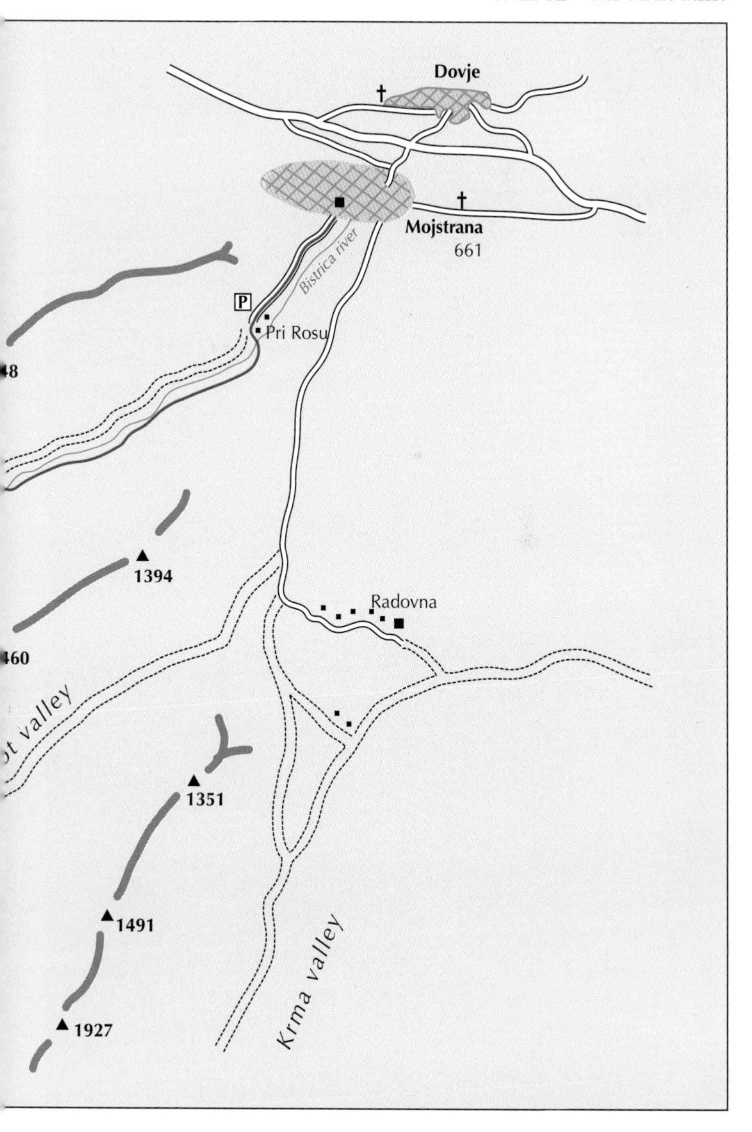
Dovje
Mojstrana
661
Bistrica river
P
Pri Rosu
1394
Radovna
valley
1351
1491
Krma valley
1927

Slap Peričnik

and you continue in the same direction. In another 10–15mins reach a landslip gully and follow the path up its right side for about 100m then cross it to reach another gully and again follow the path up its right edge to reach a rough forest track. Turn left along it for about 130m passing a signed path heading right and just beyond it reach a fork.

Take the right hand fork, with an information board about the **galleries**, shallow caves in the cliffs, now high above the river. The way leads you beneath the galleries, with the cliffs above the path sometimes dripping with water. The forest relents a little here so you can see not only the hillside of Mlinarica opposite, but also, slightly ahead, the big pyramid of Cmir with its steep rock walls. Up to the left there's a small 'window' in the ridge of Rjavina.

After the galleries continue walking along a very pleasant broad forest path, passing an old ruined building at the Poldov rovt planina and in just over 5mins rejoin the road and turn left. At a bend in the road, the summit of Triglav comes into view with its ice patch above the north wall – the remnant of the mountain's glacier. After about 5mins you are directed off the road again to the left. The river is now greatly reduced in size, and you ford it on stepping stones.

On the true right bank follow a grassy track through the trees, and in about 100m come to some more information boards in an open grassy area – these ones concern the fascinating wood ants and their nests. After reading the boards cross the river bed on a wooden footbridge and turn left on a pretty woodland path, signed Aljažev dom. Walk along the path parallel to the road for about 10min, then come to an open area, the 'hummocky meadow' at **Ancelnov rovt**, with one or two buildings, where there is a truly superb view of Triglav's north wall. Walk across the meadow, then enter woods for a short distance and pass a weekend house before reaching a broader track at a T-junction. ▶

You could also turn right here and in a short distance rejoin the road; turn left to walk through the big TNP car park to Aljažev dom (about 10mins). The first big building (Šlajmerjev dom) on the right after the car park is private.

Turn left, and in 50m reach a car park area where you turn right, signed Aljažev dom. Cross the dry river bed and in about 5mins pass another weekend house. In another 2–3mins arrive at an open area where you can see **Aljažev dom** (1015m) through the trees on the right a short distance away. Retrace your outward route back to the start.

## WALK 13

*Jerebikovec*

| | |
|---|---|
| **Start/finish** | Bus stop close to Mojstrana, 13km east of Kranjska Gora |
| **Distance** | 9.5km |
| **Total ascent/descent** | 890m |
| **Grade** | 2/3 |
| **Time** | 4–5hrs |
| **Maps** | 1:30,000 Kranjska Gora |
| **Access** | Buses run hourly from the bus station in Kranjska Gora to Mojstrana; check the times in the Tourist Information Office or at the bus stop. |
| **Parking** | On the road to Radovna/Bled, there is space to park a small number of cars on the verge just before the start of the path up to Jerebikovec and Planina Mežakla. |

Jerebikovec is a fine hill lying to the south of Mojstrana, about 13km east of Kranjska Gora. At 1593m it provides an outstanding view of Triglav and its surrounding summits, which terminate the three beautiful valleys of Krma, Kot and Vrata. The walk climbs through beautiful forest to an old planina, which nature is starting to reclaim, before reaching the summit.

Just above the road is a monument to **Jakob Aljaž** (1845–1927), who was the priest in Dovje and a pioneer of mountaineering in Slovenia. He bought the summit of Triglav for a nominal sum to keep it in Slovene ownership, and was influential in the building of many paths and huts, including the one which bears his name (Aljažev dom).

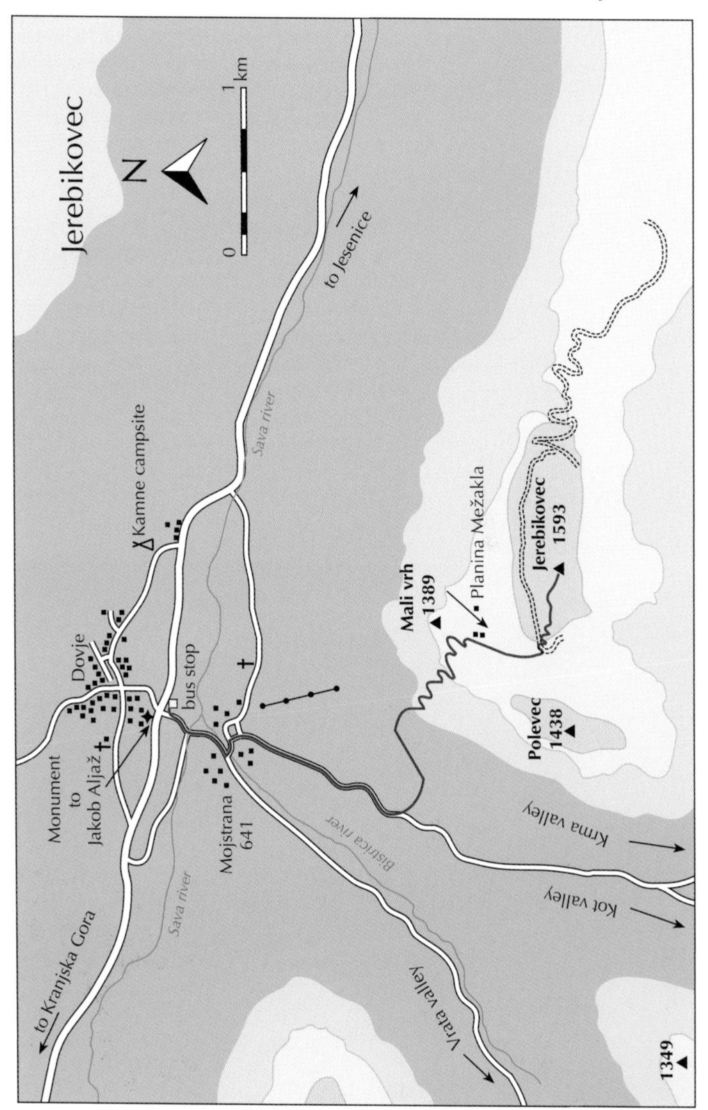
Jerebikovec
N
0
1 km
to Jesenice
Sava river
Kamne campsite
Dovje
bus stop
Monument to Jakob Aljaž
Mojstrana 641
Mali vrh 1389
Planina Mežakla
Jerebikovec 1593
Polevec 1438
Bistrica river
Krma valley
Kot valley
Sava river
to Kranjska Gora
Vrata valley
1349

From the bus stop, head down the lane towards Mojstrana. Cross the river **Sava Dolinka** on the road bridge and continue in the same direction through the village to a left turn, signed Radovna and Bled. Cross the **river Bistrica** and follow the road round to the left past the tourist information and post office, then take a right turn signed Bled. The minor road climbs steeply between the houses and bears right before it becomes broader. Continue up the road, and after about 500m pass a large metal sign saying Triglav National Park. Another 400m after the sign, look for a narrow path and painted signs saying Jerebikovec 2hrs 30mins and Mežakla, which is set back about 15m from the road on the left.

The path climbs up into the woods, and after about 150m bears left. Continue climbing for 30–40mins through the trees to reach the edge of a forested ridge. There is a good view here looking down to the village of Dovje on the other side of the valley, with the Karavanke hills behind. The path turns right and continues on

*Looking south up the Krma and Kot valleys to Triglav*

through fine beech and spruce forest for a further 30–40mins before arriving at **Planina Mežakla**, where there is a bench and a partisan memorial. The planina was abandoned in 1969.

The path continues beyond the planina, signed Jerebikovec. It soon joins a broader track which ascends gently for about 250m to reach a level col. Turn left and almost immediately take a path on the right going up into the woods, again signed Jerebikovec. Climb up through the woods for about 15mins onto the west ridge and continue along the forested crest, now rockier in places. The path suddenly emerges on to the summit of **Jerebikovec**, clear of trees, with its wonderful panorama.

As well as a magnificent view of Triglav, the peak of Stol, the highest summit of the Karavanke, is visible to the east, although other peaks of the range are somewhat obscured by trees. There is a **small bivouac hut** on the top, built by a local enthusiast, which is constructed around the trunks of two old trees.

The descent to **Mojstrana** is by the same route.

## WALK 14

*Prisank*

| | |
|---|---|
| **Start/finish** | Top of Vršič pass |
| **Distance** | 9km |
| **Total ascent/descent** | 940m |
| **Grade** | 4 |
| **Time** | 5½–6hrs |
| **Maps** | 1:30,000 Kranjska Gora, 1:25,000 Triglav, 1:25,000 Bovec-Trenta |
| **Access** | By car: park at the top of the pass (parking charge); by bus to the top of the pass from Kranjska Gora; on foot from Kranjska Gora (see Walk 5) |

Prisank (2547m), also known as Prisojnik, lies to the east of the Vršič pass. It is a huge and complex mountain with many routes on it. Its east–west ridge dominates the skyline as seen from Kranjska Gora, its most obvious feature from here being the east 'window'. In fact there are two windows on Prisank, and the route described here goes directly past the other, larger, western one (Prednje Prisankovo okno – 'the front Prisank window'). The route is not overly difficult and all the exposed sections are well protected. It is nevertheless a serious mountain route, so appropriate gear and experience are essential.

At the top of the Vršič pass, take the gravel service road leading up left past **Tičarjev dom**. Walk up the broad track and soon reach a bend and turn sharp left. A sign at the bend says Poštarski dom na Vršiču 5min, Prisank 3hrs and Razor 6hrs. Follow the gravel road as it passes between two old military defences – a huge gun emplacement to the right and a smaller pill box to the left. As you pass them and round a corner, arrive at an information board and a terrific view of Prisank's north face.

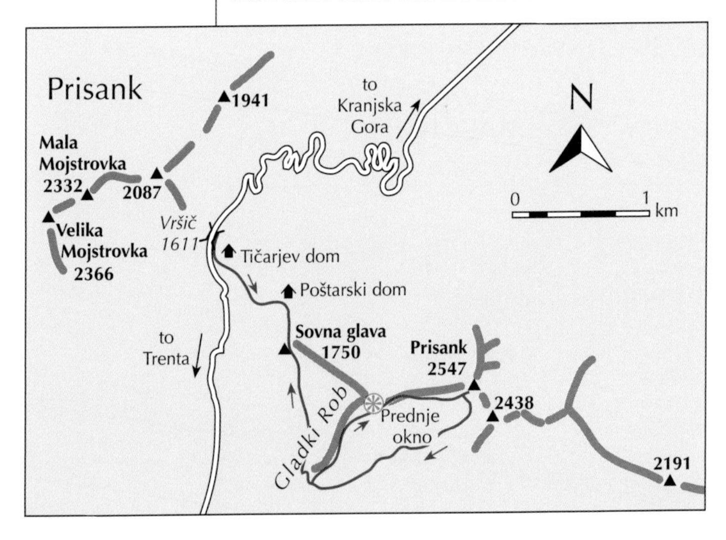

The gravel road continues on a short distance to the dom, but leave it here to the right on a narrow path signed to Prisojnik (the other name for the mountain) and Razor. ▶ Carry on through dwarf pine and then over short grass as you pass close to the little top of **Sovna Glava**, and descend to arrive at a group of boulders at a level saddle.

Another path also on the right, signed Prisojnik via Skozi Okno 3hrs 30mins, descends into the larch trees, but this leads to a difficult protected route up the north face.

The waymarked path begins to ascend diagonally across fairly extensive screes before reaching the lower rocks of the south-east ridge. Continue on, between dwarf pine again, a short distance to a junction. Turn left, signed Prisojnik – Grabenska Vratevna pot 2hrs, and begin ascending the **Gladki rob** ('smooth edge'). The path climbs very steeply at first, and after about 15–20mins the dwarf pine thins, then ceases abruptly, and you continue on the stony waymarked path. ▶

There are excellent views to the left of the crags that form the huge western spur. Mangart, Jalovec and Mala and Velika Mojstrovka are on display, while through the gap in the Vršič pass you can see into Austria.

The path keeps quite close to the left-hand side of the grassy edge, climbing steadily before bearing diagonally right as it approaches the crags. With unexpected suddenness you reach the lip of the window (**Prednje okno**). It is absolutely vast – a cathedral-sized gaping cavern, with the wind sometimes rushing up through it.

The route now leads up rocks on the right-hand side. After about 50m of easy scrambling on good rock, reach the first protected section, a steel cable heading up towards the ridge proper. Continue to follow the cables, first left and then right onto the ridge. It is quite steep and somewhat exposed in places but is well equipped.

Follow the waymarks along the ridge, initially on the left (north) side, just below the crest, which gives thrilling views of the Vršič lying almost vertically below. Some easy scrambling over rock steps helps keep the mind and body focused, but steel cables and pegs secure any difficulties.

The route continues, becoming easier as height is gained, and bears more to the right-hand side as the summit section is approached. The route appears to fork here, and a broad sloping path covered in scree continues down to the right (south gully) – this is the descent route. Continue diagonally up to the left on good rock, and just beyond some steel cables descend a few metres to the top of another cable which heads down. There are signs

*Leaving the summit of Prisank with Razor and Planja behind*

painted on the rock – straight up for Prisojnik (Prisank), and down for Vršič and Okno 2. Continue straight up on fairly steep slabby rock to reach the summit of **Prisank**.

It is 1hr 15mins from the window and 3hrs 30mins total time from Vršič to the summit, and the effort is well worth it. There is a wonderful panorama, including not just the Julian Alps but the Hohe Tauern region of Austria and even the Dolomites in Italy on a good day.

Either retrace the route in its entirety or follow the description below for the descent down the south side of the mountain.

Descend to the painted signs and steel cables. It is possible to head straight down from here, very steeply, following the Vršič and Okno 2 waymarks to reach the south gully. Or you can retrace the route, this time ascending a little at first, and then down to reach the scree-covered sloping descent path passed earlier.

Continue down the steeply sloping path on brittle scree and rock, passing waymarks after a short distance.

Traverse some minor gullies as the path descends over slabby rock and stones, then drop more steeply down the rocky left-hand side of the south gully. After about 100m the path traverses a broad ledge that leads right, across the gully. Continue over loose stony ground, then make a short descent of a rocky nose before suddenly turning right and dropping down through a notch into another smaller gully.

The route continues, bearing right, down a series of gullies with some short sections of steep scrambling, but with all the difficulties well secured. The path keeps to the left-hand side of the final gully and exits onto a rocky grassy spur. Down below you can see the path that traverses the flank of the hill and will take you back to Vršič. Continue down over grass and stones before traversing right, across the lower part of the gully, where the ground becomes easier and finally reaches the level path where you turn right and soon reach the junction of the ascent path at the foot of Gladki rob. Continue straight ahead, retracing your outward steps to the starting point.

## WALK 15

*Jalovec*

| | |
|---|---|
| **Start/finish** | Dom v Tamarju in the Planica valley |
| **Distance** | 12km |
| **Total ascent/descent** | 1540m |
| **Grade** | 4 |
| **Time** | 9–10hrs |
| **Maps** | 1:30,000 Kranjska Gora, 1:25,000 Triglav, 1:25,000 Bovec-Trenta |
| **Access** | You can walk to Dom v Tamarju from Kranjska Gora using Walk 9 in about 2hrs 15mins, or from the bus stop in Rateče in about 1½hrs. You may need to stay overnight at the dom, depending on your pace. |
| **Parking** | At Planica (parking fee). It's 45mins walk from here to the dom. |

Jalovec (2645m) is arguably the most beautiful peak in Slovenia, poised like a giant crystal guarding the head of the Planica valley. It dominates the skyline from the south too, rising proudly above the Trenta and Koritnica valleys, and the statue of the pioneer climber Julius Kugy, on the Trenta side of the Vršič pass, stands with his face turned eternally towards his favourite mountain. Jalovec holds a special place in the hearts of Slovene mountaineers, not least because of its difficulty, which is significant from all directions; it is without doubt one of the more serious routes described in this book, with a helmet, self-belaying equipment and possibly an ice axe all strongly advised.

This circular route is described in a clockwise direction but can be done either way. As described here the ascent involves long sections of steep rock, while the descent, although initially over easier-angled ledges, is covered with loose rock. The choice is yours!

A restored wheel strut stands at the start of the track, part of an American B-24 Liberator bomber that crashed on the Jalovec saddle during the Second World War.

Take the broad path behind Dom v Tamarju at the head of the Planica valley, leading right, into the forest, signed Jalovec, Mangart and Ponca. ◀ After 5mins bear left at a fork onto a narrower track signed Jalovec, zelo zahtevna pot ('very difficult route'). Walk through the woods for about 20mins until the path emerges from the trees, close to the steep walls of Ponca, and continue up the valley, gently ascending. Enter trees again for a short distance, and then begin to climb a little more steeply over gravel and scree. This area is a huge watercourse that drains the upper part of the valley and takes the brunt of torrential flows of rain and winter avalanches. The path fans out here into at least three variations at the foot of a torrent bed, but all soon merge again within 100m on its left-hand side.

Continue up for another 20mins, passing the last of the dwarf pine on the stony track, gradually steepening all the time. In another 20–25mins come to a junction of paths at a waymarked boulder, signed left for Jalovška škrbina 4hrs 30mins and right for Jalovec and Veliki kot 4hrs 30mins. About 20m further right a sign on a boulder says Kotovo sedlo – Jalovec. This marks the descent route if you make the walk in a clockwise direction – an

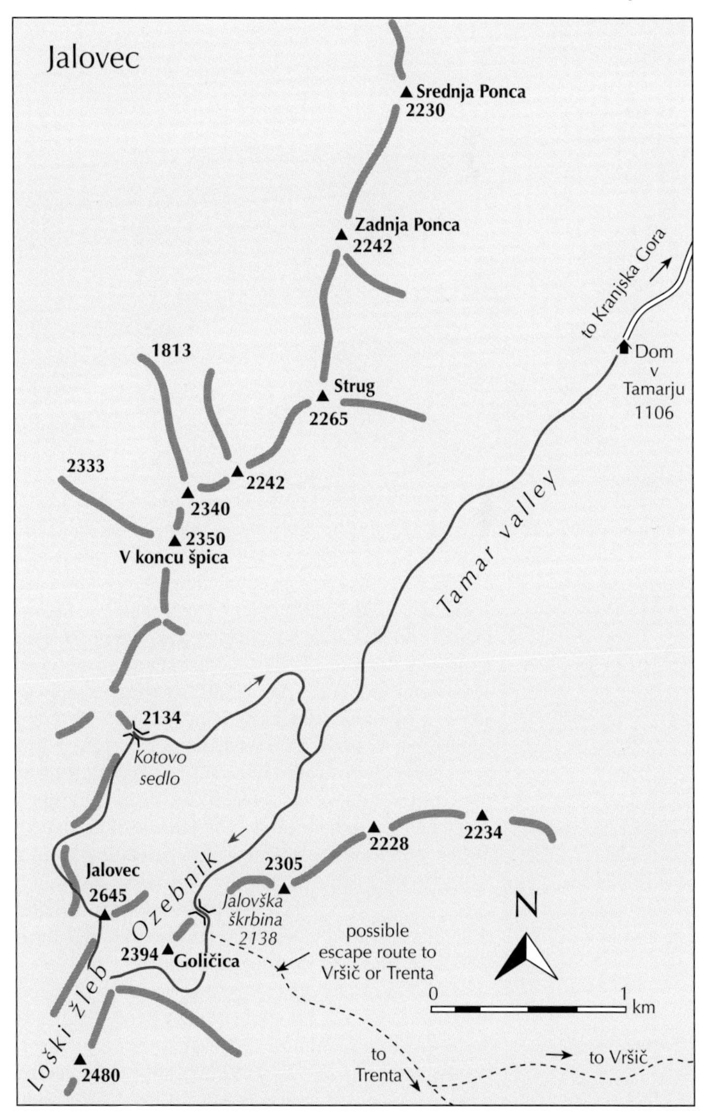
Jalovec
Srednja Ponca
2230
Zadnja Ponca
2242
to Kranjska Gora
Dom
v
Tamarju
1106
1813
Strug
2265
2333
2242
2340
2350
V koncu špica
Tamar valley
2134
Kotovo
sedlo
2228
2234
2305
Jalovec
2645
Ozebnik
Jalovška
škrbina
2138
2394
Goličica
possible
escape route to
Vršič or Trenta
N
0
1
km
Loški žleb
2480
to
Trenta
to Vršič

*Approaching Kotovo sedlo*

obvious broad ramp heading up steeply to the right with a small cave at its foot.

Take the left-hand path, climbing steeply on loose scree below the foot of crags. After about 25–30mins, notice a boulder with a prominent waymark about 25m to the left. Reach the boulder and continue up the steep scree to the foot of the precipitous north face of Jalovec, where a sign says Jalovška škrbina 3hrs to the left and Jalovec, via Kotovo sedlo 3hrs to the right. Keep left, and ascend steeply beneath rock walls on the right side of the Ozebnik couloir for about 100m, to another sign – straight on to Ozebnik, and left for Jalovška škrbina. Take the left, traversing below a large prow of rock that forms a tongue in the middle of the gully. Ascend for about 20m over a rocky rib and then descend, first to the left and then right, assisted by steel pegs, into the gully bed at the foot of the crags on the left-hand side of the couloir. ◄

This is often choked with snow until late in the season, and may require some gymnastic moves to cross.

Reach waymarks and begin to ascend with pegs and metal rungs for aid. The route initially trends right, and then bears left over a mixture of easy broken ground and steep scrambling across quite exposed but protected rock. Ascend a very steep leftward-trending ramp below slightly overhanging rock equipped with abundant metal rungs and pegs, and then continue to zigzag up the face, over gradually easier ground, to reach the col of **Jalovška škrbina** (2138m). To the right is Goličica; the route avoids its rocky summit by climbing across the steep slabs of its east face.

From the col waymarks on a rock lead south, and the path descends slightly for a few minutes to reach a junction, signed Jalovec 2hrs 30mins to the right and Vršič 2hrs 30mins to the left. The left-hand route offers an alternative, easier, descent to Vrišič should the weather close in. Traverse on the stony path to reach the rocks of the east face of Goličica. Waymarks lead up and left initially over easy ground, level or at times even descending slightly, until a steep scramble heads straight up, equipped with steel pegs and cables. Although the climbing is not too difficult there is considerable exposure in places. ▸

Amazingly, even up here Zois' bellflower and Triglav rose cling to the steep rock.

Eventually the gradient relents and the path continues up an easy-angled rocky spur. Ahead are more steep rocks, but before they are reached take a path leading left, following waymarks towards a wide easy-angled scree-filled gully. Continue up the path, making a short zigzag right to avoid some rocky slabs, and reach the mouth of the **Ozebnik couloir**. Although it offers the most direct route, the way is not recommended due to constant stonefall. The views down towards Tamar are excellent however!

Continue along the rim of the couloir to reach a small grassy col between Jalovec and the unnamed subsidiary peak marked as 2413m on the map. From here the route bears right, descending a little, and crosses the head of the **Loški žleb** gully, passing a path heading left to Zavetišče pod Špičkom – the refuge under Špiček. An ice axe could well be required here, as the snow lies late at the head of the gully. Reach the foot of the lower rocks of the summit section of Jalovec and continue easily over rocky ledges, with abundant flowers among the rocks. Although there are no real difficulties, follow the waymarks carefully as it is easy to end up on very tricky ground if you lose your concentration.

*Looking south-west to the Koritnica valley*

Follow a shallow gully with rock steps to reach the crest of the south ridge, with spectacular views of the Koritnica valley and Mangart. Continue along the ridge for about 10mins, keeping to the right (east) side when not on the crest, to reach a notch. Pass through to the left side of the ridge to meet a junction; a sign, Tamar 5hrs, and waymarks indicate the descent route, heading left. Another 5mins or so brings you to the summit of **Jalovec** at 2645m, 5–6hrs from Tamar. Allow yourself a few moments to admire the superb view of the Julian Alps of Slovenia, and the Italian and Austrian hills to the north and west.

The descent follows the north-west ridge; retrace your steps to the junction and follow the sign for Tamar. The route descends scree and rubble-covered ledges with few security aids, so be very careful. Beyond this unpleasant start, the route drops down more steeply to reach a notch in the ridge at the head of a steep gully, which is crossed with the help of a steel cable. This is soon followed by a short steep scramble up better rock to rejoin the crest of the ridge, with magnificent views down the precipitous north walls of Jalovec to Tamar.

Begin descending to the left of the crest. The way continues with a mixture of short steep sections and easier traverses, and then crosses the head of another small couloir, again protected by a steel cable. Continue descending on the left-hand side of the ridge to reach a chimney of about 25m, well equipped with pegs and cables. Descend the chimney, and then continue traversing, on fairly easy ground, with good views to the left of Bavški Grintavec and Rombon, and the village of Log pod Mangartom on the valley floor.

The route then crosses to the right-hand side of the ridge crest, dropping steeply down with pegs and metal rungs set into the rock for about 25m to reach a notch. From here descend to the left side of the crest, following a line of steel cables in a scree-filled gully. At the end of the cable follow waymarks and continue over slightly easier ground to eventually arrive at a pleasant grassy area. Bear right and head down over stone and scree towards the

Kotovo sedlo (saddle) with extremely steep drops to the left of the path. ◂

Mangart dominates the skyline view to the west, while Kotova špica rears up to the north beyond the saddle.

Reach easier ground on the rocky ridge but still with some exposure (a 50m section of the path traverses smooth slabs) and continue along it for about 400m, descending a little and heading towards Kotova špica. Reach a waymarked boulder on the **Kotovo sedlo** (2134m), where a sign says Tamar 2hrs 35mins to the right and Mangart 5hrs down to the left. Turn right, and in about 250m reach another junction. Tamar is signed both left and straight on, the left is marked zelo zahtevna pot ('very difficult route') 2hrs 45mins, and right via po melišču ('via the screes') 2hrs. The right-hand path is a possible alternative route that passes some large boulders before dropping down close to the ascent path not very far below the Ozebnik couloir. It is not recommended because the going is tedious over loose scree and stone, which can seem far more difficult in descent, particularly on the upper part if any late snow is under foot.

The other descent path, although steeper, is worth any extra time it takes because of the more stable ground and secured sections. It also deposits you considerably further down the valley. So turn left and continue over short grass amid stones and boulders for about 15mins before reaching thickets of dwarf pine that mark the top of the descent route. ◂ The path begins to descend with good views down into the Planica valley. Occasional steeper sections are secured with cables, and the path broadens a little and becomes easier as height is lost. There are no real difficulties, in spite of how it appeared from above, but it is steep enough to tax the knees at the end of a long day! Cross an easy-angled slab that water and landslides have recently exposed, and continue on scree to reach the ascent path. Turn left and continue back down the valley to **Dom v Tamarju**.

A bivouac hut is located about 40–50 metres to the left of the path wedged behind a huge split boulder before reaching the top of the descent route. It is not signed but it is marked on the sheet map.

## WALK 16

*Špik*

| | |
|---|---|
| **Start/finish** | Church in Kranjska Gora |
| **Distance** | 17km |
| **Total ascent/descent** | 1700m |
| **Grade** | 4 |
| **Time** | 10–11hrs |
| **Maps** | 1:30,000 Kranjska Gora, 1:25,000 Triglav |
| **Refreshments** | Koča v Krnici |
| **Parking** | There is a small parking area at the bridge which reduces total walking time by about 1hr. |

The shapely pyramid of Špik (2472m) is particularly evident towards the right of the great cirque of mountains viewed from Gozd Martuljek. There are no walkers' routes on the northern side but the western approach is not so precipitous, and this fine route can be completed in a day from Kranjska Gora. The route gives a close-up view of the dizzying cliffs and ridges of this northern spur of the Julian Alps, and although it is steep, with some short sections of cables and steel pegs, it is not overly difficult and self-belaying techniques are not required. It is a long and strenuous route, so an early start is advised.

From Kranjska Gora, follow the road for the Vršič pass to the south. Just before **Jezero Jasna** (Lake Jasna), cut across the car park to a walking track that goes past the lake on the right. Follow this until it rejoins the road, then continue on the road to the bridge across the **Pišnica river**. Don't cross it, but take the broad track to the left, heading south alongside the river and signed Koča v Krnici (local) route 8. After about 30mins from the bridge pass a large rock with Špik painted on it to the left of the track, and a sign reading Pot na Špik via Skozi kačji graben 4hrs; this marks the descent route. About 10mins later reach two metal gateposts (with no gate) just before a wide dry watercourse. Cross over and walk along the broad trail.

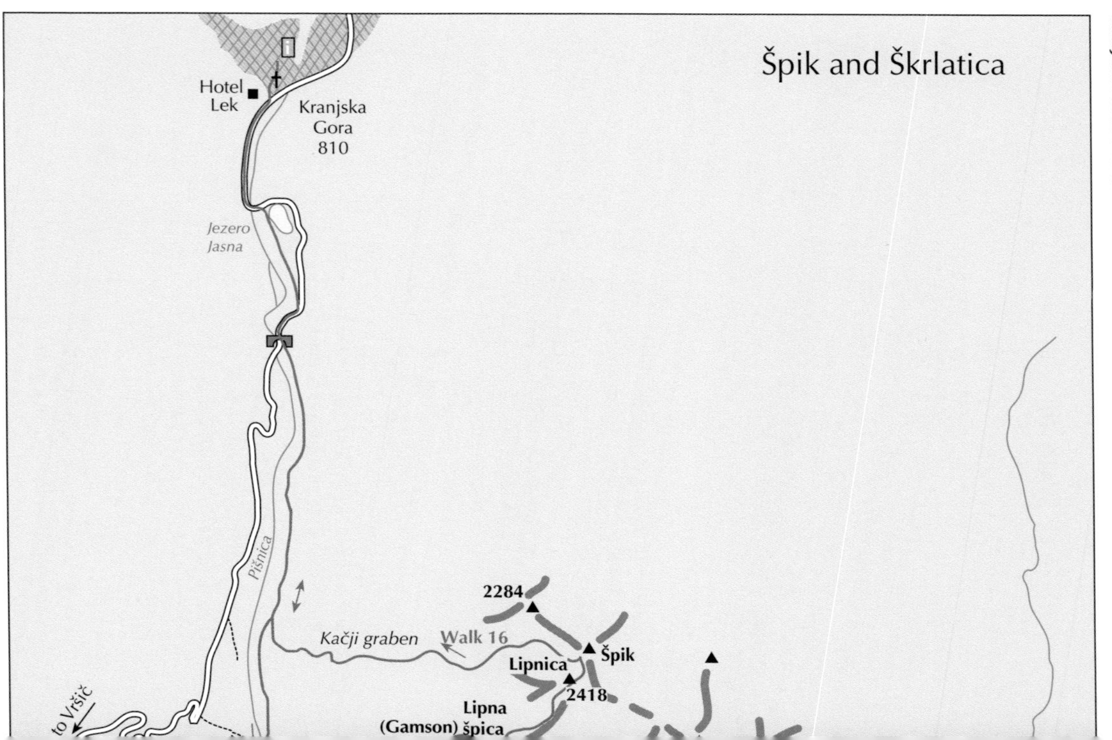
Špik and Škrlatica
Hotel
Lek
Kranjska
Gora
810
Jezero
Jasna
Pišnica
2284
Kačji graben
Walk 16
Špik
Lipnica
2418
Lipna
(Gamson) špica
to Vršič

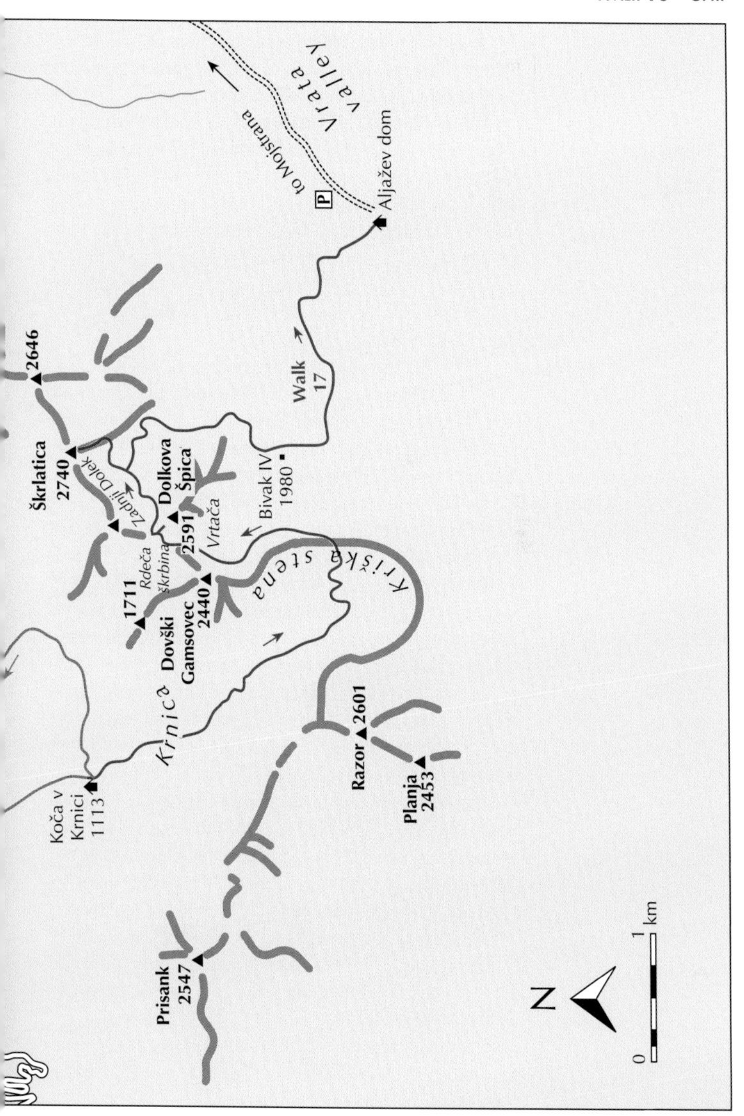
Vrata valley
to Mojstrana
P
Aljažev dom
Walk 17
Bivak IV 1980
2646
Škrlatica 2740
Zadnji Dolek
Dolkova Špica 2591
Vrtača
Rdeča škrbina
1711
Dovški Gamsovec 2440
Kriška stena
Krnica
Koča v Krnici 1113
Razor 2601
Planja 2453
Prisank 2547
N
0
1 km

Within another 150m come to a junction close to a memorial shrine, and join a track that links with the one coming down from hairpin bend 3 on the Vršič road. The track bears left, towards the dry river courses which just here are at right angles to each other; a few paces bring you to the edge. Cross the first tributary watercourse and walk for a few metres up the right-hand side (looking ahead) of the other, main, one. Almost immediately there are waymarks for a narrow path turning right into the forest, and a little further on are waymarks indicating the continuation of the forest road. Either of these will bring you to **Koča v Krnici** in 20–25mins.

At the hut the path is signed Špik 4hrs. It is well waymarked and signed throughout. The route initially heads off to the north-east, entering the wood and descending a little to cross a dry river bed. It then begins a gentle ascent through the woods before crossing another watercourse. The well-trodden path then ascends through dwarf pine on the right-hand edge of the Gruntnica valley. ◂

Looking up the valley you can see the sheer rock faces of Škrlatica and its satellite tops.

About 20mins from the koča the path bears right to cross a dry river bed, where the sound of running water coming from a rocky cleft up to the right can sometimes be heard. Continue ascending on the right of the watercourse, carefully following the waymarks on the rough scree- and boulder-covered path. As the watercourse steepens and starts to narrow, waymarks lead you across to the left-hand side, which you follow for a further 150m before finally exiting on the left.

The path now climbs up and bears sharply left, past a large boulder waymarked to Špik, and begins a long rising traverse under the crags of **Lipna špica** (also known as Gamsova špica), over scree and boulders. After the traverse, back in dwarf pine and larch, ascend a steep trough, initially staying on the right-hand side. Before reaching its head, traverse left and continue zigzagging up quite steeply to exit on the left into the upper part of the wider Tarmanova žlefa valley.

The dwarf pine have thinned out and you are now on grass and rock, with the little craggy top of Lipna špica close by on the right. Continue to a small col with an

*Looking towards the rocky saddle on the ridge between Lipnica and Špik*

amazing view into a steep chasm on its south side. Turn left and continue to another small col where the route bears left once more. The path steepens and becomes rockier and soon reaches the 20m or so of cables on Lipnica; the initial 5m are steeper than anything that follows. The angle eases again over the remaining rocks and the path broadens, decorated with bright blue gentians, to climb easily to the summit of **Lipnica**. ▸

Continue the short distance down to the rocky saddle between Lipnica and Špik, without much height loss.

Špik stands close by to the north, looking like the spear that gives it the name. There are spectacular views to the right, with the rock faces of the Škrlatica group dropping into the depths.

The route keeps to the left-hand side below the rocky crest; there are some steel cables and pegs on the traverse but it is not too difficult or exposed. Start to ascend again and pass a waymark pointing down that reads Črna voda – this is the descent route. Continue to the top of **Špik** via fairly steep rocks, taking care not to dislodge the loose stones. It is 6–7hrs to this point from Kranjska Gora, 4–5hrs from Koča v Krnici.

> The **summit** is surprisingly roomy but drops off dramatically to the north, with excellent views east to the Gozd Martuljek cirque. A little to the south is Škrlatica, then Razor and Prisank. In the Sava valley you can see Podkoren and Gozd Martuljek, although Kranjska Gora is hidden behind the ridges of Špik's north-west spur.

Five minutes from the top brings you back to the sign for Črna voda. The first 100m or so of descent from here is awkward because the scree has been run out from the top, so the ground is steep and unstable. As the more forgiving scree is reached the path begins to bear right, traversing to avoid some crags. After passing the crags it turns left and continues down. Pass some house-sized boulders which are an unusual pale reddish-brown colour, and at the end of this long descending traverse reach a stand of beautiful old larch, which marks the start of the treeline.

Continue descending pleasantly but quite steeply into the woods. There are a few short sections of cables and pegs over small rocky steps and bluffs. The descent is long and consistently steep, but eventually you hear the rushing of the river Pišnica in the floor of the valley, a refreshing sound after a long hot day on the arid mountainside!

About two-thirds of the way down, the path narrows somewhat and traverses the top of some small crags. Finally the angle eases and there is a dry rocky watercourse on your right – **Kačji graben**. Shortly afterwards cross the watercourse and carry on; ahead and to the left on the other side of the river you can see the pleasant green planina of V Klinu with its wooden buildings. Continue over stony ground with dwarf pine before entering the final section of woodland to reach the forest road. Turn right, back towards the bridge over the Pišnica, and retrace your steps to **Kranjska Gora**.

## WALK 17

*Škrlatica*

| | |
|---|---|
| **Start** | Koča v Krnici |
| **Finish** | Aljažev dom, Vrata valley |
| **Distance** | 15km |
| **Total ascent** | 1700m |
| **Grade** | 4 |
| **Time** | 10–11hrs |
| **Maps** | 1:30,000 Kranjska Gora, 1:25,000 Triglav |
| **Access** | Follow Walk 16 to Koča v Krnici from Kranjska Gora. Alternatively, drive to bend 3 on the Vršič pass and walk to the koča, following signs, in about 45mins. |

Škrlatica, the 'scarlet mountain' (2740m), named for the red aspect of its rock, is the second highest peak in Slovenia, and its mighty complex of towers and ridges is a worthy challenge for the mountaineer. This is a serious route requiring a high level of fitness and mountaineering experience. Just one protected route leads to its summit, via the south-west face, although several ways can be taken on the lower slopes of the mountain. The walk described here ascends from Koča v Krnici, and descends to Aljažev dom at the head of the Vrata valley; the route could also be done in reverse, or as a linear up and down route from either of these starting points, according to your itinerary.

An alternative starting point is Pogačnikov Dom, described in the Bovec section (Walk 40); from here climb as if to Križ and cross the Bovška vratica to the head of the Kriška Stena wall to pick up the route. It is 5–6hrs from the dom to the summit of Škrlatica.

See the route map in Walk 16.

◂ From Koča v Krnici, a sign on the hut wall says Križ 4hrs. Head south on a broad track and ascend gently through the woods for about 5mins before continuing on a slightly narrower path to the left. Follow waymarks, which after a further 10–15mins brings you to a dry watercourse. At the head of the valley you can see Kriška stena (the Križ wall). Follow the right-hand edge of the river bed and after 30m or so reach more waymarks and leave the watercourse to continue ascending through dwarf pine. A little higher up reach the torrent bed again, opposite a large boulder. Leave the bank for the dry river bed and bear right following waymarks to reach another strip of ground with dwarf pine and small larch.

The path soon becomes more defined, and after about 20mins reach another stream bed below some small crags, where it may be possible to fill your water bottle. Cross the river bed and turn right. In a few paces the path bears first left and then right, ascending between small rocky outcrops. In another 20–25mins come to the foot of the wild and rocky corrie of V Kotu, surrounded by high crags, but still with alpine flowers and, if you are lucky, a herd of chamois. Continue on the stony path for 20mins or so to reach a level area with large boulders.

The path now descends a little and then continues up steep scree towards **Kriška stena**, passing a large waymarked boulder. Looking up you can see the start of the route marked by a large waymark on the lower rocks, with a steep scree slope leading directly up to it, but it is better to bear slightly right from the boulder to ascend easier ground before turning back left to the foot of the route.

The climb initially leads left, ascending easy ground before bearing right and rising a little more steeply to where you meet the first pegs. The route continues zigzagging up the face in short steep protected scrambles, interspersed with easier going over rocky ledge paths; the main danger is the abundance of loose rock covering the ground. The scrambling on the top third of the route is on better rock with fewer loose stones. It takes about 1hr to reach the top of the face.

At the top the route initially leads right for a few paces to reach a rock with a waymark. Follow further waymarks heading east, descending a little across limestone pavement, and after about 10mins begin to bear left, past a sign on a rock saying Vrata and Škrlatica. The route descends a little more steeply to reach a junction, where you take the left fork (the right fork continues straight ahead down to Bivak 4 and Vrata).

Continue first across shattered slabs, and then over scree and stone to contour the boulder-filled bowl of **Vrtača** below the crags of Dovški Gamsovec. Eventually the path begins to ascend, climbing towards a small col on the craggy ridge. At the col a vertiginous view sweeps down to the Krnica valley. From here continue steeply over scree and rock for another 35–40mins of what must be described as a grinding slog. Finally reach the small platform of **Rdeča škrbina** (the 'red notch') at the foot of rocks that lead up to the summit of Dolkova špica (2591m).

It is worth making a detour, 15mins each way, to the top of **Dolkova špica**. Turn right and begin ascending rocks marked with a faded waymark, then bear left and up via a steep scramble for a short distance before a more level walk of 100m or so leads to the summit cairn. Apart from one waymark at the first rocks it is not signed, but there is only one way to go!

From Rdeča škrbina, the route bears left and descends steeply over the red clay-like ground that gives it the name, following steel cables at the head of a gully that drops down the west side of the ridge for a short distance. Turn right and drop into a gully on the east side of the ridge, still descending steeply over loose unpleasant ground. The angle eventually eases and the path begins to traverse the large stone- and boulder-filled corrie of **Zadnji Dolek**.

Head towards the small pointed peak of Kucelj (2372m), but before reaching it the path bears left towards

*On the steep water-worn rocks and slabs that form the crux on Škrlatica*

Škrlatica, and soon meets a junction with the path that comes up from the Vrata valley; ahead of you are the steep slabs and crags of Škrlatica's south-west face. Ascend over steep scree to reach a waymark at the foot of the broken rock wall. The route initially leads diagonally right over the easy lower rocks, and then begins to zigzag up. After about 15mins the angle steepens and you begin to ascend over rocky steps, covered with loose rock. A little further on, after a rightward traverse, meet steeper rock with some steel cables.

A short descent is followed by another level traverse to the right, and this leads you to more protection, where the route begins to ascend steeply. The scrambling in this section is enjoyable, on good rock, climbing between clefts and flakes. Reach a notch in the rocks through which the route descends for a few metres and then turns left. Ahead of you now is probably the most exposed section of the route, ascending diagonally right across bulging steep slabby rock. It is very well protected with steel rungs, pegs and cables. This is followed by easier broken ground with occasional short steep scrambles, still tending right. Look up and left to see a natural rock window. ▶

The triangular window was formed by the crumbling of part of the ridge until only a pillar remained, leaning on the rest of the ridge. It is about 3m high and wide at the base.

Soon after this, climb onto the south-east ridge. The view over the other side is of the wild complex of rocky peaks and ridges to the east of the Martuljek cirque.

Turn left and continue up the ridge; the path keeps right when not on the crest. The going is initially easier, but there is a great deal of loose rock and one or two short rock steps that add to the sense of seriousness of this high mountain ridge. A surprisingly steep but short rocky scramble brings you to the crest once more, and after another 10mins or so over rubble-covered rocky ledges you arrive at the summit of **Škrlatica**, crowned with a large aluminium cross.

The views are excellent, befitting Slovenia's **second highest peak**. The Kamnik-Savinja Alps can be seen to the east, and there is a particularly good view of Triglav's northern aspect.

Those who have parked near Koča v Krnici will need to reverse the ascent route to return to their car.

◂ Carefully follow the waymarks in descent, back to where you leave the ridge, which could be critical in poor visibility. Retrace the route down to the junction at the foot of Škrlatica's south-west face, turn left and begin to descend the Vrata path, with the steep south face of Škrlatica on your left.

After about 15mins reach a pleasant grassy area, where there is a fork in the path and a good view of the rock faces of Stenar to the south. Take the right-hand path (the left fork is a short excursion that leads within a few minutes to the mouth of a cave, passing it before rejoining the Vrata path). From the fork the path descends more steeply and begins to drop down below the east face of Dolkova špica. It then ascends a little to cross a grassy shoulder, and continues to traverse the grassy hillside with extremely steep slopes dropping away to the Vrata valley.

As you round the shoulder **Bivak IV**, an unmanned open shelter with enough room for five or six people, can be seen ahead, still about 15mins away. Just before it is reached take the left fork at a junction. Soon the path begins to descend among dwarf pine and impressive rock scenery. In another 20mins or so the path bears left, dropping down into a wide, easy-angled rocky gully. At the bottom the path reaches a grassy promontory and bears right.

Larches begin to appear among the dwarf pine, and the forest gradually thickens. The path continues down with occasional steeper sections, and eventually reaches beech woods. Continue on the waymarked path, ignoring a couple of narrower tracks that lead off to the side. Pass through another section of mixed woodland with sycamore and smaller beech trees before reaching magnificent tall open beech forest, leading to **Aljažev dom**.

If you don't wish to stay overnight at the dom then you can carry on down the Vrata valley (Walk 12) to Mojstrana, from where there are hourly buses to Kranjska Gora.

# WALK 18

*Triglav by the Tominškova pot and the Prag Route*

| | |
|---|---|
| **Start/finish** | Aljažev dom, Vrata valley |
| **Distance** | 15km |
| **Total ascent/descent** | 1900m |
| **Grade** | 4 |
| **Time** | 2 days |
| **Maps** | 1:30,000 Kranjska Gora, 1:25,000 Triglav |
| **Access** | On foot: follow Walk 12 as far as the Aljažev dom. By car: drive to the dom following signs to the Vrata valley from Mojstrana |
| **Accommodation** | Triglavski dom na Kredarici |

Three routes to the summit of Triglav, at 2864m Slovenia's highest peak, are described in this book (see also Walks 19 and 31) – this is the first, an ascent from the north. The Tominškova pot (Tominšek Route) is considered one of the more difficult ascents, and although it is well protected throughout it requires stamina and a strong head for heights; the views of the 1000m north face of the mountain are stunning. The slightly easier Prag Route is used on the descent and could also be used for the ascent, although the steep scree path would be tedious in places. Although it can be accomplished in one very long day, this description suggests an overnight stay in the Triglavski dom na Kredarici.

## DAY 1

*Aljažev dom to Triglavski dom na Kredarici*

| | |
|---|---|
| **Start** | Aljažev dom |
| **Finish** | Triglavski dom na Kredarici |
| **Distance** | 6km |
| **Total ascent** | 1550m |
| **Time** | 5–5½hrs |

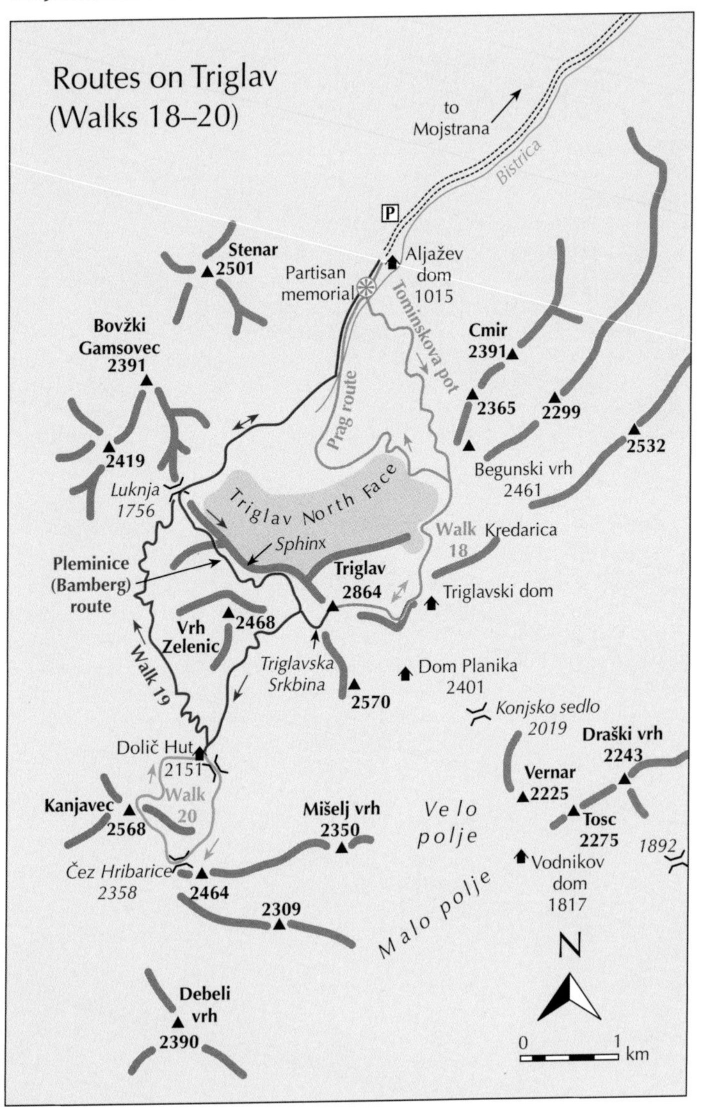
Routes on Triglav
(Walks 18–20)
to Mojstrana
Bistrica
P
Aljažev dom 1015
Partisan memorial
Tominškova pot
Stenar 2501
Bovžki Gamsovec 2391
Cmir 2391
2365
2299
2532
Prag route
2419
Begunski vrh 2461
Luknja 1756
Triglav North Face
Walk 18
Kredarica
Sphinx
Pleminice (Bamberg) route
Triglav 2864
Triglavski dom
Vrh Zelenic
2468
Triglavska Srkbina
Dom Planika 2401
Walk 19
2570
Konjsko sedlo 2019
Dolič Hut 2151
Draški vrh 2243
Vernar 2225
Walk 20
Kanjavec 2568
Mišelj vrh 2350
Velo polje
Tosc 2275
1892
Čez Hribarice 2358
2464
Vodnikov dom 1817
2309
Malo polje
N
Debeli vrh 2390
0
1
km

This is a long classic mountain route that starts in the lush forested Vrata valley. Height is gained quickly to soon reach a rocky vertiginous Alpine kingdom of bare rock and outstanding views.

From Aljažev dom, take the broad track heading south towards the huge mountain walls of Smir and Triglav, which from here look as if the only possible routes are for climbers. About 500m brings you to the well-known **memorial** to partisans and Alpinists in the shape of an enormous piton and karabiner. About 20m before the memorial is reached, cross the river bed and head up into the woods, following an obvious but narrower signed and waymarked path.

The path rises steeply, initially trending right and then continuing straight up for about an hour, crossing a steep rocky gully and gradually climbing through the different levels of vegetation, with views towards the

*The north wall of Triglav from the Tominškova pot*

Luknja pass opening out as height is gained. Enjoyable scrambling leads up a rib of broken rock, followed by more rightward traverses on ledges, and ascents over rock steps. Once out of the main forest and into the dwarf pine, the views of the north face of Triglav are second to none.

The path winds between rocks and eventually emerges onto a narrow rocky crest. The route now descends through a notch in the crest for a few metres and crosses the head of an unpleasant steep scree gully. Climb steep sloping rocks (well protected) which lead onto an exposed but level section of path, with more views of Triglav's north face. The route continues, still very airy in places, but slightly easier than before, and always well waymarked. In spite of the height and the bare rock, there are still some dwarf pine and many flowers among the rocks beside the path.

About 3hrs 30mins from Aljažev dom come to a T-junction, where the Tominškova pot joins the Prag Route. There is a metal post and sign saying Aljažev dom 2hrs 30mins by the Prag Route (used for the descent), at the top of a big scree slope with the massive cliff face of Begunjski vrh to your left. ◄

At the foot of the crag is a spring where you can top up your water bottle, although it could take a minute or two as the deliciously cold water dribbles slowly from the rock.

About 5mins from the spring is a sign to Triglavski dom (1hr 15mins) and Triglav (2hr 15mins).

Continue on the well-marked path heading right towards Triglavski dom. The route now ascends gently across a vast limestone pavement area where butterflies and cushions of flowers can be seen among the rocks. Tall metal posts, about 200m apart, mark the route when snow is lying. The route passes many rock crevasses in the karst – some of them are quite cavernous and deep. ◄ A final steep rightward-trending rise, protected with steel cables and pegs, brings you to **Triglavski dom na Kredarici** (2516m), a large building popular with walkers making the ascent from both north and south, which is the overnight stop. The climb to the summit takes a further 1hr 30mins, and is best left until morning to take advantage of the clear air and to avoid the frequent afternoon thunderstorms.

Dom Valentina Staniča can be seen on the skyline to the left.

Although busy, **Triglavski dom na Kredarici** (also known as Kredarica dom and Triglav dom) is ideally located for an overnight stay when climbing Triglav. It is well appointed and even has satellite TV. A large photograph on the wall shows just how busy it can get up here – it looks as though the entire population of Slovenia posed for it! It is also an important weather station that is manned all year. It's advisable to book in the main season.

## DAY 2

*Triglavski dom na Kredarici to Aljažev dom*

| | |
|---|---|
| **Start** | Triglavski dom na Kredarici |
| **Finish** | Aljažev dom |
| **Distance** | 9km |
| **Total ascent** | 330m |
| **Total descent** | 1900m |
| **Time** | 5½–6hrs |

Afternoon storms are common in July and August so an early evening or better still, an early morning start to gain the summit are recommended. The descent of the Prag route is steep and tiring but its alpine grandeur and views to the western peaks such as Stenar and Škrlatica are well worth the effort.

From the dom the path descends to the foot of Mali Triglav's north-east buttress. From here the route, heralded by a large waymark, starts to ascend steep rocks that are polished and smooth in places, but very well protected with plenty of steel cables and pitons. As you gain height, the exposed path traverses for a while on the left side of the buttress, where an impressive array of rows of steel pegs protect the route. Above this, it joins the ridge proper and continues, steeply in places, before the path levels where the route coming up from Dom Planika

*Descending to Kredarica from Mali Triglav*

joins the ridge close to a memorial plaque a few metres below Mali Triglav's summit.

The rocks of the summit ridge give exciting scrambling with plenty of protection, but countless ascents have left the rocks quite polished. Continue quite easily at first, with big drops to both sides, for another 15mins or so before the route steepens again. There is another short level section just before the final steep rocks, which are well protected but with considerable exposure. Notice a sign that reads 'Staničevo zavetišče 30m' pointing left – this marks a small cave that can offer emergency shelter if caught in a storm. Walk easily the final short distance to the summit of **Triglav**, marked by the metal Aljažev stolp (Aljaž's turret). In the height of the season there may be hundreds of ascents of Triglav being made on a clear day. The view, of course, is extensive in every direction.

The **turret** on the summit of Triglav was erected in 1895 on the order of a local pioneering priest from Dovje-Mojstrana, Jakob Aljaž, who had bought the summit area for a nominal sum. It was designed as a shelter, and was once furnished with three round chairs, but as it is made of metal it is advisable to make use of the Staničevo zavetišče cave instead if caught in a thunderstorm!

Retrace the route to the dom, and back down the karst plateau area to the junction below the Begunjski vrh cliffs that marks the start of the Prag Route, which is your return route. It heads down to the left, and after about 5mins a narrow, exposed, grassy promontory juts out to the right of the path, giving a good view of the top section of the Tominšek Route and down into the Vrata. After 10–15mins of easy going the stony path begins to steepen, and soon afterwards descends steep rocks with security before traversing and descending to the right across scree slopes. The path continues, descending close to the foot of crags, then reaches more rock steps with pegs and cables. Continue down, now through dwarf pine, and reach a steep crag known as the Bear's Rock – about 1hr 30mins from the junction.

The rock is so named because one of the last **bears** of the Julian Alps fell over it to its death while trying to escape from hunters. Although bears are still occasionally seen in the National Park, they are just passing through – none breed here now. The bear population of Slovenia lives in Kočevski Rog, a remote wilderness of forested hills in the south-east part of the country.

Descend steeply down the exposed rock, protected with iron rungs and pegs, for about 30m, beneath slightly overhanging walls. The path traverses on round the foot of more crags, and then begins to drop down more steeply. Soon the path turns left into a scree-filled, badly eroded gully. The waymarks direct you down the right-hand edge of the gully, through dwarf pine, but this is also becoming badly eroded. About 30m down cross back left and continue on the better path. The north face of Triglav rises dramatically to the left, with the Luknja pass directly ahead.

The scree path zigzags down through dwarf pine, then turns right to ascend a little, becoming narrower, with more steel cables. After more short ascents and descents drop down left into a loose scree gully. The angle soon eases again and the route now begins a long leftward traverse below the north face. Eventually start descending small rocky spurs and short gullies, some quite steep, bearing right, and continue down to reach the valley floor above the fast-flowing clear waters of the **river Bistrica**. Cross the river easily, and turn right on the good path that leads back down the valley to **Aljažev dom**.

## WALK 19

*Triglav by the Plemenice (or Bamberg) Route*

| | |
|---|---|
| **Start/finish** | Aljažev dom |
| **Distance** | 22.5km |
| **Total ascent/descent** | 2160m |
| **Grade** | 4 |
| **Time** | 2 days |
| **Maps** | 1:25,000 Triglav, 1:25,000 Bohinj |
| **Access** | On foot: follow Walk 12 as far as the Aljažev dom. By car: drive to the dom following signs to the Vrata valley from Mojstrana |
| **Accommodation** | Tržaška Koča na Doliču (known as the Dolič hut) |
| **Route map** | See Walk 18 |

The Plemenice Route (also known as the Bamberg Route) to the summit of Triglav via the north-west Plemenice ridge is considered to be the hardest, not least because you must climb the whole way to the summit in one day – there are no escape routes until you gain the level plateau just below the final summit section. This makes it a long and strenuous route, requiring settled weather. The ridge is steep and exposed, but with good protection on the rock sections. The route involves an overnight stay at the Dolič hut.

## DAY 1

*Aljažev dom to Dolič hut*

| | |
|---|---|
| **Start** | Aljažev dom |
| **Finish** | Dolič hut |
| **Distance** | 11km |
| **Total ascent** | 1900m |
| **Time** | 8½–9hrs |

The long relatively easy walk up the Vrata valley to reach the Luknja pass is abruptly put into perspective as the initial very steep rocks of the Plemenice route make it feel more like a cragging day in the high mountains.

From Aljažev dom, continue up the valley to reach a fork, where the path for the Prag Route heads left across the Bistrica river. Follow a sign for Luknja painted on a rock and waymarks which head right, ascending away from the river. The path climbs steadily to reach a broad rocky slope, which it crosses before descending a little as it reaches the other side and enters deciduous woodland. Begin to climb more steeply, and after 10–15mins emerge onto more open ground, with the Luknja pass visible up ahead.

The stony path continues, passing between boulders to the last larches and dwarf pine before finally heading up steep scree to arrive at the grassy saddle of the **Luknja pass** (1756m) – about 2hrs 30mins from the Aljažev dom. ▶ Follow the sign to Triglav via Plemenice (4hrs), turning left towards the crag and following the path round the right-hand side of the lower rocks. The route then scrambles steeply up for about 80m to reach a memorial plaque at the start of a very steep secured section, which is climbed on good rock for another 50–60m to easier ground.

The col is a crossroads of routes; straight on goes down to Trenta, and to the right the path leads to Bovški Gamsovec and the Pogačnikov dom.

There now follows long sections of secured scrambling alternating with ledge traverses on the grassy right flank of the ridge, which are less protected, and always offer a sense of airy exposure. Following waymarks, make a slight descent and traverse the steep hillside before ascending steeply once more. A short section of exposed scrambling along the crest of the ridge is followed by another mixture of easier ground and pleasant scrambling.

Continue for another hour or so, until you arrive at a spectacular section of the ridge where the route passes close to the **Sphinx** (Sfinga in Slovene) – a huge pillar of rock on Triglav's north face, with tremendous vertical drops to the Vrata. The route makes a brief sortie to the left of the ridge, just below the crest, above the huge void of the north wall. Steel cables lead up a steep cleft in the rock followed by more steep scrambling until you gain the ridge crest once more.

More mixed terrain, with some short descents followed by steady ascent, eventually brings you to more level ground by a large sinkhole about 30m in diameter. The way ahead now continues over the barren karst landscape of Zaplanja with limestone rock formations. ◂

The west face of Triglav's summit rocks is ahead, and nearby, just beyond the rise of Glava v Zaplanji (2556m), is the ruin of the large Morbegna barracks from the First World War.

The route continues ascending gently to reach a junction where one path leads off right to Morbegna and another goes left to the top of the north wall. Just beyond, a path bears diagonally left and up, across the scree towards the rocks, making a short-cut from the waymarked route. If visibility is poor, or if in any doubt, continue for another 200m to reach a metal post. Triglav is signed 1hr and the path now heads left up the scree to reach the rocks.

The secured route begins to ascend steeply, trending right across the polished rock, then descends a little and traverses to reach a gully. Climb the gully to arrive at a notch (**Triglavska škrbina**), where you can look across the southern face and down to Dom Planika. Step through the notch onto the east side of the south ridge and continue to ascend mixed ground with some steel cables, where eventually some steeper scrambling brings you to the crest of the ridge. You can see the popular east summit ridge to your right, strung with its

*Triglav from the west*

steel cables. A final section over rocky steps brings you to the summit area about 40m west of the Aljažev stolp on **Triglav** – 6–7hrs from the Aljažev dom and 4hrs from the Luknja pass.

To reach the Dolič hut, retrace your steps down to the metal post and sign at the bottom of the crags and follow waymarks for Tržaška koča na Doliču 1hr. The path soon begins to descend gently, leading easily across the undulating stony ground, with occasional patches of grass and small alpine flowers. After about 20mins the path becomes broader and more defined, being the former military route that led to the barracks. It is very well constructed and in places is hewn from the rock as it zigzags between outcrops.

Eventually the hut can be seen below, and the path continues to drop down, keeping to the right of a small rocky top (marked 2345m on the map). Continue zigzagging down to reach a fork with the hut signed to the left (the main path goes on down to Trenta). The path ascends a little and within 100m reaches the **Dolič hut** (2151m).

## DAY 2

*Dolič hut to Aljažev dom*

| | |
|---|---|
| **Start** | Dolič hut |
| **Finish** | Aljažev dom |
| **Distance** | 11.5km |
| **Total ascent** | 260m |
| **Total descent** | 1400m |
| **Time** | 5hrs |

This long but very beautiful descent route requires stamina after an ascent of Triglav. The route feels quite airy initially as it traverses the amazing balcony sections of an old military cart track high above the Trenta valley.

Kanjavec (Walk 20) makes a good extension to the route at the beginning of Day 2, if you are feeling fit.

◀ For the return route, from the hut follow the path signed Trenta. Once again you are descending on the excellent old military path cut into the steep rocky hillside. It traverses for a while before beginning to zigzag steadily down, past old defences, and with breathtaking views of the bulbous overhanging crags that are the lower

*Descending from Triglav en route to the Dolič hut*

ramparts of Kanjavec's northern side. (A very difficult waymarked route that leads off left traverses the crags.) Continue along the trail, ignoring a signed path heading down left to Komar, beneath huge overhanging crags (the lower ramparts of Zelenica). ▸

For a while the route keeps just above the treeline, and then begins to descend through larch trees, eventually arriving at the head of a huge gully. The path can be seen beyond, dropping steeply down in a series of unlikely zigzags. Traverse the gully and continue down the steep twisting path. At a junction, the left-hand path goes down to Trenta – bear right passing a painted sign for Luknja and Vrata and begin to ascend. Continue up the good path climbing steadily for about 45mins to reach the **Luknja pass** (3hrs from the hut). It is another 2hrs back to **Aljažev dom** following your outward route.

The old military trail is hewn out of the rock with steep drops down into the valley on your left, and is a good place to spot wildlife – ibex, marmots and lots of alpine flowers.

## WALK 20

*Kanjavec*

| | |
|---|---|
| **Start/finish** | Dolič hut |
| **Distance** | 4km |
| **Total ascent/descent** | 420m |
| **Grade** | 4 |
| **Time** | 3–3½hrs |
| **Maps** | 1:25,000 Triglav, 1:25,000 Bohinj |
| **Access** | On foot: follow Walk 19 from Aljažev dom to the Dolič hut |

The shapely peak of Kanjavec stands in the heartland of the Julian Alps, high above the Triglav Lakes and the Trenta valleys. Its ascent is described here from the Dolič hut which can be reached from Triglav (see Walk 19) or by paths from Dom Planika and the Vodnikov dom.

The ascent of Kanjavec (2568m) makes a fine addition to any of the routes that go into the Triglav area – the Triglav Lakes valley route (Walk 30) or Triglav itself (Walks 18, 19 and 31).

See the route map in Walk 18.

◄ From the Dolič hut (Koča na Doliču) take the marked, level path to the south-east and in less than 10mins reach the **Dolič saddle** (2164m) from which the hut takes its name. Turn right, signed (local) route 7 Jezero (Triglav Lakes), and descend a little on the stony path before beginning to gently climb through rocky karst scenery below the foot of the steep cliffs on the south-east side of Kanjavec. The route eventually begins to ascend more steeply, zigzagging up scree, following waymarks to the left of a boulder-filled hollow to reach the wild, stony plateau of **Čez Hribarice** (2358m).

From here there are fabulous views of Triglav and beyond to Razor and Prisank. Further to the north-west you can see into Austria with Grossglockner easily visible on a good day.

Turn right, signed Kanjavec 45mins, and soon the path begins to ascend gently. After about 15mins it steepens a little, but is without difficulty. Ascend some easy rocky steps and join the crest of the east ridge; continue easily along here for about 100m to reach a notch. Descend into the notch by a short scramble of about 5m, then continue up the easy rocks on the other side along the ridge to reach the summit of **Kanjavec** (2568m). ◄

From the summit a waymarked path signed Dolič drops down on the north side of the mountain. Descend steeply over scree and loose rock for the first 100m or so, then traverse the top of a crag for a short distance before meeting steel cables to protect a steep scramble down of about 20m. Continue over slightly easier ground, still covered with loose rock, before beginning to traverse right across scree slopes. The path then heads down over typical karst landscape, with hollows and water-worn slabs, until you see the hut below and to the right. Continue winding down between rocks, with patches of grass and flowers beginning to appear, to arrive back at the **Dolič hut** (1hr 15mins from the summit).

# 2 BOHINJ

*The statue commemorating the first ascent of Triglav at Ribčev Laz*

# INTRODUCTION

*Lake Bohinj*

Bohinj (523m) is the largest of Slovenia's permanent lakes. The glacial lake in its long valley, surrounded by high mountains, is one of the great sights of Slovenia in its own right, but the valley is also an excellent base for mountaineering in the Julian Alps. The axis of the lake is east–west – to the south lies the ridge of the Lower Bohinj mountains with their wonderful natural flower gardens, while to the north, the high mountains begin in cliffs and plateaus that rise up almost from the lake shore. The village of Ribčev Laz at the eastern end of the lake, with its beautiful stone bridge and church, is the classic viewpoint, and here too is a well-known statue celebrating the four men who first climbed Triglav.

There is no large centre for tourism here (and no town called Bohinj). Instead, a number of villages, particularly Bohinjska Bistrica, Ribčev Laz and Stara Fužina, supply visitors with all their needs – hotels, apartments, campsites, shops and tourist information. A number of tourist farms also offer accommodation. However, don't expect large hotels and apartment blocks – Lake Bohinj is firmly inside the Triglav National Park, and so development is limited. In fact a good deal of the area's charm originates in its undeveloped feel, while the villages have retained their alpine way of life. Here the old houses and barns of the villages nestle together as if to ready themselves for the harshness of the alpine winter, and the new buildings thankfully maintain a similar style.

Access to Bohinj is mainly via a good road from Bled; it takes about 25 minutes. Regular buses run from the (now closed) Hotel Zlatorog to Ribčev Laz and Bohinjska Bistrica, where you can get a connection to Bled and Ljubljana. The train from Jesenice to Nova Gorica goes through the station at Bohinjska Bistrica.

Plentiful iron ore in the area ensured Bohinj's prosperity from early times, until competition closed the last of the smelters in the late 19th century. Fortunately the opening of a railway link in 1906, which connected Bohinj with the coast, brought new opportunities for tourism and trade. The area has also been important for centuries for alpine dairy farming and cheese-making.

## THE ROUTES

Bohinj is an excellent base for all kinds of outdoor activities. The 11 walks described in this section include both easy routes which give a flavour of the valley, its villages, viewpoints and waterfalls (Walks 21–24), and harder and longer ones which include the mountains of the Lower Bohinj range on the south side (Walks 26–28) and several peaks in the Julian Alps, including Triglav (Walks 25, and 29–31). Walks 22 and 24 are river walks, and if you are interested in forests, don't miss the tree-covered peak of Pršivec (Walk 25). The ski resort of Vogel (1535m) is situated at the far end of the lake to the south, and its skiers' cable car can be utilised in the summer to gain height for some of the walks or simply to marvel at the unsurpassed view of Triglav and its mighty neighbours. There are also almost unlimited possibilities for hut-to-hut routes in the Bohinj area.

## MAPS

All the routes in this section are covered by 1:25,000 Bohinj, and all except 26–28 are on 1:25,000 Triglav.

# WALK 21

*The Tour of Lake Bohinj*

| | |
|---|---|
| **Start/finish** | Bridge at Ribčev Laz |
| **Distance** | 11.5km |
| **Total ascent/descent** | 160m |
| **Grade** | 1 |
| **Time** | 3½–4hrs |
| **Maps** | 1:25,000 Bohinj, 1:25,000 Triglav |

Bohinj is rightly one of the classic beauty spots of Slovenia, and this tour around the lake gives ample opportunity to absorb its delights. The lake shore can get busy in high season, so this route mostly follows quiet paths through the forest, which, particularly on the south side, leave the day trippers behind so that you can appreciate the wonderful natural scenery in peace. The route is described clockwise from the bridge at Ribčev Laz, but the walk may be started from either end of the lake and followed in either direction.

Walk away from the bridge on the road heading west towards Ukanc, and follow the lake shore past the car parks to the statue of Zlatorog.

**Zlatorog** is the golden-horned animal god of Slovenian legend who had his realm in the heights of Mount Triglav. Whether it was a chamois or an ibex depends on which statue you see and which story you read. Here, the statue is a chamois – at Lake Jasna in Kranjska Gora, it's an ibex!

About 100m further on there is a sign for boat hire on the right and a crag on the left, hung with fixed ropes as a sport-climbing venue. A gravel walkway by the road starts on the left, and just by it there is a yellow sign to Ukanc 1hr 15 along the gravel walkway, or 1hr 30 on a small path climbing a little into the woods above the road. Unless you are really pushed for time, take the small path, which is far more pleasant and peaceful. It traverses the hillside through attractive forest all the way to the cable-car station at Ukanc, and is delightfully shady on a hot day.

As you climb gently away from the lake, the noise of a busy summer gradually recedes until the only sounds are those of the forest. About 15mins from the lake cross a particularly pretty stream bubbling among mossy boulders on a little wooden bridge, and shortly after this pass a tiny spring on the left which tumbles over a miniature cliff. The path then continues its traverse, crossing many stream beds, usually dry, on wooden bridges. Ignore logging tracks to right and left; the path is obvious throughout its 3.5km length, and marked with yellow target waymarks.

After about 1hr reach a viewpoint where the break for some electricity cables glimpsed through the trees finally meets the path and a bench. ▸ About 10mins further on the path begins to descend gently. Cross a deep dry river bed filled with large boulders rushed down by the torrent in times of flood, and about 5mins later a yellow sign across the path directs you right and down to the **cable-car station** – you can see the car park just below.

Take a moment to admire the first good view since entering the forest; you can see the lake and the cliffs of Komarča (Walk 30) at the head of the valley.

Turn right and walk down the tarmac road at the end of the car park to a crossroads and carry straight on, about 100m along the road to the entrance to **Kamp Zlatorog**. Follow the road around a left-hand bend, and as you pass the end of the campsite grounds turn right on a track; after a short distance come to an open meadow and cross it on a path. Just after entering woods, turn left at a path junction (although right will also bring you to the river bank). Bear right at the next junction, 50m on, and then follow the river bank to a wooden bridge across the **Savica**.

Cross the bridge and turn right on a track about 30m further on, signed Ribčev Laz 1hr 30. Follow the track through trees and then pass an open area with some holiday cottages on the left to reach a junction. Turn left here, signed Lake, and after about 30m go through a gap in a

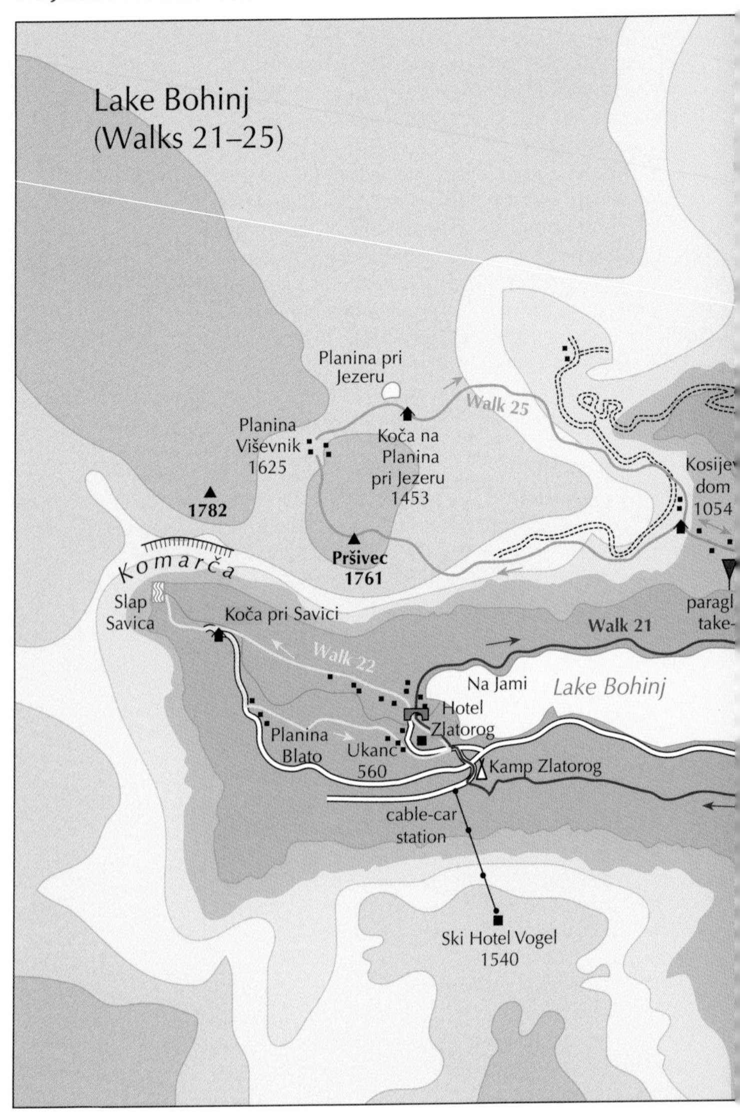
Lake Bohinj
(Walks 21–25)
Planina pri
Jezeru
Walk 25
Planina
Viševnik
1625
Koča na
Planina
pri Jezeru
1453
1782
Pršivec
1761
Komarča
Slap
Savica
Koča pri Savici
Walk 22
Walk 21
Na Jami
Lake Bohinj
Hotel
Zlatorog
Planina
Blato
Ukanc
560
Kamp Zlatorog
cable-car
station
Ski Hotel Vogel
1540

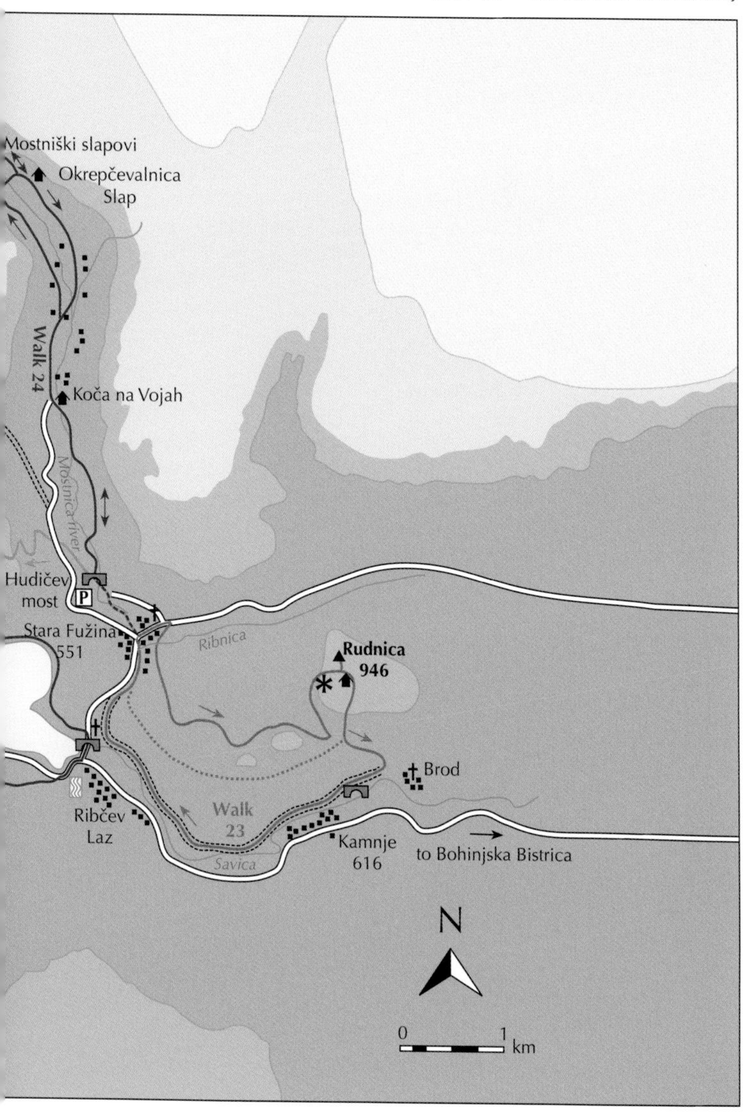
Mostniški slapovi
Okrepčevalnica
Slap
Walk 24
Koča na Vojah
Mostnica river
Hudičev
most
P
Stara Fužina
551
Ribnica
Rudnica
946
Brod
Walk
23
Ribčev
Laz
Kamnje
616
Savica
to Bohinjska Bistrica
N
0
1
km

fence and continue to the lake shore and across a bathers' area. Re-enter the trees and turn to the east, following the obvious path. ◂

Directly opposite is a good view of the span of the Vogel cable car.

Cross a couple of scree slopes, close above the deep water of the lake, and continue below massive prows of rock. About 500m from the western end of the lake come to a fork and branch left, away from the water's edge. The route now crosses a small peninsula of land called **Na Jami**.

> At times of high water a torrential waterfall bursts out from **Govic cave**, 130m above in the cliffs, bringing with it rocks and boulders which have built the land out into the lake.

Cross the (normally) dry watercourse and continue past a couple of buildings in a field on the left. At the end of the field rejoin the shore by a small beach and notice an interesting shrine on the left made of a dead tree trunk still in situ.

*The picturesque church of St John the Baptist and the old bridge at Ribčev Laz*

Continue pleasantly through the forest. About 35mins from the western end of the lake pass a series of concrete water tanks at a disused fish farm. In another 10mins the path opens out into a broad track, which you follow past a number of small beaches. Pass through another short section of woodland and continue past fields, with views of the village of Stara Fužina, and the steep slopes of Studor and Rudnica, their profiles making a textbook U-shaped valley. ▶ Cross a car park to a tarmac road which you follow for about 300m through trees before branching right across a small open area to the bridge at **Ribčev Laz**.

Looking back along the length of the lake, you can see the Lower Bohinj mountains to the left, Dom na Komni on the skyline straight ahead, and Pršivec to the right.

## WALK 22

*Slap Savica (Savica waterfall)*

| | |
|---|---|
| **Start/finish** | Bus stop by Hotel Zlatorog, Ukanc |
| **Distance** | 7km |
| **Total ascent/descent** | 240m |
| **Grade** | 1/2 |
| **Time** | 2–2½hrs |
| **Maps** | 1:25,000 Bohinj, 1:25,000 Triglav |

This beautiful waterfall is one of the main attractions of the Bohinj area and is arguably the best-known waterfall in Slovenia. The water slides for 38m down an angled gully, and then falls free for a further 51m. A smaller fall runs to the left of the main cascade. The walk starts in Ukanc and follows the main signposted route to the fall, which has a charge for entrance to the final section and viewpoint. The route returns through meadows and forest to the starting point.

This route could be happily combined with Walk 21, a tour of the lake, to make a longer day out.

▶ From the bus stop by the now-closed Hotel Zlatorog walk along the road, heading north, passing a sign on a tree that reads 'Slap Savica 1hr' and, just a few metres

See the route map in Walk 21.

beyond, another saying 1hr 20mins (!) on (local) route 3. ◂

Just to your left is the inviting Goštiče Erlah (the walk passes it on the way back).

Continue straight ahead, crossing the green river **Savica** on a wooden bridge, past pretty chalets and flower meadows with views of Vogel up to the left. Where the tarmac lane makes a sharp curve down to the left, continue straight ahead on the gravel path, signed Savica. Almost immediately cross a small stone bridge and continue along the gently ascending path. After 150m or so reach an elaborate signpost giving distance and direction to major European cities – you are apparently heading in the direction of Dublin, London and Paris, although the route descriptions are beyond the scope of this book!

The well-made gravel path continues, ascending gently past regular waymarks. About 100m past the sign notice a water trough with a picnic table and benches on the right – the sign 'pitna voda' means 'drinking water'. As you go on through the attractive forest there are occasional glimpses of the steep rock walls of Komarča through the trees, and the rush of the fast-flowing river on your left becomes louder. Ignore any paths on the left of the track, and after about 45mins from the start of the walk arrive at a trail leading up the forested slopes on the right – this is the path to Komarča (Walk 30). Continue for another 100m and cross the river on a scenic wooden bridge. ◂ Just beyond the bridge to the left is **Koča pri Savici**, but turn right and walk through the car park past the big snack bar and the small souvenir shop opposite. From here it is a further 20mins up to the waterfall. Follow the signs past the snack bar and in another 250m reach the pay kiosk, cross the bridge and continue ascending a well-made path with steps to eventually arrive at the main viewpoint for **Slap Savica**. Retrace your steps to the hut.

Wild laburnum trees hang their pendulous yellow flowers over the river in June.

Slap Savica waterfall is the source of the **Savica river**, which flows into Lake Bohinj. The outflow at the eastern end is the Sava Bohinjka, which joins the Sava Dolinka (whose source is at Zelenci near Kranjska Gora – Walk 1) just beyond Bled. Together

The Savica waterfall

they form Slovenia's longest river, the Sava, which eventually empties into the Danube at Belgrade.

At weekends in the high season the road down from Savica can be very busy, so it is better to return to Ukanc by your outward route.

◂ To return, walk past the bridge and Koča pri Savici and follow the road gently downhill, with some good views of the river through the trees. After about 15mins cross a pretty, mossy stream on a bridge, and almost immediately afterwards turn left on a gravel road passing a small building. After a further 100m the track reaches **Planina Blato** – walk between the buildings of the farm into open meadows. There are fine views of the surrounding cliffs and Vogel ski station. Go straight across the meadow to reach the end of the field at the edge of the wood and carry on, going slightly uphill into the forest, passing yellow target waymarks.

The track can be a little overgrown in parts, and soon descends into a dip that can be very boggy early in the season. If it is too wet, make your way about 20m to the left to reach drier ground and a narrow path which avoids the worst of the marshy area. In a few metres join the main path again at a fork. Take the right hand, waymarked, path and make another short ascent followed by a descent to cross a dry river bed. A little further on reach an open pasture with a couple of buildings on the left. Keep going in the same direction, passing more houses in the pretty little hamlet of **Ukanc**, to arrive back at the start of the walk where welcome refreshments can be had at Goštiče Erlah.

# WALK 23

*Rudnica*

| | |
|---|---|
| **Start/finish** | Supermarket in Stara Fužina |
| **Distance** | 10km |
| **Total ascent/descent** | 410m |
| **Grade** | 2 |
| **Time** | 3½–4hrs; 3hrs by the alternative route |
| **Maps** | 1:25,000 Bohinj, 1:25,000 Triglav |
| **Access** | By car: turn left at the crossroads where the road turns right over the bridge in Stara Fužina, and drive up the hill for about 700m to a car park (parking fee in summer) |

The low top of Rudnica (946m) divides the eastern end of the Bohinj valley into two. The northern half, overlooked by the sentinel peak of Studor, contains the villages of Stara Fužina and Srednja vas alongside the west-flowing river Ribnica, while in the southern half of the valley the Sava Bohinjka river flows east past the villages of Kamnje and Bohinjska Bistrica. The summit of Rudnica stands between, and from the little planina near its top, an excellent viewpoint of the lake and surroundings can be gained.

There are numerous ways up and down the hill, and a circular route is described here, starting in the beautiful village of Stara Fužina and climbing to the top of Rudnica in just over an hour. It then descends the opposite side of the hill to the village of Brod and returns along the excellent cycle track by the Sava Bohinjka river.

See the route map in Walk 21.

▸ From the small supermarket in Stara Fužina walk north for a few metres past the village noticeboard and turn right to cross the bridge over the **Mostnica river**. Continue up the road through the extremely attractive village, and just before you reach the *gasilski dom* (fire station) and church, take a minor road to the right which is signed Planinska pot Rudnica.

The road crosses pastures between *toplars* – Slovene double hayracks – and soon arrives at a bridge. Cross the **river Ribnica** and continue straight ahead on a broad gravel track which begins to climb. Within 5mins the track forks; take the left, as the right fork just leads to a nearby pasture building. In another 5mins arrive at a crossroads of tracks and continue straight ahead, following a sign on a tree for Rudnica.

The track climbs through a mixture of woodland and attractive flower meadows with occasional small wooden farm huts. After 30–40mins of steady climbing arrive at a level pasture with a building to the right. You will come back to this meadow again on the descent. The track bears sharply left here and continues quite level for about 150m before steepening once again.

Another 15mins of climbing brings you to an open sloping pasture just below the summit of Rudnica. The track forks - the right fork leads to a wooden hut just 50m away, which used to be a popular rest stop where refreshments were served, but alas, it is now closed. Take the rutted left fork of the track, which skirts the edge of the meadow and then swings right to reach another small wooden hut near a stand of trees. There is a picnic table and log bench below the trees, painted with yellow and white target waymarks.

This is a **lovely place to relax** for a few moments. The lake lies below, with the Vogel ski station and its mountains on the left, and on the right the plateau of Fužinarske planine and the peak of Pršivec. The U-shaped form of the Bohinj valley, where it was formed by the glacier, is very obvious from here.

Continue to the top of the planina on the narrow path to reach the trees. Enter the woods and in another 100m reach a junction; ignore the wooden sign pointing right to Brod, and continue in the same direction as the path edges along the steep crags of Rudnica, and soon arrives at a magnificent viewpoint. ◂

Below lie the villages of Srednja vas and Bohinjska Češnjica and the undulating agricultural land between them. Directly above Srednja vas you can see the high Zajamniki planina, with its row of herders' huts, on the Pokljuka plateau.

About 20m behind a bench lies a small stone cairn among the trees with a visitors' book in its metal box that marks the summit of **Rudnica**.

*The wonderful view of Lake Bohinj seen from the little pasture below the summit of Rudnica*

Retrace your steps back to the picnic table and log bench on the pasture, and continue straight down on the narrow path to reach the edge of the wood about 50m above and to the left of the lower planina hut. Signs saying Razglednik (viewpoint) 100m, Brod, and Bohinsko jezero direct you onto a path into the forest above the cliffs which drop away on the south side of the hill. Walk over tree roots and rocks on the narrow path as a wonderful panorama view opens to your left, where you can look down to Bohinjska Bistrica, the river Sava Bohinjka, and two little villages directly below, Brod and Savica.

The path continues quite level on through the forest, keeping the cliffs to the left. After around 200m it begins to descend. After about 10mins of descent, still following the line of the cliffs, come to the level pasture that you passed on the way up, with the building visible over to the right. Just as you enter the little meadow, notice a signed path a few metres to your left. ▶

The alternative return route back to Stara Fužina goes straight on here.

Take this path, which after about 20m becomes more distinct and waymarked, and soon begins to descend diagonally to the left. Walk below crags, with steep forested slopes down to the right. The path begins to move away from the crags and crosses a scree slope with views of the villages below. Continue down quite steeply to the bottom of the hillside, where you meet a track at a T-junction and turn left. The track almost immediately becomes a tarmac road and passes houses of the village of **Brod**. This road curves round to the right to reach a bridge over the river Sava Bohinjka which leads to the village of Savica.

It is about 5km from here to Ribčev Laz, all the way on a pleasant tarmac cycle track. Don't cross the bridge, but continue straight ahead across the fertile agricultural land between the river and the hill. After about 1km the track enters the trees and continues, with the river on your left, through woodland and pasture. Pass a climbers' crag, and soon after reach a picnic area with a wooden roofed structure offering shelter to walkers and cyclists.

Continue along the pleasant, quiet route, with occasional views up to the high Julian Alps. Go up a short rise, marked 10% for cyclists, and then begin to descend, catching a glimpse of the church of Sveti Janez (St John the Baptist) in Ribčev Laz ahead through the trees. The track curves round to the right and soon afterwards passes some houses; you can leave the track here, signed to the lake, or turn right to Stara Fužina. At the edge of the village the cycle track turns right and continues to Studor, but cross the river Ribnica on a bridge and enter **Stara Fužina**, following the lane to meet the main road through the village; turn left and cross the bridge over the river Mostnica to return to the starting point.

### Alternative route back to Stara Fužina

Continue straight ahead across the meadow and in 100m reach another sign, Bohinjsko Jezero, at the edge of the wood. Follow the narrow path into the wood as it initially meanders through quite densely planted small conifers before passing through small open glades. Yellow waymarks and direction arrows confirm the way as the path bears left, beginning to descend more steadily. The path becomes broader, and although there are no views to be had in this section the pleasant shade of the trees will likely be very welcome on hot summer days.

About 20mins after leaving the level pasture, arrive at a small patch of open ground where a track branches left. Ignore this and continue straight down on a broad stony track, within 25m passing a signed path to Rudnica that leads up right. In another 100m the track forks; take the left fork and begin a short ascent, with a view of the Triglav massif high above the tree tops straight ahead as the path levels out once more. Continue for another 10mins over undulating ground before reaching a small meadow, which you cross before entering the trees again. The path now makes a gentle descent through shady deciduous woods and soon arrives at another junction; one track is signed left to the small top of Peč and another unmarked path continues straight ahead.

Ignore both of these and take the path which bears to the right, continuing quite steeply down a forested ridge, passing waymarks and gaining a view further right through the trees to Stara Fužina. Soon the path swings left and makes a series of short zigzags down through the wood before emerging at another small meadow.

Walk down the left edge of the meadow to arrive at a minor tarmac road. Straight ahead is a bridge that crosses the Mostnica river and leads to the main Stara Fužina road, but turn right along the cycle track just before the bridge. Continue alongside the river and across open meadows with a good view of Debeli vrh (2390m) ahead to the left. Where the cycle track swings sharply right, signed Srednja vas, cross the bridge straight ahead over the river Ribnica on the edge of **Stara Fužina**. At the next junction turn left and in 100m cross the bridge over the Mostnica river and turn left to arrive back at the village noticeboard and supermarket.

# WALK 24

*Korita Mostnice*

| | |
|---|---|
| **Start/finish** | Hudičev most ('the Devil's bridge') |
| **Distance** | 11km |
| **Total ascent/descent** | 300m |
| **Grade** | 2 |
| **Time** | 3½–4hrs |
| **Maps** | 1:25,000 Bohinj, 1:25,000 Triglav, 1:30,000 Bled |
| **Refreshments** | Koča na Vojah and at Okrepčevalnica Slap |
| **Access** | By car: go left at the crossroads where the road turns right over the bridge in Stara Fužina, and drive up the hill for about 700m to a car park (parking fee in summer). Take the trail signed local route 7 for Slap Mostnica and walk along the level path for about 250m to arrive at the bridge. |
| **Route map** | See Walk 21 |

This lovely walk follows the river Mostnica to the head of the Voje valley. The first section runs alongside the deep gorge which has been cut by the river (there is an entry charge in summer). The route then goes on to visit the waterfall at the end of the valley before circling back through the open planina area with its wooden buildings and flower meadows. The route is beautiful throughout, varying between woods and open land, and is full of interest, with wonderful views of the surrounding peaks.

**If you arrive on foot in Stara Fužina**

From the supermarket in Stara Fužina walk north and go straight ahead at the crossroads, following a yellow sign to Hudičev most with the river on your right and passing pretty houses on both sides. After crossing the river turn left at a T-junction and walk up the lane; soon after the large Rabič apartment building on your left, go through an iron gate, where the track is joined by another from the right, and continue round to the left across a small open pasture to reach the bridge.

▸ From Hudičev most walk up the track on the west bank of the **Mostnica river** for a short distance to a big orientation sign describing the gorge (unfortunately in Slovene only), and take the path straight on, descending slightly into the woods, with the gorge falling away to your right. Walk pleasantly through the forest to the pay kiosk, and then cross a bridge, with more views down into the deep gorge. Further along from this bridge the gorge becomes much shallower and the path runs to the right of the extremely pretty river.

The Mostnica gorge is much deeper than expected as you look down from the bridge!

The phrase '**crystal clear**' is somewhat overused to describe rivers but this one genuinely merits it – it sparkles like diamonds, and in places is so clear that you have to look twice to see if there is any water there at all. At times it reflects startlingly green where the bottom is sandy, while elsewhere there are potholes, small rapids and little waterfalls. At a sign that says 'Slonček' ('elephant rock'), pointing the 10m or so towards the river, there is an enchanting deep green pool with a little natural rock arch.

The path continues through beech woods, bending slightly away from the river, and the gorge gradually deepens again. Reach a viewpoint which shows the gorge with the rocks almost overhanging – the top ones are barely a metre apart. Further on another bridge takes you back onto the west side, again with good views into the depths, where you take the path climbing steeply away from the river into the forest, signed (local) route 7, Slap Mostnice and Voje. Follow the waymarks on a northward trail, with the noise of the river on your right.

About 10mins from the bridge emerge at a second orientation sign, where the path joins a lane coming up from Stara Fužina. Turn right and within a few paces there is the first glimpse of the beautiful view of the head of the Voje valley and the peaks beyond. About 200m further on reach **Koča na Vojah**, where you can refresh yourself with a drink while gazing at the view out into the open

Koča na Vojah

valley with its buildings and forests, and the shapely peak of Draški vrh in the background.

After the hut the road becomes unmade and you continue north along it. After about 5mins ignore a track which goes up to a house in the woods on the left, and carry on along the main track to a building where the track forks; the right-hand trail is signed to Voje Slap and Uskovnica, while the left is signed to Velo polje and Triglav.

Take the left fork, which keeps to the left-hand side of the valley and emerges near the valley head in an open area. A little further on come to a sign on a tree, 'Slap 450m', indicating a path heading right. Take this narrow track and soon reach a bridge; cross it and continue straight ahead for about 100m to come out opposite Okrepčevalnica Slap, where you can get refreshments. Turn left onto a broad path and walk for about 5mins to the viewpoint for **Mostniški slapovi** (the Mostnice waterfalls). ▸

The falls are in two tiers, falling into deep green pools deeply shaded by the trees.

Return down the path, and continue straight on, past **Okrepčevalnica Slap**, and on through the delightful open planina of Voje, with its wooden buildings and short sections of forest. At the end of the planina the road enters the forest once more and soon crosses the river to return to the building where the track forks on the outward route. Continue the way you came back to Koča na Vojah, and carry on down the gorge again to return to **Stara Fužina**. Alternatively take the road, which is slightly longer but may be easier walking; turn left at the signpost to 'Hudičev most' soon after emerging from the woods into some pastures, as the road makes a longer detour before reaching Stara Fužina.

# WALK 25

*Pršivec*

| | |
|---|---|
| **Start/finish** | Hudičev most ('the Devil's bridge') |
| **Distance** | 17km |
| **Total ascent/descent** | 1260m |
| **Grade** | 3 |
| **Time** | 7–8hrs |
| **Maps** | 1:25,000 Bohinj, 1:25,000 Triglav |
| **Refreshments** | Kosijev Dom na Vogarju and Planina pri Jezeru hut |
| **Access** | By car: turn left at the crossroads where the road turns right over the bridge in Stara Fužina, and drive up the hill for about 700m to a car park (parking fee in summer). Take the trail signed local route 7 for Slap Mostnica and walk along the level path for about 250m to arrive at the bridge |
| **Route map** | See Walk 21 |

If you like walking through forests, then this mountain is for you. Almost the entire trail is through the trees, the mixed woodland of the lower slopes gradually giving way to pine, spruce, larch and finally dwarf pine. It is even better in the autumn, as the larches begin to shed their needles in a golden rain against the impossibly blue skies, and the beeches burn red and orange in the valley. The views from the summit are even more rewarding for the lack of them on the way up – when you finally emerge from the trees, the panorama is startling in its extent.

It is perfectly feasible to climb Pršivec and return the same way, but it is worth making the circular route described here. Although the return trail is slightly longer, the charms of Planina Viševnik with its shepherds' huts tucked beneath the cliffs, and Planina pri Jezeru with its beautiful lake, will more than repay the extra effort.

**If you arrive on foot in Stara Fužina**

From the supermarket in Stara Fužina walk north and go straight ahead at the crossroads, following a yellow sign to Hudičev most with the river on your right and passing pretty houses on both sides. After crossing the river turn left at a T-junction and walk up the lane; soon after the large Rabič apartment building on your left, go through an iron gate, where the track is joined by another from the right, and continue round to the left across a small open pasture to reach the bridge.

At Hudičev most, take the track on the west side of the river and walk uphill, following a sign for Vogar. At an information board about the Voje valley, don't take the track that leads down right to Korita Mostnice, but keep walking up the road, signed for Vogar. Keep on the gravel track as it gently climbs to meet a minor tarmac road. Turn right, and walk up the road for about 30m to the waymarked track that continues on the left-hand side. There are fine views of the attractive peaks of Tosc and Draški Vrh at the head of the valley. Follow a sign saying Kosijev dom 1hr and Pršivec 3hrs 30mins.

Walk up between wire fences on an open grassy pasture and then climb up through the woods; it's steep but the height gain is a pleasure because of the well-laid stones of the old mule track that still survive in many places. Eventually, as the gradient finally eases, a path leads left, signed Spomenik (memorial), which leads to a launch site for paragliders. It is worth the 30m detour to get an excellent view of the lake.

Return to the main path and continue up it, passing a small pasture with two beautiful old planina buildings. The broad track continues past a water drinking trough and between more attractive buildings at the lower end of the Vogar planina, all of them roofed with the traditional wood shingles of the area. Soon arrive at **Kosijev Dom na Vogarju** (the Vogar dom) where rest and refreshments can be found. ▶

The walk to the dom is a pleasant walk in itself, taking about 2hrs 30mins for the round trip from Stara Fužina.

Continue up and past the hut, and then level out near more buildings to reach a signed junction. The broad track bends sharply to the right here but leave it to the left on a path, signed Pršivec 2hrs 30mins. The path is narrow and almost immediately leads into the forest, heading uphill. It continues to rise gently and very enjoyably through primarily beech forest, and becomes almost level. After about 20mins arrive at a fork in the track and,

A small stream flows into this flat glade from the right and is the reason for this little marshy habitat.

ignoring a path that leads steeply up to the right, continue straight ahead, passing a boulder signed Pršivec. In another 5mins or so arrive at a small open marshy glade filled with butterburs with their broad, rhubarb-like leaves. ◂

The track crosses the glade and on the other side begins to climb steeply again. Follow the waymarks, ignoring any tracks off to right or left. The path levels and bears sharply left while another broader muddy track swings up to the right into the wood. Stay left on the waymarked path as it skirts a bracken-filled hollow about 50m wide, the delightful woodland route giving enjoyable walking.

The forest gradually begins to change, with increasing stands of conifers. In about 10mins turn left onto a broader track with a red sign for Pršivec. After another 20mins the path bears sharply to the right and soon arrives at another marshy area with more butterburs. Just as you enter this small boggy glade you get your first glimpse of the peak, with its craggy southern aspect just visible above the tree tops. As you leave this clearing the path steepens; take care to follow the waymarks showing the direct route, as various short-cuts can be misleading.

Twenty minutes of steep ascent through surprisingly lush vegetation brings you to a junction where an overgrown path heads off right to Planina Viševnik, but continue straight ahead following a sign on a rock for Pršivec. Just 25m beyond the junction, the path crosses the top of a steep gully bounded on its left by a huge prow of rock, offering precipitous views down to Ukanc. Beyond this, there are some short steps of easy scrambling with no real difficulties; nevertheless, there is a feeling of exposure and care should be taken if the rock is wet.

The view really opens out now, and the path continues over easier ground, still covered with lush plant growth and small trees whose twisted roots and branches encroach on the path. After 10mins further ascent the narrow path passes a small rise or subsidiary top and continues between rocks and small larches for another 5mins before arriving at the open summit of **Pršivec** (1761m).

The **top of Pršivec** is marked by a stone cairn and the metal box containing the summit book and stamp. There is a fabulous 360° panorama, all the better in a way for the restricted outlook on the way up. To the west is Bogatin and the Komna plateau, and to the north is Triglav. Continuing clockwise the Karavanke ridge stretches away into the distance towards the Kamnik-Savinja Alps, while to the south is Vogel and the Lower Bohinj mountains.

The route leaves the summit to the north, following a narrow path and sign on a rock for Viševnik, and drops down through the dwarf pine. The waymarked path descends over typical limestone rock steps with many small crevices, and care should be taken if it is wet, as it is easy to twist an ankle on this terrain. About 10mins after you leave the summit, pass the entrance to Majska jama, one of the deepest caves in the Pršivec area, which has been explored to a depth of over 592m. Special equipment is needed for exploration of the cave. About 100m further on, the path rises briefly before dropping down through the interesting limestone landscape. ▶ This area is called Prišivski kras on the Bohinj 1:25,000 map.

In spite of the rocky ground, the trees still manage to flourish with a great variety of plants nestled in the rocky niches.

Around 25mins brings you to **Planina Viševnik** – an extremely scenic little planina nestling under the cliffs

*Approaching the delightful shingle-roofed buildings of Planina Viševnik*

*Planina pri Jezeru with its herders' huts and dom*

of Griva, with six or seven wooden huts topped by shingled roofs, one of which offers refreshments in summer. A sign at the planina reads Dom na planina pri Jezeru 45mins, but this time is overestimated and contradictory to the following signs. Leave the planina on the same path and within another 100m arrive at a fork. Both paths are waymarked and signed Planini pri Jezeru – take the path to the right, signed 25mins. Continue on into the wood, the path soon dropping steeply over rocks and gnarled tree roots to skirt beneath a large crag, and reach **Planina pri Jezeru** with its charming lake, herders' huts and big dom.

Take the broad track that leads away from the dom, signed Planina Vogar 1hr, which enters the wood after 100m. In another 150m reach a signed junction where a narrow path heads right, signed Planina Vogar 1hr 45mins, and the main track goes straight on for Stara Fužina and Planina Vogar 1hr 30mins. Either way can be taken – the right-hand path visits another attractive planina, Vodični vrh – but the way described here continues straight on along the broad stony track. In another 5mins go through a gate and continue down, passing log benches where a path heads steeply down to the left.

About 30mins after leaving the dom, reach a junction at a sharp left-hand bend in the track, where a path is signed to the right, Planina Vogar 1hr. Take this, descending into the wood, and in about 15mins pass a sign that now says Planina Vogar 30mins – more confusion with regard to timing.

In another 50m leave the track for a narrow path that bears right, signed Vogar. The path runs quite level as it passes through beautiful mature beech woods, and in another 15mins emerges onto a broad forest road. From here Planina Vogar is signed 20mins and Stara Fužina 1hr 20mins, so continue along the road and soon pass a small planina with two pretty weekend cottages. About 200m after this arrive at a junction, leave the forest road and continue straight ahead on a broad gravel track signed Koča na Vogu 10mins.

Pass more attractive cottages as you enter the upper end of Planina Vogar, and arrive back at the junction 5mins from the Vogar dom, where the path to Pršivec leads off into the forest to the right. Continue along the broad track the short distance to the Vogar dom, and from here reverse the ascent route back to the start.

# WALK 26

## *Vogel*

| | |
|---|---|
| **Start/finish** | Top station of the Vogel cable car (Ski Hotel) |
| **Distance** | 10.5km |
| **Total ascent/descent** | 600m |
| **Grade** | 3 |
| **Time** | 4–5hrs |
| **Maps** | 1:25,000 Bohinj |
| **Refreshments** | Planina Zadnji Vogel |
| **Access** | The bottom cable-car station is near Ukanc at the western end of Bohinjsko jezero and is signed from the road. |

The ascent of Vogel (1922m) is made easy by using the ski-resort cable car, which also runs in summer (check opening times with the Tourist Office or on www.vogel.si). Most people who arrive at the Ski Hotel only look north, at the admittedly magnificent view of Triglav and the Julian Alps, as the view south to Vogel is made unpleasant by the ravages of the ski lifts and runs that are so popular in winter. However, the mountain massif of Vogel is complex, and there are places to be found with views and alpine meadows that are as beautiful as anywhere in the Julian Alps.

This tour descends slightly from the cable-car station before climbing to the summit of Vogel via a stunningly beautiful secluded valley. The return is by a high-level balcony path that avoids the ski slopes until the very last section, making an excellent short mountain day. It's not worth trying to tackle the walk up from the valley floor – the ski slope is miserably steep to ascend in places.

From the top cable-car station, walk past the Ski Hotel Vogel and continue on the broad ski service road and past a pizzeria. About 200m from the cable car turn right at a junction, signed Komna, Vogel and Zlatorog. Soon afterwards pass a right-hand junction which is the way down to the valley, after which the track, signed Planina Zadnji Vogel, bears slightly right and down. Don't take

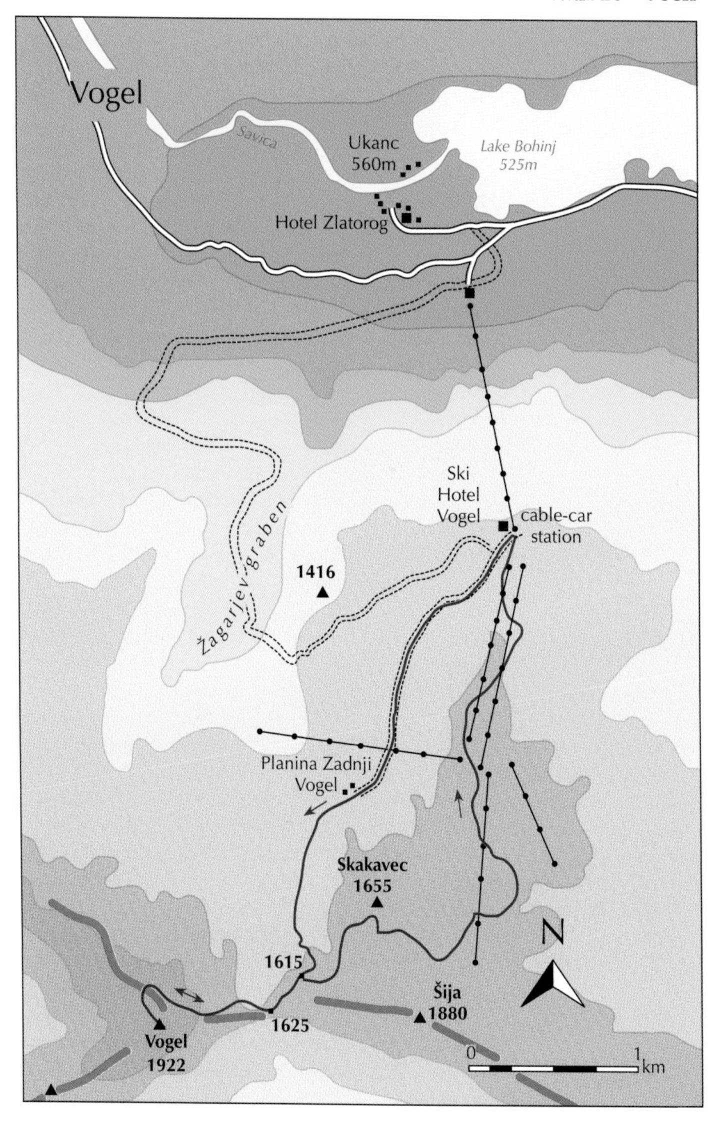
Vogel
Savica
Ukanc
560m
Lake Bohinj
525m
Hotel Zlatorog
Ski
Hotel
Vogel
cable-car
station
Žagarjev graben
1416
Planina Zadnji
Vogel
Skakavec
1655
1615
1625
Šija
1880
Vogel
1922
N
0
1
km

this track, but instead head uphill for a short distance on an old track bearing left, which brings you to a sign for Planina Zadnji Vogel indicating a narrow path entering the forest to the right.

This very pretty path lined with flowers and old trees, predominantly beech, gives a pleasant 10mins alternative to the service road. All too soon it begins to descend a little and you can see the service road below, which you eventually rejoin, continuing in the same direction. Another 10mins on the service road brings you to **Planina Zadnji Vogel**. Leave the forest road, which heads down to the right, and cross the open area past the *sirarna* (cheese-making building) continuing straight ahead on the now grassy track.

**Bohinj cheese** is famous in Slovenia – cheese-making was restarted at this planina in 2009, after a decline following the Second World War. Cheese and other dairy products are made and sold, and the building is also a mountain hut with food and accommodation.

Shortly afterwards come to a prominent rock, signed to the left Vogel 2hrs and, straight on, Komna 5–6hrs.

Head left on the narrow path, through dwarf pine, alpine flowers, and larch and spruce trees. After a few hundred metres enter a small, open valley with steep rocky sides covered with trees, while flowers of all hues carpet its floor in what can only be described as an alpine garden. Walk due south across the valley and ascend the rocky path at its head. Half an hour's delightful walk brings you almost to the top of the valley and another prominent boulder, signed Vogel to the left, which you follow actually in more or less the same direction. ◄

Pause a moment to look back at the excellent view of Triglav, looking vastly bigger than its companions of the Julian Alps. The lower peak of Pršivec (Walk 25) is straight ahead on the other side of the Bohinj valley.

A further 10mins climbing brings you to a path crossroads (by spot height 1615m on the sketch map). To the left is the return route to the cable car, while to the right the path winds all the way to Komna. Continue straight ahead to Vogel, as the path traverses the left-hand side of a rocky scoop. On the skyline is a dramatic notch on the craggy ridge, and further to the right along the ridge is the summit pyramid of Vogel. After 10mins reach the ridge at a col and get the first view to the Primorska (south) side, which is much steeper and craggier.

The path turns right and continues on the northern side below the ridge.

The ridge path is signed '1', and is the **Slovene high-level route** (see *Trekking in Slovenia –The Slovene High Level Route* by Justi Carey and Roy Clark). It starts in Maribor in the north-east of the country and wanders across various mountain ranges of Slovenia – Pohorje, the Kamniško-Savinjske Alpe, the Karavanke and the Julian Alps – to finally arrive, after several weeks, at the coast.

Looking back now you can see along the ridge of the Lower Bohinj mountains. The path continues, keeping well below the crest to the right-hand side, and in about 10mins brings you to a second col, with the bulk of the summit of Vogel right in front. Make a short scramble up the lower rocks of the ridge; it is not difficult but it is a little exposed, and protected by a steel cable. The path then traverses across screes, again on the northern side, before turning left at a junction to reach the western ridge which it follows to Vogel's summit.

The **view** from the wonderfully airy summit is spectacular: to the south-east a stratified ridge links Vogel to nearby Žabiški Kuk (1844m). The hills of the Spodnje Bohinjske gore (Lower Bohinj mountains) continue towards Bogatin (Walk 29), while Triglav and his companions dominate the view to the north. To the east stretches the enticing ridge which leads all the way to Črna prst (Walks 27 and 28).

Retrace your steps back to the path crossroads at 1615m, and turn right onto the return route to the cable car (signed Orlova glava). ▶ The path traverses

As an alternative return route, follow the high-level route 1 which follows the ridge east to Šija, where you turn left to descend the ski slopes.

*Approaching the summit ridge of Vogel*

the hillside through dwarf pine and alpine flowers with excellent views to the north and west. A short uphill section takes you to the crest of a ridge (of the subsidiary top of **Skakavec**) covered with a thicket of dwarf pine, which edges the last side valley before the main ski area. To avoid the descent and ascent of an ugly ski slope, turn right where the path divides, signed Šija, and traverse round the head of the rocky valley. ▶

A side path from the head of the valley makes a short diversion to the summit of Šija (15–20mins to the top).

Continue round and pass under the ski lift, close to its top, and shortly afterwards see a sign on a rock signed Ski Hotel. Continue on the path, which winds down through limestone rock formations and dwarf pines. Meet the ski lift again, and then unfortunately the ski slopes can no longer be avoided. Ascend slightly, passing underneath the ski lift, and make your way down following the pistes. You can see the Ski Hotel below, along with wonderful views of Triglav, one reason why the slopes are so popular in winter. It is about 20mins from here back to the top cable-car station.

## WALK 27

*Črna prst*

| | |
|---|---|
| **Start/finish** | Main crossroads in Bohinjska Bistrica |
| **Distance** | 12km |
| **Total ascent/descent** | 1400m |
| **Grade** | 3 |
| **Time** | 6hrs |
| **Maps** | 1:25,000 Bohinj |
| **Refreshments** | Orožnova koča, on the way up, and Dom Zorka Jelinčiča na Črni prsti, just below the summit |
| **Access** | By car: drive up to Ravne and park just before the forest road enters the woods. Walk up the road for a few hundred metres and turn left at the rock marked 'Črna prst 2hrs30'. |
| **Note** | The path is easy but often rocky and can be slippery after rain. |

The real beauty and attraction of this mountain lies in the fact that its flanks and summit are home to a diverse collection of flowers, which start at around 1400m and continue all the way to the top at 1844m. The route passes through them as if through a perfectly planted border, carefully tended by expert gardeners. Here, though, the only gardeners are natural selection and climate, combined with unusual soil conditions – the name Črna prst means 'black earth'. There are wonderful views, too – north towards Triglav and the white limestone Julian Alps, and south across Primorska with its softer, steep-sided, tree-covered hills.

The route starts in Bohinjska Bistrica and is very well waymarked and signed throughout. However, if you have a car you won't miss anything (except muddy boots!), and you will gain 300m in height, if you drive up to the ski slopes at Ravne. This reduces the total walking time to around 4½–5hrs.

From the main crossroads in Bohinjska Bistrica, looking south towards the Lower Bohinj mountains, turn left and walk along the road, round a right hand bend, to the house at 10 Jelovška cesta. Turn right and take the rough track on the right, signed Črna prst, up past some gardens and across a field to reach a military cemetery.

The **military cemetery** has 285 marked graves of soldiers of different nationalities. Between 1915 and 1917 Bohinj was an important military base behind Austro-Hungarian lines in the high mountains of the Krn front, and there were two military hospitals in Bohinjska Bistrica. Patients were transported to hospital by rail, and the dead were buried here in late 1917.

Continue across more fields, following a grassy track which brings you to a forest road, where you turn right and immediately see a sign for Črna prst pointing up the hill towards the south. Walk quite steeply up the rutted and usually muddy track for 15 minutes, then level out in a tiny field and continue in the same direction on a narrow path. Another 15mins climb brings you to a wide track where you turn left. This quickly turns into a path

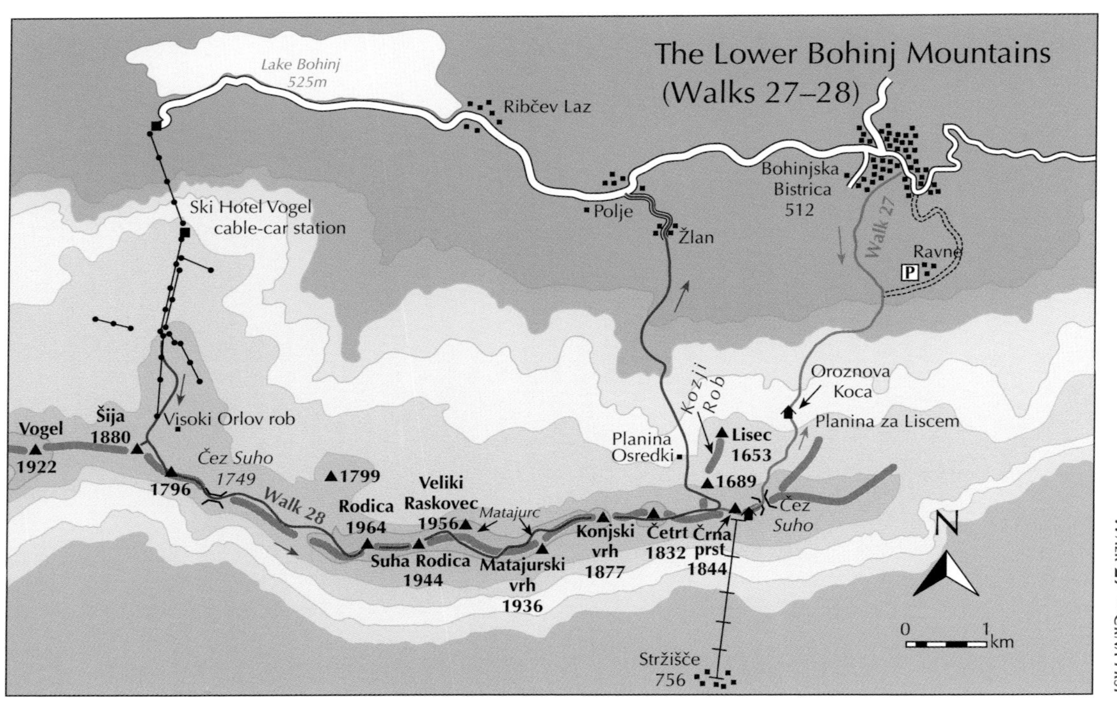

The Lower Bohinj Mountains
(Walks 27–28)
Lake Bohinj
525m
Ribčev Laz
Bohinjska
Bistrica
512
Polje
Žlan
Ski Hotel Vogel
cable-car station
Walk 27
Ravne
P
Oroznova
Koca
Planina za Liscem
Kozji
Rob
Lisec
1653
1689
Planina
Osredki
Visoki Orlov rob
Šija
1880
Vogel
1922
Čez Suho
1749
1796
1799
Walk 28
Rodica
1964
Veliki
Raskovec
1956
Matajurc
Suha Rodica
1944
Matajurski
vrh
1936
Konjski
vrh
1877
Četrt
1832
Črna
prst
1844
Čez
Suho
N
0
1
km
Stržišče
756

This path for the lower section is not marked clearly on the sheet map, although it is obvious on the ground.

across a small pasture and comes out on another wide track. Turn left again, and after a few paces reach the forest road. ◂

Turn right this time and after about 150m pass a sign on a rock, 'Črna prst 2hrs30', and just after this, turn left onto an obvious path heading up left into the woods. After about 5mins the route makes a slight detour as it crosses a scree-filled gully – in 2014 the original line of the path was covered in fallen trees, the result of a major ice storm. Within 40m join the original path again and climb steadily on this pleasant trail, trending diagonally right across the forested hillside.

After about 30mins the path looks as if it carries on traversing, but waymarks direct you up quite steeply to the left. About 5mins more brings you to the upper forest road, where Črna prst is signed to the right. Within 100m you see the hill Lisec straight ahead, looking like a forested cone from here, and as you round the next corner, Črna prst looms into view to the left of it.

Continue on the forest road for about 5mins to a tree with a waymark, signed Črna prst and Orožnova koča to the left, but also Črna prst and Planina za Liscem along the forest road to the right. The route now goes left up into the forest, directly south towards Črna prst. After 15–20mins of steady climbing come to a more level section through mixed woodland with thick undergrowth, and in another 5mins reach some small crags where there is an extraordinary pair of trees, a conifer and a beech, growing tightly together on top of a rock. The path continues, still climbing but more easily now, past the crags to some final zigzags up to the planina.

The original koča was the very first hut owned and used by the Slovene Alpine Club, built in 1894 and destroyed in 1944.

Just before the trees part to reveal the planina, a path goes right, down towards Lake Bohinj (signed Jezero, meaning 'lake'), Bohinjska Bistrica and Polje. On the return this could provide an alternative descent route to the valley. Just up ahead you can see **Orožnova Koča**, rebuilt in 2004. ◂ In front of the koča is the basin of **Planina za Liscem**, with a tiny pool in the bottom, Lisec on the right (not quite as cone-shaped now) and Črna prst up ahead.

*Leaving Orožnova koča at Planina za Liscem*

Follow waymarks left into the wood and pass a Triglav National Park sign and information boards about the special flora of the area.

> Around the signs, notice the wild mixture of **plants**, each carefully marked with small signs giving the Slovene and Latin names. These unobtrusive and useful signs are used along the path almost to the summit crags, to help identify the rich variety of plant life.

The track quickly gains height and then begins to level out a little as it traverses the rocky side of the high planina, and you walk through a mass of different perennials and small shrubs, mostly above knee height. ▶

It pays to linger along this beautiful balcony path through the flowers, with extensive views north towards Triglav.

You are now at the bottom of the summit slopes – the gardens continue up quite steeply to the base of the crags. As the height increases the species gradually change, but there is always the same incredible range of colours. The path continues pleasantly up, and just below the summit crags it traverses to the left beneath them.

Looking down you can see the planina with the koča, Bohinjska Bistrica on the floor of the valley, and behind that the Pokljuka plateau. Planina Zajamniki with its row of herders' cottages can be seen in the distance straight ahead, while behind is the dark forested ridge of Debela peč and the peaks of the Julian Alps, with Triglav very much in charge. Over to the right is the inevitable line of the Karavanke, always on the edge of view, and then the Kamniško-Savinjske Alpe. Babji zob, the craggy top above Bled, marks the gorge of the Sava Bohinjka where it divides the plateaus of Pokljuka and Jelovica.

The path begins to traverse away from the summit cliffs, heading left along a rocky ramp, which soon enters a small thicket of low trees and plants. Keep traversing left and then come out into the open again where a path signed to Planina Za Črno goro continues straight ahead. Turn right here and ascend the final few metres to the small col of **Čez Suho**. Now you can see the summit not far away, with Dom Zorka Jelinčiča beneath it on the south side. Turn right along the ridge, and the last 10–15mins is a pleasant stroll along the south side, with excellent views to Primorska down an amazing, uniformly steep, grassy slope, still covered with lush vegetation. The hut supply cableway, coming up from the little village of Stržišče, can be seen. Behind the dom scramble up easy rocks a few metres to the top of **Črna prst** for a truly panoramic view.

To descend, retrace your steps of the ascent.

# WALK 28

*Spodnje Bohinjske gore (the Lower Bohinj mountains)*

| | |
|---|---|
| **Start** | Top station of the Vogel chairlift |
| **Finish** | Polje on the road between Bohinjska Bistrica and Ribčev Laz; or Bohinjska Bistrica |
| **Distance** | 17km (for either descent route) |
| **Total ascent** | About 600m |
| **Total descent** | About 1300m |
| **Grade** | 3 |
| **Time** | 9hrs |
| **Maps** | 1:25,000 Bohinj |
| **Refreshments** | Dom Zorka Jelinčiča |
| **Access** | Take the cable car at the western end of Lake Bohinj to the top station and continue on the chairlift which runs directly from the top station, just outside the café. |
| **Return to start** | You will need to take a bus (several buses a day run from Bohinjska Bistrica to Bohinj Zlatorog – check times at the Tourist Information Office) or taxi back to the start or have a group with two cars and place one at the end before you start. |

This excellent high-level ridge walk marks the southern edge of the main Julian Alps. It runs from Vogel to Črna prst, never quite reaching 2000m but never falling below 1700m. The walk makes use of the Vogel cable car and chairlift to gain height, and then follows the Lower Bohinj mountain ridge from Šija to Črna prst. Apart from the excellent views to north and south, a major attraction of these mountains is the wonderful variety and abundance of flowers, which catch the eye on every side. There is a narrow section on the ridge just beyond Rodica, which can feel quite airy due to the very steep grassy slopes particularly on the south side, but apart from this there are no major difficulties. However, check the weather forecast before you go, as the ridge is no place to be in a thunderstorm.

▸ From the top of the chairlift, walk up the path through the dwarf pine to reach a junction, where waymarked paths go left and right – turn right for Šija.

See the route map in Walk 27.

Follow the stony track, between the piste fences and over the little top of Orlova glava, to eventually reach the top of the second chairlift at **Visoki Orlov rob**. The path continues just to the right of the little cabin here, at first descending slightly and then beginning the ascent of **Šija**. Reach a junction with route 1, which traverses the hillside, signed left to Rodica and right to Vogel, but for now go straight on and continue climbing steadily. Reach the grassy summit after about 30mins walk from the cabin, with good views to the south and along the ridge east to Rodica and west towards Vogel.

Return to the junction with route 1 and turn right for Rodica. The path traverses the hillside, descending gently for about 10mins, and then climbs over a few rocky steps and dwarf pine roots to reach the broad grassy ridge. The path continues along the gently rising ridge, which is covered with flowers, including edelweiss, and even a few varieties of mushroom.

Another 10mins brings you to the unnamed top at **1796m**. From here the rocky path drops down between dwarf pine to reach the grassy col of **Čez Suho**. To your

*The path weaving up the flanks of Rodica*

left are two large karst sinkholes (marked on the sheet map), and there are good views to the north down into the forested valley, with Triglav and the Julian Alps in the distance. Just beyond the col there is a cairn at a T-junction, where you keep straight on, signed Rodica, route 1. ▶

A possible escape route here turns left to go down Zadnja Suha to Planina Suha, where a waymarked path continues down to Ribčev Laz at the eastern end of Lake Bohinj.

The path continues easily along the broad grassy ridge with its abundance of wild flowers. Ribčev Laz can be seen down to the left. Eventually, the path drops a little to wind between two more karst sinkholes, and from here another 20mins or so of ascent brings you to the summit of **Rodica** (1964m).

From the summit the ridge ahead narrows, but a good path continues along the crest with steep slopes to either side. After about 100m the path drops down a little to the right-hand (southern) side and continues just below the rocky crest. A little further on briefly join the crest again to avoid a short steep impasse. The path soon takes to the left-hand (northern) side to pass below the craggy top of **Suha Rodica** (1944m), and continues more easily now as the ridge begins to broaden out again.

Begin to ascend once more and cross back to the south side of the ridge to traverse below the summit of **Veliki Raskovec** (1956m). From here you can see Črna prst with its hut in the distance. Continue, rejoining the crest for a short while, before dropping back to the north side, just below the crest. The path traverses well below the summit of the next peak, **Matajurski vrh**, with the large stony corrie of Matajurc on your left. Pass another big sinkhole to the left and join the grassy crest again, carpeted with flowers.

The next section is one of the most pleasant parts of the walk, wandering along easily to the right of the level ridge, with an airy feeling of space above the steep grassy slopes falling uniformly down to the forest in the valley. The path follows either the crest or the right-hand side of the ridge, and passes below the summit of **Četrt** (1832m). The village of Stržišče can be seen down in the valley to your right. ▶

As you approach the unique plant habitat of Črna prst, the flowers become more colourful, larger and more varied.

A brief scramble up some rocky steps brings you to a short section of steel cable as a handrail and a painted sign on a rock, Koča Črna prst 20mins. Continue steeply up, with more cable handrail on the eroded path but no real difficulties, to reach the crest of the ridge, noticing a path going down on the north side signed Bohinjsko jezero which you will take on your return. To reach Črna Prst and Dom Zorka Jelinčiča, just below the summit, continue ascending east along the ridge for another 15mins.

Return to the path mentioned above, signed Polje, Žlan and Planina Osredki as well as Bohinjsko jezero. Begin the descent from the ridge through dwarf pine and shrubs and within 10mins reach a grassy notch at the foot of the satellite ridge that leads to Lisec. Pass through the notch and descend the stony path, still surrounded by the tall lush plants. ◄ About 20mins from the notch, the path passes through a level open area of grass about 100m across. Pass a small cattle watering hole, as the narrow path enters thickets and shrubs and then descends again. The two attractive wooden buildings of **Planina Osredki** come into view, sitting on a grassy rise above a small

You may see and hear marmots in the boulder- and scree-filled corrie to your left.

*Beginning the descent from the ridge*

pool with the beautiful backdrop of Triglav and the Julian Alps behind.

Walk down the small planina where you may need to step over/under a wire cattle fence before you enter mixed forest, with clumps of small shrubs and trees lining the quite overgrown path. This gives way to beautiful open beech woods, and after 25mins of steep descent from the planina, cross a forest road, following waymarks and a sign on a tree (Polje), and continue down the path. After another 15mins pass a track going off right to Planina za Liscem and Orožnova koča, and continue straight ahead to reach a fork in the path in another 5mins or so. This fork can be easily missed as the track is quite overgrown at this point with tall grasses and shrubs. Turn left here and continue down, to soon reach a broad gravel road which is crossed to follow the continuation of the path, signed Polje, jezero. ▶

If you miss the left fork, continue straight down to reach the gravel road and turn left, and after 100m turn right down the path mentioned above to Polje, jezero.

Continue down the now broad forest track, which in 150m crosses a dry stream bed on a concrete ford as it bears right. After a further 15–20mins of descent, notice an old ruined stone building amid the trees below to the right. In a few more metres the track ends and you continue down, bearing left, on a narrower path into the wood.

In a few more minutes reach a dry watercourse that crosses the path. Straight ahead is another stony watercourse. Follow the waymarked path on its right bank for a few metres that soon heads further to the right into the woods, before bearing left across a small clearing. Pass through a band of saplings to arrive at another grassy clearing with an attractive weekend cottage. Just as you are passing the cottage, notice a waymarked tree to the left and follow a narrow path that heads down towards trees. A temporary cattle fence may need to be negotiated here but continue to follow waymarks on the narrow path that descends through the wood and bears left.

The roofs and small fields of Žlan soon come into view below and the path emerges at a gravel turning point. Within a short distance the gravel road becomes tarmac and passes between the houses and old wooden toplars of the pretty village of **Žlan**. Continue down the road for almost 1km to reach the main road at **Polje**, just by the bus stop.

### Descent to Bohinjska Bistrica

From Črna prst descend east to reach the grassy col Čez Suho then follow signs for Orožnova Koča and Bohinjska Bistrica. The path leads down left then bears right as it traverses above Planina za Liscem before arriving at the koča. From the hut, zigzag down through the woods following waymarks and signs for Bohinjska Bistrica.

The path soon forks – take the right fork and follow the path as it passes below small crags and through shrubby undergrowth before descending steadily for about 10–15mins to reach a forest road. Turn right along the road and in 5mins take the waymarked path on the left that leads steeply down through the forest for another 20mins to meet a forest road again. ◂ Turn right and continue along it for about 150m before turning left and heading down a track that becomes a path as it crosses a small open meadow just below the road.

Continue along this forest road to reach Ravine, if you have left a car there.

Continue down following waymarks on a track, then turn right onto a path, signed Bohinjska Bistrica, passing another small meadow then dropping down more steeply on a rutted track to come out into the open at a gravel road. Turn right, then within a few metres turn left and head down a grassy track across a field and pass a WW1 military cemetery before reaching a road (Jelovška cesta). Follow the road as it bends left to reach the main crossroads in Bohinjska Bistrica.

## WALK 29

*Bogatin and Mahavšček*

| | |
|---|---|
| **Start/finish** | Koča pri Savici, west of Ukanc |
| **Distance** | 21km |
| **Total ascent/descent** | 1400m |
| **Grade** | 3 |
| **Time** | 8½–9½hrs |
| **Maps** | 1:25,000 Bohinj, 1:25,000 Triglav, 1:25,000 Bovec-Trenta |
| **Access** | Koča pri Savici can be reached by bus or car from Ukanc, or by a walk of 30–40 minutes (described in Walk 22). |
| **Accommodation** | Dom na Komni and Koča pod Bogatinom |

Bogatin (1977m) is closely linked with one of Slovenia's favourite legends, that of Zlatorog, the goldenhorn. The treasure he guarded was supposed to lie under this mountain, and so is close to the hearts of Slovene mountaineers. Local stories aside, it is a shapely mountain and combined with its close neighbour, Mahavšček, introduces the walker to the area around Komna to make a fine day out from the Bohinj valley. The route is described from Koča pri Savici, at the western end of Lake Bohinj.

Walk through the car park past the big snack bar where a sign points towards the Savica waterfall and to Dom na Komni, 2hrs 30mins. Just before the waterfall pay kiosk the path branches left, again signed Dom na Komni and Bogatin. Walk up the good path through the beech woods, quickly gaining height in sweeping hairpins. There are a couple of places where it is possible to get a good view of the lake. At the top of the hairpins the path continues, heading through the wood.

For a while the hut cableway can be seen overhead, but it later disappears into the trees as the route to the

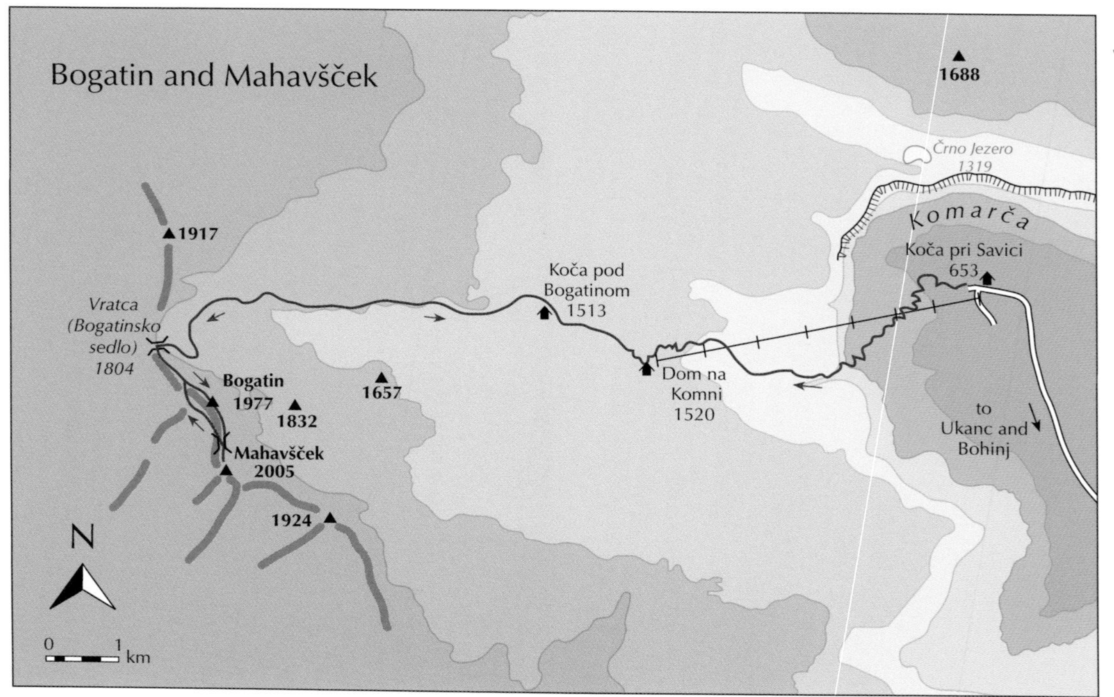
Bogatin and Mahavšček
1688
Črno Jezero
1319
Komarča
Koča pri Savici
653
Koča pod
Bogatinom
1513
▲1917
Vratca
(Bogatinsko
sedlo)
1804
Bogatin
1977
1832
1657
Dom na
Komni
1520
to
Ukanc and
Bohinj
Mahavšček
2005
1924
N
0
1
km

hut meanders away from it. Look out for a glimpse of Dom na Komni through the trees, ahead and on your left. After about 2hrs 20mins the route emerges from the trees to reach a junction signed Dom na Komni 5mins and Koča pod Bogatinom 15mins. Follow the sign for the koča or make the short detour left to Dom na Komni for refreshments.

The **view** opens out and is stunning – although you are now above the beech and spruce, there are still plenty of dwarf pine and rowan, and the bare tops on the skyline are reminiscent of the Scottish Highlands. All the peaks above Komna can be seen across a tree-filled valley, with the summits of Mahavšček and Bogatin to the left of the Vratca saddle (Bogatinsko sedlo).

Reach **Koča pod Bogatinom** and continue on along an excellent path which was once a military

*Mahavšček seen from the summit of Bogatin*

Concrete and stone defences can be seen around the koča – which was used as a military hospital for a while during WW1 – and below the pass.

road. ◂ Just below the **Vratca saddle** the path divides, with a steeper path heading up to the right and traversing some rocky outcrops to the saddle, while the main path keeps left and makes an easier zigzag; you can take either way. At the saddle there is a signpost and an old military building. From here, bear left and begin to climb the ridge.

Climb quite steeply but easily up the ridge, although care should be taken as the rock is loose and broken. Look back over your left shoulder for good views of Triglav. The path levels for a while before the final steep section, which is narrow for about 40m with steep drops on both sides, and while it is without real difficulty it might seem intimidating on a windy day. It is 1hr 30mins–2hrs to the top of **Bogatin** (1977m) from Koča pod Bogatinom.

From the top the **vista** is excellent – all the northern Julian Alps can be seen, and a very clear view of Lake Bohinj. To the south-east the ridge continues towards Vogel and the Lower Bohinj mountains, and in the distance are the Karavanke, the Kamniške Alpe and beyond.

Mahavšček (2005m) lies enticingly close to the south, and its ascent offers excellent views of the deep Tolminka valley and surrounding peaks that cannot be seen from Bogatin. It takes at least 30mins each way from the summit of Bogatin. The path drops down, quite steeply at first, from the summit of Bogatin, with a few rocky steps, before reaching easier, though still loose and broken, ground. This brings you to a **saddle** between the two peaks. Continue easily up the rocky ridge, which is not quite as steep or narrow as that of Bogatin, to reach the summit of **Mahavšček**.

Retrace your steps to the saddle. You can avoid ascending to the summit of Bogatin again by taking an easy path from the saddle which traverses the western side of Bogatin below the summit that leads back to the Vratca saddle. Reverse the route of ascent back down to the valley, or stay overnight in either of the two mountain huts, Dom na Komni and Koča pod Bogatinom.

A circular route heading south-east down the ridge from Mahavšček and then east via Planina Govnjač to Dom na Komni looks enticing on the map but is not recommended. The route is little used and therefore quite overgrown in places, making route-finding awkward, especially in poor visibility.

## WALK 30

*Triglav Lakes valley and Veliko špičje*

| | |
|---|---|
| **Start/finish** | Koča pri Savici |
| **Distance** | 23km |
| **Total ascent/descent** | 1750m |
| **Grade** | 4 |
| **Time** | 2 days |
| **Maps** | 1:25,000 Bohinj, 1:25,000 Triglav, 1:25,000 Bovec-Trenta |
| **Access** | Koča pri Savici can be reached by bus from Ukanc in the summer. Alternatively follow Walk 22 as far as the turn-off to the Komarča path (just before Koča pri Savici). |
| **Accommodation** | Koča pri Triglavskih jezerih (Triglav Lakes hut) |

The Triglav Lakes valley, containing a string of seven lakes, is one of the highlights of the Julian Alps. Each lake, surrounded by steep mountains and, in the lower part of the valley, by rich mixed forest, has its own character. This route comprises a half-day's walk up to the Triglav Lakes hut (Koča pri Triglavskih jezerih), followed by the ascent of Veliko špičje (2398m) by its north-eastern ridge and the return on Day 2. For a more leisurely tour, you could stay a second night at Zasavska Koča na Prehodavcih. Don't be daunted by the grade 4 given for this walk: although there are some sections of scrambling which are somewhat exposed, they are short, and competent hillwalkers should not find any serious difficulties.

## DAY 1

*Koča pri Savici to*
*Koča pri Triglavskih jezerih*

| | |
|---|---|
| **Start** | Koča pri Savici |
| **Finish** | Koča pri Triglavskih jezerih |
| **Distance** | 5.5km |
| **Total ascent** | 1050m |
| **Time** | 3–3½hrs |

The wall of crags that rise up behind Koča pri Savici can look daunting but a well laid out route makes relatively easy work of the ascent. From the top, the waymarked path leads gradually through fine woods until Koča pri Triglavskih jezerih is reached in its glorious Alpine lakeland setting. If you don't have much time to explore the Triglav Lakes valley, this route as far as the hut makes an enjoyable day's walk from Bohinj.

From the car park at Savica, a sign directs you over the bridge – to Črno jezero 1hr 45mins and Koča pri Triglavskih jezerih 3hrs 15mins. About 100m past the bridge reach the sign on the left for the Komarča path and take it, climbing steadily through beautiful beech forest. Ignore a path to the left that leads to Savica waterfall (Slap Savica), and after about 20mins reach the foot of the first rocks, dripping with water.

The path branches left and continues climbing steadily below crags in the trees, and shortly afterwards reaches another sign for Komarča. Continue up, zigzagging through the trees towards the crags before beginning to ascend the **Komarča** cliff face. The path is very well constructed, with steel cables as a handrail in places and occasional steel pegs.

The **Komarča** ('ladder') face was first explored towards the end of the 18th century, and at that time spruce trees, with their branches cut like the

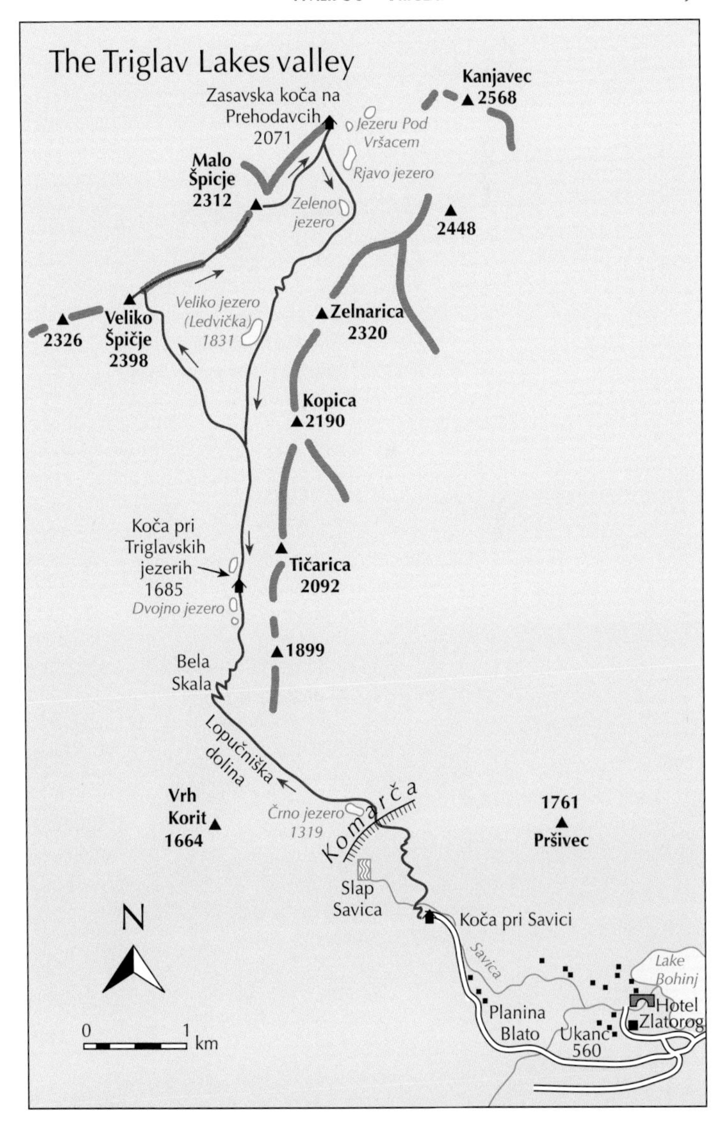
The Triglav Lakes valley
Zasavska koča na Prehodavcih 2071
Kanjavec 2568
Jezeru Pod Vršacem
Rjavo jezero
Malo Špicje 2312
Zeleno jezero
2448
Veliko jezero (Ledvička) 1831
Zelnarica 2320
2326
Veliko Špičje 2398
Kopica 2190
Koča pri Triglavskih jezerih 1685
Tičarica 2092
Dvojno jezero
1899
Bela Skala
Lopučniška dolina
Vrh Korit 1664
Črno jezero 1319
Komarča
1761
Pršivec
Slap Savica
Koča pri Savici
Savica
Lake Bohinj
Hotel Zlatorog
Planina Blato
Ukanc 560
N
0
1
km

rungs of a ladder, were laid over the most difficult places, giving the face its name.

About three-quarters of the way up, the route meets a fast-flowing stream in a steep gully, and ascends on some metal rungs for a few metres to the left of it. There are occasional glimpses through the trees to the end of the lake and across the valley to Vogel. The path is steepest near the top, a fact that is particularly noticeable in the descent. At the top the path levels out and enters a forest of beautiful tall spruce and beech, reaching **Črno jezero**, 'the black lake', in less than 10mins. ◀

The lake is surrounded by trees and flanked on its northern edge by the huge crags of Stador and by steep rock walls to the south.

The waymarked path branches right just before the lake shore is reached. In another 50m reach a sign on a tree pointing to the left, saying 'Koča pri Triglavskih jezerih 1hr30'. The path continues through the woods above the right-hand side of the lake, below the crags – keeping it away from the shore helps to conserve the lake's sensitive ecosystem. Just before the end of the lake reach another junction, signed left to Komna, but the route described here keeps straight on to Triglav Lakes.

*The Triglav Lakes hut with Lepa špica behind*

The rocky path continues through pine and shrubs along a narrow valley known as **Lopučniška dolina**, gradually changing to tall spruce with occasional beech. After about 1.5km the path passes underneath a wet overhanging wall and begins ascending gently along the foot of the rocks of **Bela Skala** – 'the white cliff'. Pass a water trough that collects the refreshing water from the crags, and in another 5mins or so swing sharply right and begin to zigzag up more steeply.

Soon the zigzags relent and the path continues climbing steadily. Reach a sign for the koča (15mins) to the left at a junction. The trail becomes easy, passing through larch trees and soon reaching the pretty twin lakes (**Dvojno jezero**) with the koča at the far end. Continue along the right-hand side of the lake to reach **Koča pri Triglavskih jezerih** in its dramatic setting with the towering cliffs of Tičarica on the right.

## DAY 2

*Koča pri Triglavskih jezerih to Koča pri Savici*

| | |
|---|---|
| **Start** | Koča pri Triglavskih jezerih |
| **Finish** | Koča pri Savici |
| **Distance** | 17.5km |
| **Total ascent** | 750m |
| **Total descent** | 1750m |
| **Time** | 9–10hrs |

This is a full mountain day that entails a very long descent if returning all the way to Koča pri Savici. The superb walk along the high ridge contrasts perfectly with the gentler descent past the shimmering turquoise waters of the Triglav Lakes valley.

From the koča the path leads off on the right-hand side, close to the pools of the next (man-made) lake with its small dam. The path climbs gently up between boulders and over limestone pavement slabs for about 25mins to a sign for Velika špičje (2hrs) at a left-hand fork. This path is narrower, and after about 5mins it descends a little to a karst hollow sometimes filled with water, 80–100m in length. Skirt the hollow by the western end and continue, following waymarks. Soon begin to ascend gently again, around karst sinkholes and through the lush vegetation and occasional larch trees. Through the trees you can see Lepa špica ahead. After a while the path begins to ascend more steadily, to the left of outcrops of rock topped with dwarf pine. ◂

There are good views behind you, of the ridge opposite, and back down the valley with the Lower Bohinj mountains on the skyline.

Pass through a shallow rocky channel, being careful to follow waymarks left, and soon afterwards begin to climb more steeply over more limestone pavement towards the rocky grassy spur that is the ascent route. The path winds its way up this spur for the next 10–15mins to reach a steel cable which protects a short but quite exposed traverse across a steep section of rock, and then ascends rocky steps to reach easier ground again on the crest of the spur. There is an abundance of flowers beneath your feet. Continue on to reach the crest of the main ridge, where you turn left and follow the path for about 100m to the summit of **Veliko špičje**. ◂

The views from the summit are excellent; the position of Veliko špičje between the Bohinj and Trenta peaks ensures a panorama across the whole Julian Alps, and beyond into Austria and Italy.

Retrace your steps from the summit to the path junction, and follow waymarks along the ridge towards Prehodavci. In a short distance the path drops a little to the right-hand side of the ridge, with a good view of the Triglav Lakes valley. The path momentarily joins the crest again, with a view down a vast chasm to Trenta on the other side, and then continues along the ridge, keeping mostly on the right-hand side.

> The excellent views are maintained along the length of the **ridge** as the path traverses pleasantly over short grass and rocks painted with deep blue gentians, Zois' bellflower and cushions of Triglav rose. The ridge is also a regular haunt of ibex.

Make a short descent before beginning to climb again towards the peak **Malo špičje** (2312m); the path

*Descending the Triglav Lakes valley towards Veliko jezero (Ledvička)*

bypasses the summit but you can make a 2–3min detour, signed left, to the top for a spectacular view back along the ridge, and on towards the next koča.

After this the path soon begins to descend, bearing left at first before turning right again and continuing down over fissured limestone rock, avoiding steep crags that bar the continuation of the ridge from Malo špičje. Eventually turn right at the edge of a slabby white limestone pavement for about 30m, then turn left again as you climb up onto the slabs and cross them. Reach a junction, signed right for Triglavska koča 2hrs (go this way if you wish to shorten the route a little, avoiding Zasavska koča na Prehodavcih) and left for Prehodavci. Turn left, and about 100m past the junction reach another one with a path going down left to Trenta on the old military road; continue on for another 200m to reach **Zasavska koča na Prehodavcih**.

From Zasavska koča you can see the highest of the seven **Triglav Lakes**, Jezero pod Vršacem (1993m), lying in the hollow beneath the steep cliffs of Kanjavec. It is unusual among the seven lakes in that its water does not flow into the Triglav Lakes valley, but towards the Soča. All the other six lakes are connected underground, and their level fluctuates widely throughout the year.

These upper reaches of the Triglav Lakes valley are the epitome of an alpine wilderness – there are no trees and the ground is a turmoil of jumbled limestone, although still with some grass and hardy colourful flowers.

Continue descending on the waymarked path, with **Rjavo jezero** ('brown lake') about 200m to the left, enveloped by the massive crags of the surrounding mountains – Kanjavec and Vršaki. The path continues descending to **Zeleno jezero** ('green lake') with its fantastic backdrop of the Zelnarica crags. Here a path heads left to Čez Hribarice, but keep straight on for Koča pri Triglavskih jezerih (the Triglav Lakes hut) (1hr 30mins). ◂

There are some similarities to a North American landscape in this part of the valley, with the rocky peaks and larches beyond the lake.

The path continues easily down the valley and eventually some thickets of dwarf pine mark where you drop down to **Veliko jezero (Ledvička)**, the largest and deepest of the lakes, named 'kidney lake' for its shape. ◂ The path passes above the water on the left-hand side, below the screes of Zelnarica, and continues down the valley, eventually meeting the first larches. As the trees begin to thicken, you reach the junction for Veliko špičje, and continue past it to regain the **Triglav Lakes hut**. It is about 3hrs from here back down Komarča to Savica.

## WALK 31

*Triglav – the southern approach*

| | |
|---|---|
| **Start/finish** | Supermarket in Stara Fužina |
| **Distance** | 34km |
| **Total ascent/descent** | 2500m |
| **Grade** | 4 |
| **Time** | 2 days |
| **Maps** | 1:25,000 Bohinj, 1:25,000 Triglav |
| **Accommodation** | Dom Planika |

The landscape of the southern approach to Triglav (2864m), the highest point in Slovenia, offers a contrast to the stark faces of the northern side; the walk in is longer, but the slopes are generally gentler, and the route is considered to be easier than those from the north (see Walks 18 and 19). However, this is still a big mountain and not to be undertaken lightly. The approach used here is through the Voje valley from Stara Fužina, then the route climbs up to Vodnikov dom and then to Dom Planika (2401m), where you can spend the night. The dom is well positioned for making the final ascent of Triglav's summit rocks in the (hopefully!) clear air of the morning, before retracing the route back to Stara Fužina.

## DAY 1

*Stara Fužina to Dom Planika*

| | |
|---|---|
| **Start** | Supermarket in Stara Fužina |
| **Alternative start** | Drive to Koča na Vojah on a toll road in summer – turn left onto it just past the supermarket (reduces length of walk by about 3km/1hr) |
| **Finish** | Dom Planika |
| **Distance** | 16km |
| **Total ascent** | 1855m |
| **Time** | 7–7½hrs |
| **Access** | By car: go left at the crossroads where the road turns right over the bridge in Stara Fužina, and drive up the hill for about 700m to a car park (parking fee in summer). Take the trail signed local route 7 for Slap Mostnica and walk along the level path for about 250m to arrive at Hudičev most. |

This is a long walk with a big height gain. It starts off quite gently, along the beautiful Mostnica valley, and then becomes a steady ascent that finishes at the foot of Triglav's steep southern rock wall.

From the supermarket walk north and go straight ahead at the crossroads, following a yellow sign to Hudičev most

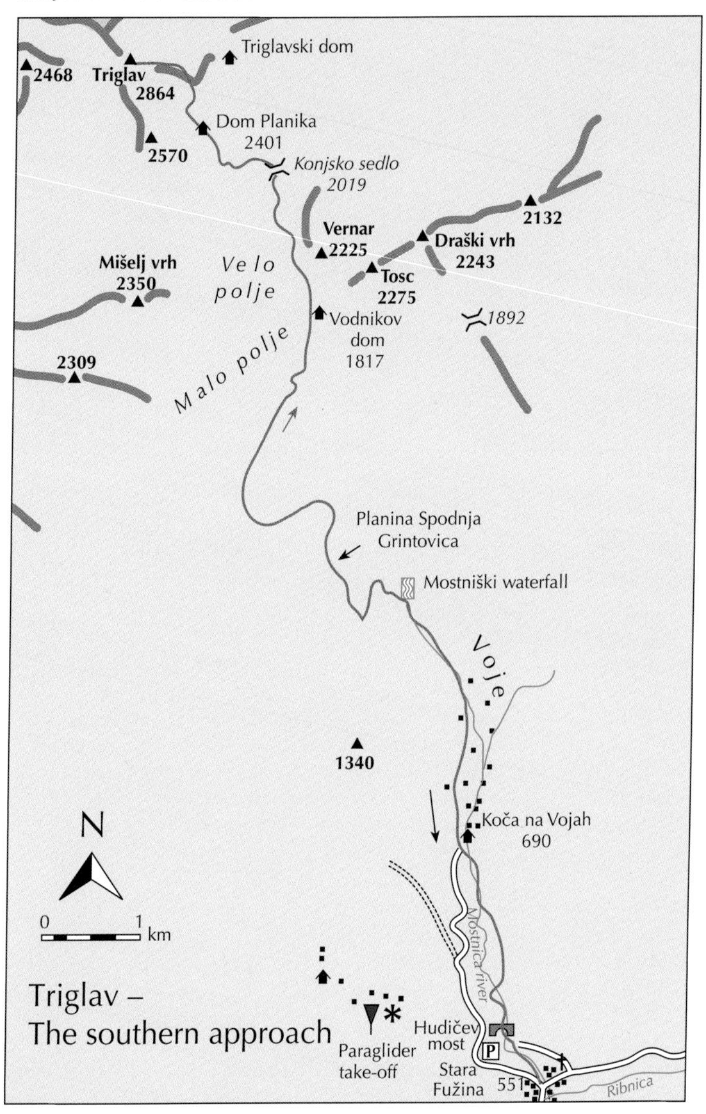
Triglavski dom
2468
Triglav
2864
Dom Planika
2401
2570
Konjsko sedlo
2019
2132
Vernar
2225
Draški vrh
2243
Mišelj vrh
2350
Velo polje
Tosc
2275
Vodnikov dom
1817
1892
2309
Malo polje
Planina Spodnja Grintovica
Mostniški waterfall
Voje
1340
Koča na Vojah
690
N
0
1
km
Mostnica river
Triglav –
The southern approach
Paraglider take-off
Hudičev most
P
Stara Fužina
551
Ribnica

with the river on your right and passing pretty houses on both sides. After crossing the river turn left at a T-junction and walk up the lane; soon after the large Rabič apartment building on your left, go through an iron gate, where the track is joined by another from the right, and continue round to the left across a small open pasture to reach the bridge.

Walk up the track on the west bank of the **Mostnica river** for a short distance to a big orientation sign describing the gorge (unfortunately in Slovene only), and take the path straight on, descending slightly into the woods, with the gorge falling away to your right. Walk pleasantly through the forest to the pay kiosk, and then cross a bridge, with more views down into the deep gorge. Further along from this bridge the gorge becomes much shallower and the path runs to the right of the extremely pretty river.

The path continues through beech woods, bending slightly away from the river, and the gorge gradually deepens again. Reach a viewpoint which shows the gorge with the rocks almost overhanging – the top ones are barely a metre apart. Further on another bridge takes you back onto the west side, again with good views into the depths, where you take the path climbing steeply away from the river into the forest, signed (local) route 7, Slap Mostnice and Voje. Follow the waymarks on a northward trail, with the noise of the river on your right.

About 10mins from the bridge emerge at a second orientation sign, where the path joins a lane coming up from Stara Fužina. Turn right and within a few paces there is the first glimpse of the beautiful view of the head of the Voje valley and the peaks beyond. About 200m further on reach **Koča na Vojah**, where you can refresh yourself with a drink while gazing at the view out into the open valley with its buildings and forests, and the shapely peak of Draški vrh in the background.

Continue past the koča on the unmade track for about 1km to a fork by a building. Take the left-hand track, signed Vodnikov dom, Velo polje and Triglav, and continue (ignoring the first waterfall sign) to a wooden sign at a fork, where you bear left signed Velo polje. The broad stony path immediately enters the woods and begins to ascend quite steeply in hairpins up the steep hillside at the head of the valley. After about 1hr the path reaches a little open alp, **Planina Spodnja Grintovica**. Follow the waymarked path across it, passing a spring and water trough about 20m to the left. ◂

There are excellent views to the north of Tosc and Draški vrh.

Re-enter the woods and continue to wind up through the forest, quite steeply in places, for another 30mins or so before the ground begins to level out. Pass some small outcrops to your left, and then descend a little, with steep forested slopes down to your right where Planina Vrtača lies in the valley below before beginning to ascend again. In the summer the lush vegetation encroaches on the path, quite surprisingly so considering this is one of the main paths to Triglav. Continue on, winding between boulders and karst hollows.

Notice the subtle changes in the **alpine scenery** as you gain height. Spruce, larch and rowan trees give way to dwarf pine among tall larch trees, which gradually begin to thin out. The flowers, too, change with height, but always with the same rich range of colours.

Eventually reach a major junction where the path levels, signed Uskovnica to the right. Turn left, and the path immediately forks again; this time take the right fork, signed Vodnikov dom and Triglav. After another 20m or so you get an uninterrupted view of Triglav, showing its classic three-headed profile which features on the Slovene flag. The path traverses high above Malo polje ('small pasture'), the highest karst polje in Slovenia, and reaches **Vodnikov dom** in about 10mins (5hrs from Stara Fužina). ◂

There is a wonderful view of Mišelj vrh (2350m) to the west, a fine rocky peak that looks like it has been displaced from Yosemite!

Immediately after leaving the dom the path forks; take the right-hand path, signed Dom Planika, which you can see on a rocky shoulder (still a long way above!). The path traverses through dwarf pine and in less than 15mins a handrail leads across the rocks of the lower slopes of **Vernar** (2225m). The route then climbs quite steeply across a scree slope to pass beneath the rocky summit. Soon reach the foot of rocks with steps cut into them, and more steel cables for a handrail.

The path climbs on, skirting the foot of crags, over increasingly rocky terrain. About 40mins from the dom the path passes through a karst hollow area, quite level and pretty with flowers, and then drops down a short gentle descent towards **Konjsko sedlo**. A number of paths head off from the saddle – take the signed path to Planika, heading north-west, following the waymarks carefully, especially in poor visibility, as a number of older worn paths criss-cross the quite featureless terrain.

The route climbs fairly steeply from the saddle and then begins a long rising traverse across the rocky hillside. About 40mins from the saddle reach the top of a shoulder and turn right. Continue up, heading north, again being careful to follow waymarks over increasingly barren ground. Another 15mins brings you to a rocky scoop or bowl in the hillside. The hut is just above, and the waymarks lead to the right of the bowl to reach the overnight stop at **Dom Planika** (2401m) in 10mins or so.

## DAY 2

*Dom Planika to Stara Fužina*

| | |
|---|---|
| **Start** | Dom Planika |
| **Finish** | Supermarket in Stara Fužina |
| **Distance** | 19km |
| **Total ascent** | 465m |
| **Total descent** | 2320m |
| **Time** | 7–8hrs |

From Dom Planika, the route soon becomes more serious as it is impossible to avoid the exposed scrambling that leads up to Triglav's airy ridge and summit. The descent to Stara Fužina involves huge height loss and requires stamina (walking poles recommended!).

*On Triglav's summit ridge*

From Dom Planika take the waymarked route, signed to Triglav on a stone. Head across fairly level scree, initially in a north-north-west direction, for about 200m, and then over steeper rocky ground as the route begins to ascend towards the south-east spur. Continue over scree and rubble, and more easy rocks, which bring you to the foot of steeper crags. The route turns right and passes through a cleft in the rock where you meet the first steel cables (about 20mins from the hut).

Reach the end of the cleft which forms a notch with a gully dropping down the other side, and head straight up the fairly easy-angled rock following steel cables and pegs. After a few metres the route trends left again for a short distance and then continues up to reach steeper rocks with more pegs. Shortly afterwards reach a shoulder, with Triglavski dom na Kredarici visible to the right below. Close by on the south side of the Mali Triglav buttress you can see the long rows of

*An early morning view to the west from the summit of Triglav*

steel pegs that mark the bold traverse line on the route from Kredarica.

The path goes left and up again, with no major difficulties but some exposure, following steel cables all the while. After a final scramble over easy rock steps join the ridge where the route comes up from Kredarica. The south-east spur joins the ridge a few metres below the summit of Mali Triglav, at a junction close to a memorial plaque. The rocks of the summit ridge give exciting scrambling with plenty of protection, but countless ascents have left the rocks quite polished. Continue quite easily at first, with big drops to both sides, for about 15mins or so before the route steepens again. There is another short, level section just before the final steep rocks, which are well protected but with considerable exposure. Then walk easily the short distance to the summit of **Triglav** (2864m) (1hr 20mins from the hut). ▶

The view is excellent if the air is clear. Triglav's considerable height difference is obvious as you survey, below you, all the other peaks of the Julian Alps.

Return to Stara Fužina the same way.

**ALTERNATIVE ENDINGS**

There are numerous alternatives to an immediate return to Stara Fužina once you have reached Triglav's summit. You could stay in the high-level huts such as Dom Planika, Triglavski dom na Kredarici, or Koča na Doliču, to ascend other peaks and/or return to a different valley – down the Triglav Lakes valley to Ukanc, down the Vrata to reach Kranjska Gora or down Zadnjica to Trenta.

*Looking towards Stenar from Bovški Gamsovec (Walk 42)*

# INTRODUCTION

*Mangart and Jalovec seen from Log pod Mangartom*

The large village of Bovec (460m) lies in a wide flat basin called Bovška kotlina at the foot of Rombon, which forms, along with the rest of the Kanin range, a steep, impressive mountain backdrop. The valley lies at the confluence of two rivers, the Soča and the Koritnica; the former flows west from its source high in the Trenta valley, and the latter comes down from the north. Steep slopes rear up on every side, and Bovec even has its own 'Matterhorn' – Svinjak, a mountain of comparatively modest height but impressive profile which guards the head of the valley between the two rivers. Routes to the high peaks of Krn, Mangart, Rombon and Kanin are all described in this section.

Bovec has a plethora of companies offering guided outdoor activities, and it is easy to see why. As well as the mountaineering possibilities, the river Soča, which flows through the valley, is considered to be one of the finest in the whole of the Alps, with enormous potential for canoeing, rafting and canyoning. The ski resort of Kanin (2202m) is Slovenia's highest and only true alpine ski area – its height ensures a long season and it is justifiably popular. The gondola which lifts skiers to the heights in the winter is employed during the summer to spare walkers the grinding slog up nearly 1600m of slopes to reach the ridges and high hanging valleys of the Kanin peaks (Walks 37 and 38). In 2014 the gondola, and therefore the ski resort, had been out of action for two years following an accident – attempts are being made to get it up and running again. Tandem paragliding is also offered from Kanin, and mountain bikers can take the cable car to station B (979m) for a long forest road descent back to Bovec. Caving is another popular sport; the area around Bovec is riddled with caves and potholes. There is a small airfield, too, that offers pleasure flights.

The Bovec area is steeped in history; this is the land that took the brunt of the fighting during the First World War on the Soča (Isonzo) front. Many of the local settlements were evacuated (and at least partially destroyed) as the soldiers from both the Italian and Austro-Hungarian armies took over hillside and pass. Local walks are littered with old gun emplacements and fortifications, and two of the routes described here specifically visit First World War defence positions (Walks 33 and 35).

Although Bovec is relatively small, it has a sporty, upbeat atmosphere and is well used to visitors, with all the usual tourist requirements easily fulfilled. There are a number of hotels, restaurants and supermarkets, and a helpful Tourist Information Centre in the village. There is a campsite about 500m from the village centre.

Bovec is comparatively remote; there are no trains, although there are regular buses. The main access by bus or car is from the south, on the 102 road which follows the Soča valley up from Tolmin and Nova Gorica. To the north the Vršič pass links Bovec to Kranjska Gora via Trenta, and several buses a day run during the summer season. In winter the pass is closed from about December to April. Another pass, the Predel, also to the north, provides access to Italy, and links to Tarvisio on the Italian/Austrian border. The Predel pass is usually open all winter.

## THE ROUTES

The 13 routes described in this section offer a varied selection of possibilities for the Bovec area. Walks 32 and 36 visit water features in the area around Bovec and, with the peak of Svinjak (Walk 34), provide a good orientation to the area. Walks 33 and 35 visit First World War sites, and Walk 39, the Soča Trail, which starts high up in the hills at the top of the Vršič pass, follows ancient tracks alongside the river Soča to various points of interest. Two groups of high-mountain walks, those of Kanin (Walks 37 and 38) and the Križ area above Trenta (Walks 40–42), are followed by routes up two mountains that stand alone – Krn (Walk 43) and Mangart (Walk 44).

## MAPS

The 1:25,000 Bovec-Trenta map covers all the routes in this section. Walks 39 and 40–42 are also on the 1:25,000 Triglav and 1:30,000 Kranjska Gora maps.

# WALK 32

*The Bovec Basin*

| | |
|---|---|
| **Start/finish** | Tourist Information Office, Bovec |
| **Distance** | 9km |
| **Total ascent/descent** | 160m |
| **Grade** | 1 |
| **Time** | 2½–3hrs |
| **Maps** | 1:25,000 Bovec-Trenta |

This pleasant orientation walk explores the flat-floored Bovec basin, skirting the airfield to reach the Soča river and then wandering along the far side of the river to visit the tiny hamlets of Uštinc and Jablenca. A detour is made to the scenic Soča gorge and the springs at Zmuklica before returning to Bovec across pastures.

From the Tourist Information Office in Bovec walk along the main road heading west. After about 100m take the first left by a small supermarket and walk down this pleasant road, cross the Gereš stream and continue to a crossroads with the Bovec bypass road. Cross over, and on the left take the path that goes behind a shrine and continues along the edge of a field. The track bears round to the right, skirting the airfield which is a regular landing place for paragliders, and after about 500m enters a thicket for a short distance. Once in the open again bear left on a vague track towards a wooden signpost and bench at the edge of woodland. ◂

There are fine views of Kanin up to the right and, all around, of the flat meadows of the Bovec valley, contrasting with the steep mountains on every side.

At the bench the track bears left and downwards, through woods which are full of birdsong, to reach a tarmac road where you turn right and cross the bridge over the luminescent green **river Soča**.

There's no need to enter the village of Čezsoča unless you want to; turn left onto a signed track that takes you east along the south bank of the river. Continue along the good track, with the river on your left, to reach

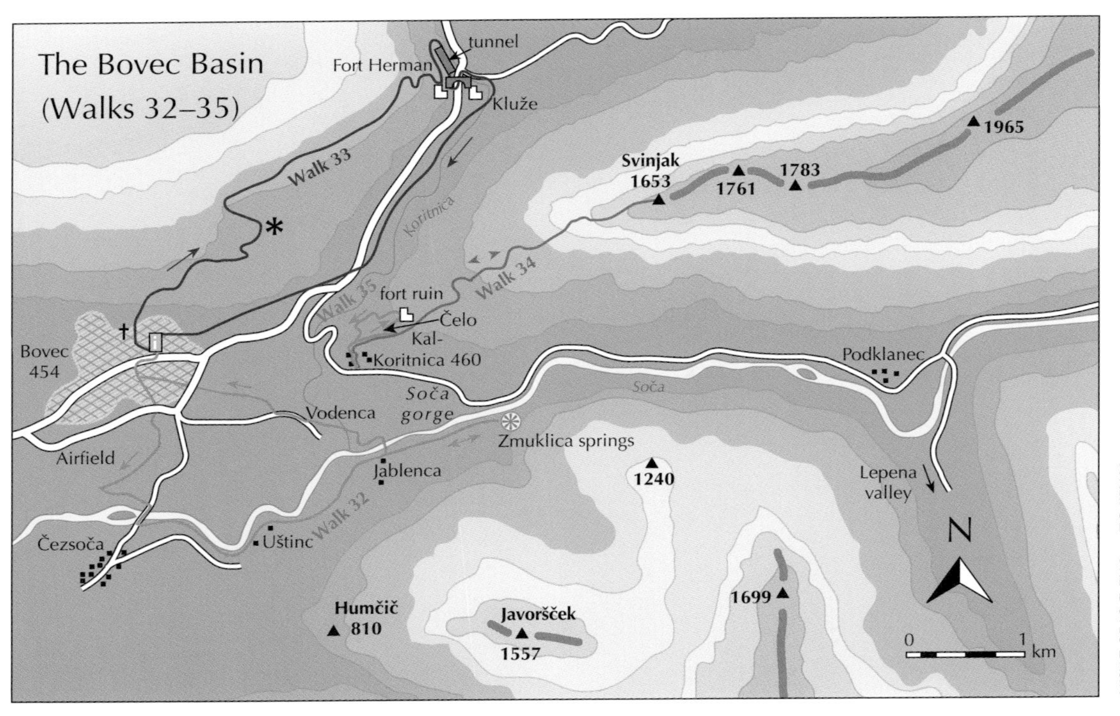
The Bovec Basin
(Walks 32–35)
tunnel
Fort Herman
Kluže
1965
Walk 33
Svinjak
1653
1761
1783
Koritnica
Walk 34
Walk 35
fort ruin
Čelo
Kal-
Koritnica 460
Bovec
454
Podklanec
Soča
Soča
gorge
Vodenca
Zmuklica springs
Airfield
1240
Jablenca
Lepena
valley
Walk 32
Čezsoča
Uštinc
N
1699
Humčič
810
Javoršček
1557
0
1
km

*The pretty lane on the south side of the Soča*

a road bridge over the tributary river Slatenik. The route now continues along the tarmac road, still with the Soča river on your left. After about 300m cross another, smaller bridge over a tributary stream and continue along the road, ignoring a track that goes down to the water's edge on your left. Shortly afterward reach a fork and take the left, signed Jablenca, to reach the small settlement of **Uštinc**.

Walk through the pretty hamlet with good views up to Svinjak, which looks considerably less like the Matterhorn from this angle, and continue alongside the Soča for about 1km to the next hamlet, **Jablenca**. Here the road swings round to the left and then bears right, signed by an orange marker on an old building. As you leave Jablenca a path heads down to the left, signed Vodenca B1 – this is the return route, but for now continue on to visit the Soča gorge and Zmuklica springs.

Reach another little group of farm buildings and houses, cross a stream on a small wooden bridge and continue gently uphill, now on a narrow path which skirts a field with a stone wall on your left. Drop down a little to cross another stream and keep straight on, ignoring side paths, to a path crossroads and continue straight ahead, signed Kršovec. In a short distance reach another junction and turn right, signed Zmuklica. Soon afterwards merge with a forest road, and walk down it for about 100m before turning back into the wood on a path signed with a wooden post. This takes you to the edge of the impressive gorge with the remains of an old suspension bridge. The path rejoins the forest road, still on the south side, with views of the gorge on your left. Reach the curious scenic springs at **Zmuklica**, where the water emerges directly from the moss-covered boulders on the right-hand side of the track to flow across it and down into the river.

From here, retrace your steps along the south bank of the river to the path turn-off just past Jablenca. Turn right here to reach a suspension bridge and cross high above the river. On the other side turn left, signed Vodenca, and climb gently through the woods, parallel to the Soča. Follow the path round to the right at the confluence with the **river Koritnica**, turning away from the Soča and now keeping the Koritnica on the left, and continue for about 200m to another suspension bridge which you cross to the complex of campsites at **Vodenca**. Walk across the campsites to reach the access road and turn right, walking gently uphill for a few minutes.

As the road levels out take a track, signed Bovec, to the right, which enters woods after about 50m. The track passes between the two small knolls of Stržišče and Ravelnik, then comes out into fields with good views of Kanin and Bovec straight ahead. Follow cart-tracks across the fields towards Bovec, and reach the main bypass road opposite a church. Cross over to a sign for the town centre and walk up the track, crossing a stream, through a small flower meadow to a parking area and a bar. Turn right and follow a minor road to the centre of **Bovec**.

# WALK 33

*Kluže*

| | |
|---|---|
| **Start/finish** | Tourist Information Office, Bovec |
| **Distance** | 13km |
| **Total ascent/descent** | 440m |
| **Grade** | 2 |
| **Time** | 3–4hrs |
| **Maps** | 1:25,000 Bovec-Trenta |

This walk (local route B4) climbs above Bovec to walk through beautiful forests on the lower slopes of Rombon and visits two military forts – Fort Herman and Kluže. The original wooden stronghold at Kluže was erected as early as 1420, and subsequent buildings have guarded the valley and the Koritnica bridge for centuries. The present fortress is a museum. The return walk follows the valley of the Koritnica river through woodland and pastures back to Bovec.

See the route map in Walk 32.

◄ From the Tourist Information Centre walk west along the main street and turn right, passing the Post Office, up towards the **church** of Sveti Urh. At the church take the right-hand fork, signed Ravni Laz – this minor road passes between the church and a volleyball sports centre. In just 200m, as the road turns sharply left, take the tarmac track heading right, signed Razni Laz and Višna. Within 50m leave the tarmac lane, which just leads to a house, and take a gravel track to the left. Walk through a gate, and after another 50m ignore a track signed left for Višna and continue on through the woods. The path rises gently through the woods, passing a stone sheep barn which has a yellow target sign and a number 4 on it. ◄ After 10mins or so go through a gate and pass some farm buildings, then continue, fairly level, to reach another gate a little further on; 50m after this second gate reach a junction where you turn left up a broader track, signed Plajer B4.

Up to the left are views of the rocky lower slopes of Rombon.

The track bears left before curving round a right-hand hairpin bend and continuing straight on to pass some craggy boulders and a farm building. Continue a short distance to reach a house on the left.

This is a good **viewpoint**, with Bovec and its airfield on the floor of the valley and Svinjak at its head. Straight across is Javoršček, with a huge rock scar caused by a landslide in 1950, and higher up you begin to see into the complexity of the Krn massif.

The track becomes a narrow path with a stone wall on your right, and in about 50m, as you reach the corner of the wall, notice two flat limestone rocks with yellow markers directing you uphill to the left. The path becomes a little indistinct as it doubles back just above the house and continues on over short grass with rocks and many varieties of small alpine flowers. After a short distance it turns sharply to the right as it ascends below the right hand end of a small rocky outcrop, following waymarks. Within another 100m, enter a mixture of pine and oak woodland where more yellow markings on the rock indicate the route on the now more distinct path.

After a winding ascent through the woods, arrive at the edge of a very obvious scree slope where a signpost at a T-junction points left to Višna and right to Kluže, heading across the scree slope. Beyond the scree slope the path traverses the hillside through the attractive mixed woodland and in another 10mins reaches a fork in the track where you go right, signed Kluže. Occasional open sections of more scree and small outcrops offer views down the steep slopes to the right. After about 40mins, the path begins to make a steady descent through beechwoods and very soon joins a track, turning right and down, signposted Kluže B4. After another 15mins of descent come to **Fort Herman**.

**Fort Herman** is the upper fortification at Kluže, and is now very overgrown, but a suggestion of the part it played during the First World War is still

*The ruined Fort Herman is slowly succumbing to nature*

present in its eerie atmosphere. It was completed in 1900, but despite its heavy defences of four cannons, four howitzers and eight heavy machine guns it was badly damaged by the Italians during the very first attack in 1915. Excavation work has been carried out at the fort in recent years and information boards erected, but take care exploring the structure as some of the interior floors have now collapsed.

Turn left and head into the wood on a path signed Kluže, away from the building. This was the supply line between the upper and lower fortifications. The route goes gently downhill, alongside crags which have additional strongholds hewn out of the cliff face. Continue to a right-hand hairpin and double back at a lower level to reach a **tunnel**, which is lit by movement sensor lights. The entrance is waymarked, leading first into a room cut out of the hill. Walk through for about 200m; when you emerge you can see **Kluže**, the lower fortification, over the road not far away, and the bridge over the Koritnica gorge. Walk a few hundred metres along the track to reach it.

> The present **Kluže fortification** was built in the early 1880s by the Austrians, in the same spot as previous defences, and was defended by 180 men with three cannons and four heavy machine guns. It played an important role as a command and control facility for the Austro-Hungarian forces in the First World War, and was also used in the Second World War. It is now a museum with a small entrance fee; there is also a refreshment bar.

To continue the walk, cross the road bridge, built in 1946 over the surprisingly deep gorge. On the other side of the bridge turn right, signed Bavšica, and walk along this minor road for about 5mins to take a track on the right, signed Šunik. Ignore a track doubling back, which just leads to a house, and continue straight ahead for about 200m to a right-hand hairpin.

A further 150m brings you to a fork. Both ways are signed B4 and either will continue the route; the left is a broader track favoured by mountain bikers, whereas the right is only suitable for walkers. The right-hand path goes alongside the northern bank of the Šunik river, gradually descending and finally making a few steep zigzags to the river. However, the water's edge, when you reach it, is actually the **Koritnica**, which is crossed by a wood and iron suspension bridge about 50m upstream. On the other side pass a ruined stone building and continue on to meet a crossroads of paths. The route then carries straight on through the woods, signed B4, to emerge by a road bridge which goes to a house – this is where the left-hand path, which follows the southern bank, joins up again.

Continue on the rough vehicle track in the same direction, south-west, to eventually meet the main road. About 30m ahead on the other side of the road you can see the wooden signpost indicating the path continuation, signed Bovec. Continue along the narrow path through the woods to reach a diagonal crossroads with a vehicle track and go straight on, following a sign for Mala Vas. Continue through open hay meadows, passing a number of buildings. Cross a track which serves some houses and carry on across more meadows, passing a number of vegetable plots and a small orchard to reach a bench by a signpost where the main track swings left.

Continue straight ahead along another track towards Bovec, signed B4. The main road and the industrial zone are visible on the left. Continue past more small buildings as the track becomes a narrow path passing through woodland to emerge at fields on the edge of Bovec (Mala Vas) where you join a tarmac lane. At the next junction, just past house No. 47, turn left across a stream and walk down through the village towards the main road, then turn right to walk back to the starting point in **Bovec**.

## WALK 34

*Svinjak*

| | |
|---|---|
| **Start/finish** | Bus stop in Koritnica village |
| **Distance** | 8km |
| **Total ascent/descent** | 1200m |
| **Grade** | 3 |
| **Time** | 5hrs |
| **Maps** | 1:25,000 Bovec-Trenta |
| **Access** | On foot: you can walk from Bovec by reversing Walk 32 as far as the campsite; cross the river Koritnica on the suspension bridge, and where the path turns left to continue alongside the Soča, turn up the hill and walk for about 500m to reach the main road close to the bus stop. By bus: from Bovec. |
| **Parking** | There is limited parking in Koritnica 200m past the bus stop heading east, just adjacent to the gostilna on the left. |

Svinjak (1653m) is the very shapely peak at the head of the valley as seen from Bovec; from this angle its magnificent pyramid form dominates the skyline. However, from other viewpoints it is not so satisfyingly shaped all the way round, but is in fact merely a point on the end of the long ridge of Bavški Grintavec. Although Svinjak is not as high as other mountains around Bovec, it offers a fine walk and an excellent airy viewpoint.

▸ From the bus stop, follow the sign to Svinjak into the village of Koritnica, and continue along the narrow street until it bends round to the left, heading to Kolovrat. At the bend is a water trough that is waymarked, with a sign to Svinjak (3hrs). There is also a little graphic showing someone rock climbing, but walkers should not be put off!

See the route map in Walk 32.

Leave the tarmac road here and start ascending gently on the grassy track that crosses a small stream and continues up a narrow field. At the top of the field go through a gate and walk on with a dry stone wall to the right and a steep wooded stream gully on the left, until you come to a signpost close to a concrete bunker with a metal door. This is part of the water distribution system for the valley, which becomes very important in years of low rainfall.

Svinjak (still 3hrs) is signed to the right. The path going left leads to a crag popular with rock climbers – hence the pictures on the sign at the fountain. The path climbs pleasantly and after about 200m passes through a small gate and continues for another 5mins to the junction for Walk 35, Čelo. The path continues straight ahead, gently ascending at first and then making some zigzags and heading up left to join the crest of the ridge (about 40mins from Koritnica). There are some good glimpses down into the Koritnica valley through the trees.

Turn right along the crest. After about 50m a right fork in the path heads down the hillside, but continue straight on and up. Further on the path leaves the crest and keeps to the right-hand side of the ridge, zigzagging up through the woods in dappled sunlight and shade until it rejoins the crest at a short rocky step. Because the ridge is quite

*Heading up the path towards Svinjak and Čelo*

long the gradient is not as steep as it appears from Bovec. Continue following the adequate waymarks, weaving up through the woods. The path always takes the right-hand side of the ridge when it is not on the crest. Pass through an area of forest that was devastated by fire that swept the hillside in summer 2003, but is now recovering as native trees are once again regaining a foothold. Not long after this, a little more than 2hrs from the start of the walk, a splendid view opens out quite suddenly to the right. ▶

The turquoise Soča river can be seen on the valley floor, with the strange mound-like hill of Črni vrh just beyond and to the right of the hamlet of Podklanec. Javoršček and Krasji vrh lie to the south.

The path now skirts a small crag and continues ascending quite easily. Soon the trees begin to thin and an excellent view of the Bovec basin and the Kanin range opens up behind you. You are now on the final steep rise – there are no real difficulties but there is a feeling of airiness and space as the grassy slopes fall away steeply to the valley. By the dry stump of an old dead larch there is a rocky step which requires an easy scramble. Quite suddenly, as you crest the last short rise, a rocky cairn confronts you, and 100m beyond that on the level ridge is the true summit of **Svinjak** (1653m) with its visitors' book (3hrs from Koritnica).

On the summit here are blue gentians and many other **alpine flowers** with a myriad of vibrantly coloured butterflies. The views are panoramic – along the ridge is Bavški Grintavec with its stratified precipices, and behind Jerebica and Rombon you can see the rocky, lofty heights of the Jof Fuart group in Italy.

Retrace the route for descent.

# WALK 35

## *Čelo*

| | |
|---|---|
| **Start/finish** | Bus stop in Koritnica village |
| **Distance** | 2km |
| **Total ascent/descent** | 190m |
| **Grade** | 2 |
| **Time** | 1½hrs including exploring the defences |
| **Maps** | 1:25,000 Bovec-Trenta |
| **Access** | On foot: you can walk from Bovec by reversing Walk 32 as far as the campsite; cross the river Koritnica on the suspension bridge, and where the path turns left to continue alongside the Soča, turn up the hill and walk for about 500m to reach the main road close to the bus stop. By bus: from Bovec |
| **Note** | You'll need a torch to visit the bunkers at Čelo. |

This walk visits old defences on Pot miru, the Walk of Peace, which is almost 100km in length, starting near Log pod Mangartom and finishing in the south near the town of Most na Soči. This section of the trail lies on the lower slopes of Svinjak and makes for a short but very interesting walk if time is limited for the high hills above Bovec. It could also be done as a brief excursion (about 20mins) on the descent of Svinjak (Walk 34) should you still have enough energy!

See the route map in Walk 32.

◄ From the bus stop, follow the sign to Svinjak into the village of Koritnica, and continue along the narrow street until it bends round to the left, heading to Kolovrat. At the bend is a water trough that is waymarked, with a sign to Svinjak 3hrs, and a sign for Čelo with the Pot miru peace dove motif.

Walk up the grassy track between the houses and within 50m cross a stream on a footbridge. Continue up the field, through a gate, to soon arrive at a signpost in front of a concrete bunker that is used for the local water supply system. Follow the signs, right for Čelo – Pot miru, that lead you up the stony path, climbing pleasantly, with hawthorn and sloe bushes, heavy with ripe berries in autumn, overhanging the path. After about 200m, go through a small gate and continue for just over 5mins to arrive at a junction. The Svinjak path carries straight on, but turn left here, signed Čelo – Pot miru.

The path begins to wind its way up through small shady beech trees, with an enormous variety of colourful plants covering the woodland floor, and soon emerges by the ruins of a long stone building and a trench-like corridor with an information board about the site.

These First World War defences are the remains of an important Austro-Hungarian fort which was part of the **Bovec basin defences** (the Sperre Flitsch), built to prevent the Italian forces attacking from the Soča. Two large gun emplacements were linked by almost 200m of stone and cement trenches that included a kitchen and dormitories. There are also a number of underground tunnels and bunkers cut into the hillside behind the fort.

Walk between the narrow walls of the trench, following an arrow, as you are led under a door lintel into

*Looking out over the Bovec basin from the ruins of the Austro-Hungarian fort at Čelo*

a long room that was a dormitory for 40 men. The route leads you out briefly onto open ground before descending back into the trench, and leads past the first of two large gun emplacements. ◀ In another 30m you reach the end of the trench (which is also the end of the fort) as it passes the second gun emplacement, and the path climbs a stone step and passes through a small doorway.

Large European green lizards and smaller common wall lizards like to bask on the now peaceful warm crumbling walls.

To visit the bunkers, continue straight ahead and descend the stony path, with a cable fence line to your left safeguarding a steep drop down the wooded hillside. After just 25m, pass the entrance of a dark bunker. In just a few more metres the path forks, with a route heading down to the left, but continue straight on a short way to a second bunker entrance in the hillside. The two join inside the hill in underground passages and rooms.

The route ends here, so return to the small doorway at the end of the fort but do not return through it; instead, follow a narrow path to the right as it ascends above the outer wall of the gun emplacement and onto open grassy ground. There are good views towards Rombon and the Kanin range, but at this point the view down to the Bovec basin is obscured by trees and scrub. From here, the path bears right as it descends diagonally below the upper part of the fort, and in 100m it passes the end of the lower eastern section. ◀

The view from here is truly spectacular with the whole of the Bovec basin visible, so it's an excellent place to linger for a while.

The path now heads right for a few metres before turning left down a short steep section and then continuing as it makes a descending traverse of the steep hillside. Pass more bunkers and descend for another 5mins to reach a fence line with a small gate. The path becomes a little vague here but in 50m bear right, through a low-lying band of rock and stone with faded direction markers, and continue down through thickets of small trees where the path becomes more distinct again.

Soon the path drops down onto more open ground with a steep slope to the right. As the rooftops of Koritnica come into view below, reach the stony grassy slope just above the concrete water system bunker and the signpost at the fork in the track. Continue down to reach the stone wall and gate and return to the start point.

# WALK 36

*Izvir Glijuna and Slap Virje*

| | |
|---|---|
| **Start/finish** | Ski gondola car park, Bovec |
| **Distance** | 6.5km |
| **Total ascent/descent** | 180m |
| **Grade** | 1 |
| **Time** | 2–2½hrs |
| **Maps** | 1:25,000 Bovec-Trenta |
| **Access** | From the centre of Bovec, follow the main road that leads west and take the right fork opposite a petrol station into the ski gondola car park. |

This is a short walk in terms of distance, but there is plenty of interest here to keep you out for a good two or three hours. The route wanders pleasantly through woodland and pasture within 3km of Bovec to visit three water features – a reservoir and man-made water channels, the extraordinary source of the river Glijun, and Slap Virje (Virje waterfall). The route continues through the charming village of Plužna before returning to Bovec through attractive woodland and pastures near the ski gondola.

Cross the ski gondola car park to a track which leads west, signed Plužna B2. Continue easily along the track for just under 1km, with good views up towards the craggy peaks of the Kanin range; the top station of the gondola is also visible. The track enters some woodland, and opposite a clearing reach a left-hand fork, signed Pod Turo B2. Follow this downhill for about 150m before reaching a second fork where you turn right, descending more steeply but still easily. After a few hundred metres the track joins a forest road; turn left onto it and continue to a T-junction with a vehicle road, opposite the second hole of Bovec golf course.

Turn right here and cross the little river Ročica, then immediately turn left, signed Jezero (lake) (the Plužna track continues to the right). After 50m or so cross the

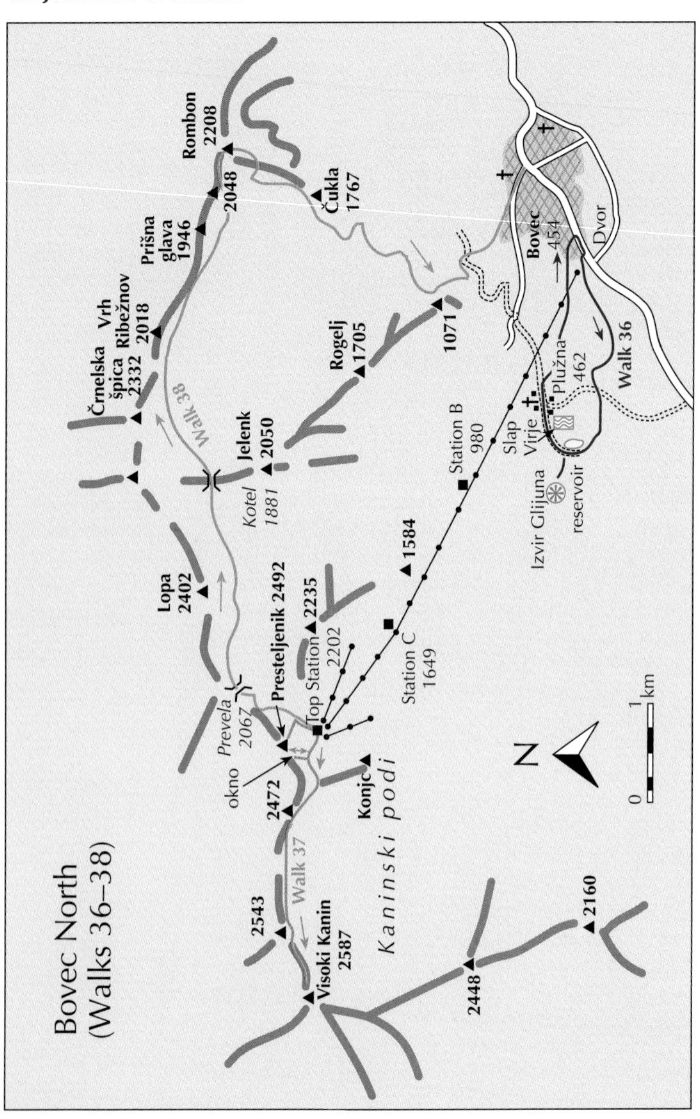
Bovec North
(Walks 36–38)
Rombon
2208
2048
Čukla
1767
Prišna
glava
1946
Vrh
Ribežnov
2018
Črnelska
špica
2332
Walk 38
Jelenk
2050
Rogelj
1705
1071
Kotel
1881
Lopa
2402
Presteljenik 2492
2235
Top Station
2202
Prevela
2067
okno
2472
Konjc
Kaninski podi
Walk 37
2543
Visoki Kanin
2587
2448
2160
Station C
1649
1584
Station B
980
Slap
Virje
Izvir Glijuna
reservoir
Plužna
462
Walk 36
Bovec
454
Dvor
N
0
1
km

*The pretty reservoir on the way to Izvir Glijuna*

river Glijun on an attractive stone-built humpbacked bridge. Pass a house, and continue on a narrow path uphill, skirting the golf course, into more woodland. After about 500m the path emerges onto a level concrete walkway which is actually a covered water channel. Turn right and walk along it to a small man-made reservoir.

The **reservoir** forms part of a water-collection system which supplies a hydroelectric power station built when the area was under Italian rule and still working today. Although the reservoir is man-made, it is very scenic, with two cottages to one side and wonderful views across the valley to Svinjak and the Polovnik ridge. Signs warn that fishing and bathing are forbidden.

The route skirts the western side of the lake and then continues along the concrete walkway to reach a dam and sluice gate complex just before **Izvir Glijuna** – the source of the river Glijun.

The unusual **source of the river Glijun** is one of those features that make limestone country so interesting. The river rushes along among attractive moss-covered boulders, but a few metres above it there is – nothing. The water gushes directly out of the rocks, and although the inclination is to go and look for the water descending from above, perhaps around a bend, it is just not there. The emerging water has a steady year-round temperature of 5.5°C, and changes in the level of the water table can be seen in the different types of mosses on the rocks and how wet they are.

Retrace your steps a short distance to a path leading down left to a bridge over the river, then continue across the bridge and up the made road on the other side. After about 100m there is a sign on the right for **Slap Virje** (Virje waterfall), 5min. Follow the broad track down and round to the water's edge in front of the beautiful waterfall. ◂

It is possible to swim in the pool, but it is very cold.

Return to the tarmac road and continue uphill, past a chalet on the left, and then on along the scenic lane with excellent views up to Kanin, to reach the pretty village of **Plužna**. Turn left past the war memorial, and take the road leading up towards the church, signed B2 Bovec. Just past the last houses, and before the sign saying you are leaving the village, take a track leading down to the right, signed Dvor. After about 100m leave the track for a path on the right, signed Dvor B2b.

Cross a stream in a damp wooded gully, then continue through the woods heading down quite steeply in places. About 5mins after the stream the path makes a sharp right, then bears left again, still descending, to reach a deep stream bed which it follows for a few metres before continuing on the other side. Cross a third stream and join another path on the far side, signed Bovec. This wider track eventually crosses a fourth stream on another little bridge.

Pass a weekend cottage in an open pasture on the right, then merge with another track, signed Dvor, before walking beneath the **gondola cables**. After yet another stream turn right onto a vehicular track, signed Dvor, and continue to a tarmac road and houses; the road soon meets the main road at a T-junction. Turn right and walk 50m or so to the ski car park, or turn left to walk back along the main road to Bovec.

## WALK 37

*Visoki Kanin and Prestreljenik*

| | |
|---|---|
| **Start/finish** | Top station of Kanin ski gondola, near Bovec |
| **Distance** | 7km (to Visoki Kanin); 2.5km (to Prestreljenik) |
| **Total ascent/descent** | 385m (Visoki Kanin); 300m (Prestreljenik) |
| **Grade** | 4 |
| **Time** | 3½–4hrs (to Visoki Kanin); 1½hrs (to Prestreljenik) |
| **Maps** | 1:25,000 Bovec-Trenta |
| **Refreshments** | Café at the top station of gondola |
| **Access** | On foot/by car: follow the Tolmin road west out of Bovec and turn right opposite a petrol station to reach the gondola. The car park is at 439m, and the gondola ride takes about 30mins. |
| **Route map** | See Walk 36 |
| **Note** | In early 2013 an accident rendered the gondola inoperable, and in 2014 it had still not been replaced. Without the gondola these walks involve a long, long slog from the valley, with no huts available. Currently, it is possible for walkers and mountain bikers to buy a ride in a pickup to the middle gondola station. Ask at the Tourist Office for information and prices. |

The two peaks of Visoki Kanin and Prestreljenik stand at the western end of a long ridge to the north of Bovec which marks the state boundary with Italy. The ridge is bounded on both sides by huge basins and plateaus of karst limestone, with their fissured surfaces reminiscent of a glacier. Access is made easy by the Kanin ski centre gondola, which lifts summer walkers up to 2202m – hence the short walking times. The gondola is not open every day, so check with the Tourist Information Office first. The routes to the two mountains do not link up, so they are described separately here.

**Visoki Kanin (2587m)**

At the top station of the gondola, just outside the building, are signs for several local mountains painted on a rock – follow the one for Kanin over rocky ground heading north-west. Pass a small ski bar and follow waymarks a little further to reach a junction where a path is signed left to Dom Petra Skalarja. The Kanin path bears right, traversing a steep scree slope. Watch for the okno (window) on Prestreljenik, coming into view on the right.

Shortly after the turn for the path heading up to the window, reach rocks and the first steel cable. After the cable the path bears right and climbs the rocky rib in an easy scramble with occasional steel pegs. Continue over broken ground onto a rocky shoulder, where a short distance across scree and stone brings you to the edge of an enormous corrie, the **Kaninski podi**. From here the line of the path can be seen all the way to Kanin, following the foot of the crags along the rim of the corrie.

The Kaninski podi is a distinctive example of **high mountain karst**. In recent decades very deep potholes have been discovered. Four of these have been explored to depths greater than 1000m – the deepest is 1538m – and the largest vertical entrance shaft in the world, at 643m, has also been discovered here.

The landscape is bleak but extremely impressive. The distinct path follows waymarks across scree and rocks round the rim of the bowl for a good 30mins. Towards the end the route begins to ascend and arrives at the foot of crags. Waymarks lead left and up the rocks to reach the ridge – there are some pegs and cables to assist the easy scramble. At the crest turn left, with views down impressive drops to the equally bleak Italian side to the north.

The route continues along the broad ridge quite easily for a few minutes before descending to a notch, where a gully drops steeply away to the left. A steel cable and a few pegs protect the step across. Continue along the crest over slabs of broken rock. Reach a minor top (Kaninski Vršič 2530m) with a border post and cairn, and a sign saying 'experts only', which marks the top of a steep via ferrata on the Italian side.

From here the route descends slightly across slabs for a short distance before rising again. Continue easily, then descend a little on the left-hand side. ▶ From here scramble down steeply to the left for about 20m (steel cables), then ascend again almost immediately to another notch below a big overhanging prow of rock. Continue up the ridge and look back for a view of the enormous chasm in the ridge. The route carries on easily along the crest of the ridge, following waymarks over shattered ground with occasional rock steps. Finally a large wooden cross comes into view, which is the summit of **Visoki Kanin** (2hrs).

To the right is a curious karst feature in the form of a massive hole in the ridge.

Retrace your steps for about 40mins back along the ridge to the scree path above the Kaninski podi. At the end of the scree path where it meets the rocky shoulder, be sure to follow waymarks and signs to Žičnica ('gondola') – the right-hand path goes to the dom. Return across the rib to the junction of the Prestreljenik window path and turn left to visit the **okno**.

The route climbs up the scree quite steeply to the rocks below the window, where waymarks direct you slightly left at first and then right, traversing the rocks. It is quite loose and not particularly pleasant. Bear left round a corner and then up the left-hand side of a small gully. At the head of it turn right and scramble up steeply over loose rock a short distance to the window. There is

*The window on Prestreljenik*

an exciting view through the window down into Italy. Return the same way and continue down to the gondola station.

**Prestreljenik (2499m)**

Just above the top gondola station, follow signs to Prestreljenik. Slog up the ski slope, over scree and stones, for about 10mins and bear right at the top, passing beneath the chairlift cables to reach the saddle which is on a subsidiary ridge. Turn left and cross under the cables again, then begin to ascend on the right-hand side of the ridge on an easy broad path, signed Prestreljenik. Reach a short level section, 10mins from the col, and then continue more steeply up the ridge. Climb a few easy rock steps and walk along the stony path, still on the right-hand side of the ridge. ▶ Eventually the route starts to bear left, over easy rock steps, and joins a subsidiary ridge from the north to continue left up to the summit of **Prestreljenik**.

As you gain height the ground becomes more grassy, liberally scattered with cushions of pretty flowers.

There are fine views of the Reklanska valley in Italy, with the Jof di Montasio range to the north. The summit also has the added interest of a **tiny tower**, about 40cm high, which is a replica of the stolp on Triglav. The visitors' book is inside.

Return to the top station the same way.

# WALK 38

*Rombon*

| | |
|---|---|
| **Start** | Top station of Kanin ski gondola, near Bovec |
| **Finish** | Bovec |
| **Distance** | 15.5km |
| **Total ascent** | About 400m |
| **Total descent** | 1750m |
| **Grade** | 3/4 |
| **Time** | 8–9hrs |
| **Maps** | 1:25,000 Bovec-Trenta |
| **Refreshments** | Take plenty of refreshments with you as there is no mountain hut on this walk and only one tiny spring. |
| **Access** | On foot/by car: follow the Tolmin road west out of Bovec and turn right opposite a petrol station to reach the gondola. The car park is at 439m, and the gondola ride takes about 30mins; check running times with the Tourist Office. |

Starting from the top of the Kanin gondola, the ascent of Rombon (2208m) is a glorious high-level walk, hugging the 2000m contour most of the way. It crosses a fascinating landscape; with textbook examples of karst geology, a veritable garden of alpine flowers and, strewn along its length, an array of artefacts from the First World War, there is something of interest around every corner. The 1750m descent down Rombon's southern flank winds past countless military caves and tunnels, built when the front line ran right across the mountain.

There are no real difficulties on this route, but it merits its 3/4 grade by its length – 5 hours to the summit from the gondola, followed by the very long descent, which will probably give your knees something to say the next day!

See the route map in Walk 36.

◂ Outside the top gondola station, Rombon is signed on the rock slab – head up the ski slope for about 10mins to the col, as if for Prestreljenik. At the col the route continues over the other side, signed for Rombon, beneath the cables of the highest chairlift. Follow waymarks down, over classic limestone pavement, with extensive views across the Julian Alps to the right and the line of the path seen contouring the huge bowl ahead. The summit of Rombon is visible behind the ridge of Pri Banderi.

The path descends fairly steeply at first before levelling out a little and bearing right above the **Prevala col** (2067m), with some First World War trenches by the turn. It then descends gently, and curves back left to reach the grassy saddle, about 35–40mins from the gondola. On the far side of the col you can look down to the ski station of Sella Nevea in Italy. ▶

Below the steep face just a little further ahead there are the remains of military buildings cut into the rock.

Several paths leave the col in different directions; one heads roughly south-east, down to Bovec, and one north-west down to Italy. Another heads north past the military buildings and over the western shoulder of Lopa into Italy. Your path heads east, following a faded sign to Rombon; it ascends a little between boulders, and then contours high above the Krnica valley.

*Walkers approaching the Prevala col, where the path begins its long traverse to Rombon*

Even now you can see how well the path was engineered as a **military supply route**, with built sections to take the easiest line. Flowers abound in every crevice – moss campion, thyme, Triglav rose, harebell, Zois' bellflower and edelweiss to name but a few.

Pass below the peak of **Lopa** (2406m) and continue traversing, with good views to the right into the valley and beyond to the Soča river. After about 50mins from the col reach a vast karst hollow, marked **Kotel** (1881m) on the map. The path goes round to the left of it, weaving up and around boulders and karst formations. It then descends slightly to pass more military buildings before climbing up to a **col** on the subsidiary ridge that links the peaks Pri Banderi, Jelenk and Vratni vrh.

Follow waymarks over the col, past heaps of barbed wire embedded in the ground, and see ahead an even more jumbled karst plateau, with limestone pavements and sinkholes, some of which are known to be over 1000m deep. The path follows a complicated route between the chasms, but is well waymarked. ◂ After about 30mins you reach a junction for the peak of Črnelska špica. Rombon is signed bearing slightly right, and the path continues through the limestone scenery for another 15mins or so to reach a col at 1955m. Here there are more remains of military buildings, one of which has been made into a bivouac shelter (Zasilni). The first views down the north side look into Korita Prodi at the head of the Možnica valley.

All around is evidence of the war – food tins, boot soles, barbed wire and twisted metal.

From the col the path ascends steadily and shortly passes a path on the right signed to Rupa, which eventually joins the descent route to Bovec. ◂ Just after the junction the path ascends more steeply before traversing the upper slopes of **Vrh Ribežnov**. Just here the route traverses close to the crest of the ridge and the views down the almost vertical north walls to the floor of the Možnica valley are breathtaking. Pass just below the rocky top of Prisna Glava, and then bear right and descend a little for about 100m. Pass a sign for 'voda' (water) at a tiny spring,

If you don't want to go all the way to the summit of Rombon, the descent from here would curtail the walk by about 2hrs 30mins.

right by the track. The path continues among shattered limestone boulders, and soon after begins the ascent to the summit of Rombon.

Reach a sign, Veliki vrh (Rombon) 1hr, and turn left, ascending man-made rock steps which zigzag up the hillside on a well-constructed path to just below the crest of the ridge, and on to reach an obvious entrance tunnelled into the hillside. ▸

It is worth a look inside the tunnel for its observation window with an amazing view to the north. The villages of Log pod Mangartom and Strmec can be seen, with Mangart and its military road, still used today, behind.

The path continues close to the crest of the ridge, over a small rocky top, and ascends a few easy rock steps, with the last summit section of Rombon ahead. Looking right, across the boulder-strewn corrie below, filled with the warning cries of marmots, you can see the descent gully dropping from the south ridge.

The path descends a little to the right-hand side of the ridge and traverses for 100m or so before climbing once more to the crest. A short descent passes the foot of rocky outcrops, with a short easy section of scrambling protected by a handrail. The path continues across

*Looking back along the high level traverse that leads to Rombon*

shattered slabs and then begins to ascend, following waymarks up the steep slope of rocks and grass. Just below the summit reach a notch and cross to the north side of the ridge for the last easy walk of 50m or so to the top of **Rombon**.

> Just beyond the notch there is another gun emplacement and tunnels in the rock – even up here. The view from the **summit of Rombon** is considered one of the most extensive and beautiful in all the Julian Alps, due more to its unique position than its height, which is relatively modest.

The path continues over the summit, following waymarks and a sign for Bovec. It soon turns right and heads south, descending easily down the south ridge, with a fine outlook to Krn and Krasji vrh, and a bird's-eye view of Bovec 1700m below. About 20mins from the top descend an awkward little rock step to the top of a large gully on the right, signed BC. Head down here to reach the boulder-strewn corrie and turn left at the bottom to continue down unpleasant steep scree and stones below the crags.

As the path levels, cross a boulder field, seeing ahead the grassy top of Čukla (1767m), crowned with a stone memorial. Continue down past a complex of defences to a sign, Čukla 5mins, where a short detour to the left visits the First World War monument erected in 1997. After the junction pass yet more defences, with crumpled sheets of rusting corrugated iron, and continue descending, with the vegetation gradually changing as you reach the dwarf pine.

Eventually the path swings left and begins to drop down into thicker beech forest. After about 25mins in the woods, exit onto clearer ground bearing right, then ascend a little before dropping down and turning left past a small building. Soon after, begin to descend quite steeply through pleasant beech forest, finding relief in its cool shade. After about 45mins of descent cross waterworn slabs and continue down steeply. The path becomes rocky and descends steps cut in the rock through small outcrops. Eventually the gradient eases a little and the stony path winds down to the left of a boulder-littered scree slope. It then bears left and continues down over loose stones to reach a rough gravel road at a water trough and spring (3hrs 30mins–4hrs from the summit of Rombon).

Follow the sign left for Bovec, and immediately take the track to the right, signed B3a, for about 50m. Go through a gate at the side of a building and begin to descend, following a dry stone wall. The path continues between two fences, goes across a field, through a gate, and then enters woods. Here it soon becomes a broad track which you follow for about 100m before turning left once again onto a narrower track by an orange waymark on a tree. Keep descending through the woods to a fence at the edge of a field, where the path turns left and crosses a small stream. Another 50m brings you to a sign at a gravel road saying 'centre'. Follow this to the tarmac road, and then turn left to reach **Bovec**.

## WALK 39

*The Soča Trail*

| | |
|---|---|
| **Start** | Top of Vršič pass |
| **Finish** | Trenta village |
| **Distance** | 11km |
| **Descent** | 1000m |
| **Grade** | 2 |
| **Time** | 3½–4hrs |
| **Maps** | 1:25,000 Bovec-Trenta, 1:25,000 Triglav, 1:30,000 Kranjska Gora |
| **Refreshments** | Koča pri Izviru Soče |
| **Access** | Several buses a day cross the Vršič pass between Bovec and Kranjska Gora, and can drop passengers at the top of the pass. Pick up the same bus route in Trenta to return to Bovec. |

The Soča river may be short, at 96km, but it is without doubt one of the most beautiful in the Alps. Its most notable characteristic is its incredible luminous green colour, which is difficult to credit from pictures until you see it for yourself. The valley and the river have been an important trade and access route since early times, and were of vital strategic importance during the First World War. As a result there are many historical as well as natural sights to be seen along the way.

The Soča trail was created by linking several age-old routes through the valley, and is well signposted with information boards. This walk descends the Vršič pass, and then follows the first part of the Soča trail to finish in the small village of Trenta (Na Logu). After walking down the pass into the Zadnja Trenta valley, the route visits the source of the Soča (Izvir Soče) before passing the Kugy monument and a short diversion to the Juliana Alpine Garden, and then continues to the village of Trenta, where there is limited accommodation if required. The Soča Trail continues beyond Trenta, following the river downstream.

The walk can be combined with Walk 5 to make an excellent route to link Kranjska Gora and Bovec.

From the top of the Vršič pass head south, past the souvenir kiosk and the path leading left to the **Tičarjev dom**. ◄ Walk down the road and 150m or so from the top of the pass cross a stream on a bridge. Immediately afterwards take a path to the right, which simply cuts off the bend and brings you to hairpin bend 26. Continue down the road and about 200m past bend 26, just beyond a set of crash barriers, there is a painted sign on the right saying 'Trenta Izviru Soče 1hr' by steps going down and the path just below. Once you are on it there are arrows and waymarks, and the path runs parallel to and below the road, descending gently.

Mala Mojstrovka is the mountain on the right (Walk 10), and Prisank (Walk 14) is on the left.

The route passes mostly through forest, crossing numerous streams, and gradually leaves the road behind. There are occasional good views up to the right to the Mojstrovka ridge. After 10mins or so cross a stream and join the old road, now a grassy track, at a hairpin bend. Turn right and down to a couple of benches and a memorial. The track curves round to the right a few paces after

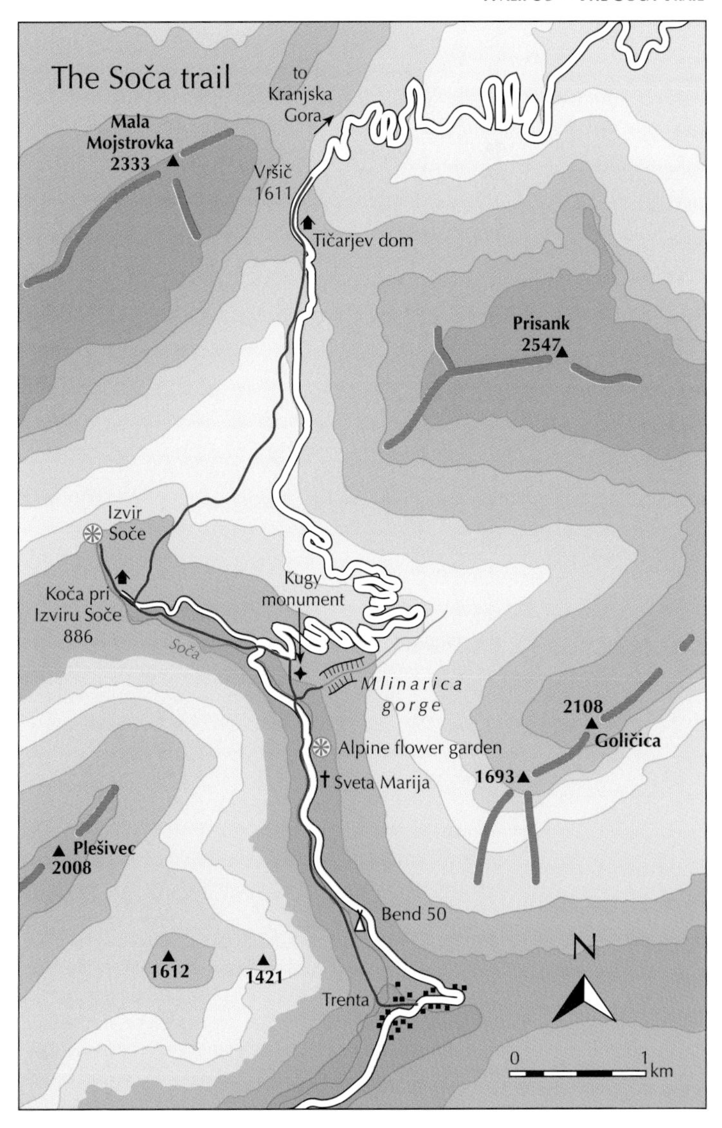
The Soča trail
to
Kranjska
Gora
Mala
Mojstrovka
2333
Vršič
1611
Tičarjev dom
Prisank
2547
Izvir
Soče
Koča pri
Izviru Soče
886
Soča
Kugy
monument
Mlinarica
gorge
2108
Goličica
Alpine flower garden
Sveta Marija
1693
Plešivec
2008
Bend 50
N
1612
1421
Trenta
0
1
km

the bench, but follow a waymark for the path marked straight ahead. This rejoins the track a little further down, where you carry on walking in the same direction, with good views to the hills above Trenta. After another 5mins look for a waymark directing you to a path heading down to the right. Walk down here, still descending gently, and 2–3mins further on meet another broad track. Turn right onto it and continue down.

Reach a fork and take the left, signed with the Alpe Adrija logo, descending gently at first as the track curves round to the right. The path continues down, more or less steeply, and in a short while begins to descend in hairpins.

On the outside of one of the left-hand bends there is a sign on a rock which says 'voda' (water) by an attractive mossy **spring** which comes out of the rocks only to disappear almost immediately into the gravel. The water is very cold and fresh.

Continue down, passing a house-sized boulder on the left with a coat of arms dated 1915 engraved on the side of it. Carry on down more hairpins and emerge from the trees to finally reach a wonderful viewpoint over the Zadnja Trenta valley. As you descend you begin to hear the river Limarica on the right, which you eventually cross on stepping stones. The path now levels out, passes some weekend cottages and continues between two stone walls for a short distance to a tarmac road, where you turn right to **Koča pri Izviru Soče**.

The source of the Soča is signed behind the hut, 15mins. The path climbs easily up to a viewpoint (*razgledna*), where you turn right and then left to climb more steeply over rocks fashioned into rough steps, with a handrail. The last section to the river's source, **Izvir Soče**, is on a steep narrow ledge above a drop into the river and is not for the faint-hearted; it can be slippery and the handrail is very welcome. The river emerges from a cave in a deep green pool in a cave with very variable water levels; the mouth of the cave can only be approached at low water.

Retrace your steps to the koča, then head left down the road for about 250m to a lay-by with an information sign and a turn-off to a path on the right. The path enters woodland and continues with the **Soča river** to the right, some distance below. ▶ As the path descends a little you begin to get some views of the river, the rushing pale green water contrasting with the darker green of the forest trees and the mountains and crags behind.

There are good views through the trees of the mountains closing in all around.

After 20mins on this pleasant path come to a junction where the route turns left and up. In a short distance rejoin the minor road from the koča, turn right and walk 200m or so to join the main road at bend 49. Turn left; unfortunately the next short section is up the road, but it is less than 5mins to bend 48 and the **Kugy monument**. Walk the short distance from the road to the statue which shows Julius Kugy looking up to Jalovec, his favourite mountain. There are excellent views of the surrounding peaks.

**Dr Julius Kugy** (1858–1944) was a pioneer climber of the Julian Alps and one of the early mountain authors, writing in German. He originally came here as an amateur botanist but fell in love with these mountains and set out with local Trenta guides to explore them. One of his most famous quotes was 'Triglav is not a mountain, Triglav is a realm.' The monument was built in 1953.

*Julius Kugy eternally looks towards his beloved mountains*

Walk around the back of the monument, following a sign for Korita Mlinarice (Mlinarica gorge), and take a path through a flower meadow past some buildings with typical shingled roofs. Enter the forest and drop down almost to the water's edge, then come to a footbridge which crosses the river (Soča). Do not cross, but continue straight on to the **Mlinarica gorge**. A short walk on a well-made footpath brings you underneath the cliffs to a viewpoint. ◂

The Mlinarica river has a very steep gradient, falling 300m for every 700m of its length, and this awesome power has eroded the narrow gorge.

Walk back to the footbridge over the Soča, and cross it this time to walk along the road for 2–3mins. Just before a bridge, the trail branches off to continue on the right-hand side of the valley to the village of Trenta.

It is well worth a short detour at this point to visit the **Juliana Alpine Garden**, 200m further down the road across the bridge. This garden was created in 1926 and consists mostly of flowers from the Julian Alps, the Karavanke and the Kamnik-Savinja Alps, although some flowers from the western Alps and the Pyrenees have also been planted. There is a small entrance fee.

Pick up the route again by crossing the footbridge opposite the church 100m or so further down the road.

The trail soon narrows to a path which is not waymarked but is easy and obvious all the way. About 5mins walking brings you to an open area by a footbridge opposite the small church of **Sveta Marija**. ◂ Continue along the path with the river to the left, through sections of forest and flower meadows filled with butterflies. After about 20mins descend a little to a small pasture with some derelict buildings on the left; just beyond them is another footbridge which leads to the **Trenta campsite**.

The church dates back to 1690 and has amazing painted 'alcoves' on its completely flat walls, creating an extraordinary optical illusion.

About 100m further on the path begins to climb for about 5mins to top a rib. Descend the other side in easy steps and hairpins, down to the river again, and turn left at a junction to cross the Soča on a footbridge constructed in 2004. Walk up the path on the other side to a field and a track heading left, past a building on the right and then alongside the river Krajcarica. After 200m reach the main road and turn right into Trenta – the bus stop is opposite the Dom Trenta visitor centre in the centre of the village.

## WALK 40

*Pogačnikov dom and Kriški podi*

| | |
|---|---|
| **Start/finish** | Bend 50 on the Vršič pass road, about 700m from Trenta village centre and bus stop |
| **Distance** | 16km |
| **Total ascent/descent** | 1450m |
| **Grade** | 3 |
| **Time** | 7½–8hrs |
| **Maps** | 1:25,000 Bovec-Trenta, 1:25,000 Triglav, 1:30,000 Kranjska Gora |
| **Refreshments** | Pogačnikov dom |
| **Parking** | Turn off at the bend and drive a short distance on the gravel road where it is possible to park on the right. There is also a small car park at the far end of the gravel road but spaces are limited and it's usually best to park as suggested and walk up the road – maximum 1.5km. |

The ascent to Pogačnikov dom (2050m) makes a fine walk, and its spectacular position on the edge of the extensive karst plateau of Kriški podi, with its limestone pavements, three mountain lakes and magnificent cirque of craggy peaks, makes it well worth a day trip, even if you don't intend to go on and climb any of the surrounding summits (see Walks 41 and 42).

It is a fairly long day walk, at around 4½hrs for the ascent and 3hrs for the descent by the same route, but it gives the walker an opportunity to reach a high-mountain environment without any major difficulties. The height gain is considerable and the path is steep at times, but the continuing interest of the forest vegetation and the spectacular unfolding views make the effort worthwhile. This is a lovely walk for late spring and early autumn, as it is in the sun all the way when not under trees.

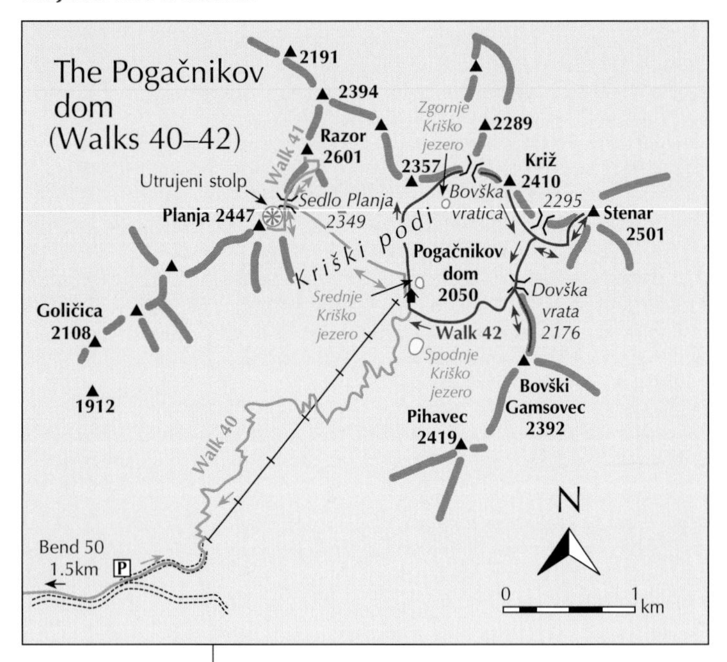


From bend 50, follow the gravel road, signed Pogačnikov dom 4hrs, for about 20mins to reach a small car park on the left. From the car park bear left and follow the forest track up the hill for 10–15mins to arrive at the goods cableway that is used by the hut – an information board about Kriški podi (the limestone lake area around the hut) is also found here. Follow a narrow path which sets off steeply into the trees, signed for the hut.

The path zigzags in hairpins high above the river, giving tremendous views of steep rock walls all around. The path is a well-engineered First World War mule track, built up with stone in certain sections, and although the hairpins make the gradient seem quite gentle you gain height quickly. There are numerous short-cuts at the bends, but on the whole it is probably best to stick to the main path. Throughout the route there are places where it can feel somewhat exposed, although the path is always wide enough for comfortable walking.

There are several river canyons to cross which could be dangerous after heavy rainfall. After about 1hr the path passes below rock outcrops where the hut can be seen far ahead perched on the skyline; about 10mins further on, pass a shrine on the left, and in 5mins more reach the biggest of the water canyons. Each crossing brings you further round to the right-hand side of the valley, where you eventually cross beneath the line of the cableway.

The path winds up steep hairpins beneath a crag, and then continues above it as the vegetation gradually changes with the increased altitude. Eventually you emerge from the dwarf pine onto an open slope with excellent views of the steep rock faces all around and the valley now far below. The track continues across steep scree and passes small rock outcrops up to a spring with a stone trough that lies a few metres to the right of the path. From here you can see the hut, looking not too far away, but this last section can feel like hard work, especially on a hot day!

As you round the next bend, a sign points to the right marking a short detour of about 100m to visit the first of three mountain lakes along the route, **Spodnje (lower) Kriško jezero**. This is the lowest in altitude and the largest of the lakes, 120m long and 9.5m deep.

Return to the track and continue through more open ground. Below the final crag you can go left or right to the **Pogačnikov dom** – the right-hand route is waymarked and is a little less steep than the left.

**Pogačnikov dom** (2050m) stands on the rim of the huge limestone corrie of Kriški podi, a paradise for geologists. It is surrounded by a ring of peaks – from left to right, Planja, Razor, Križ, Stenar, Bovški Gamsovec and Pihavec. Ibex can be seen here and a small herd often passes close to the hut.

From the hut it is about 30mins to visit the middle lake, Srednje Kriško jezero, which interestingly was formed by water erosion not glacial

*Looking down into the Trenta valley from Pogačnikov dom*

action. Cold air collects in the hollow formed by the lake and snow can remain late into the season. The upper lake, Zgornje Kriško jezero, is over 200m higher up, and is the highest lake in Slovenia. There is no path to it from here: it is best seen from the ridge that leads to Križ (Walk 42).

**ROCKFALL**

If you are planning to tackle any of the surrounding peaks from the hut, note that the peaks in this region appear to be more prone to rockfall and landslides than other mountains of the Julian Alps. Recent rockfalls near the summits of Razor, Križ and Pihavec have affected the normal ascent paths.

To descend from Pogačnikov dom return the way you came.

## WALK 41

*Planja and Razor*

| | |
|---|---|
| **Start/finish** | Pogačnikov dom |
| **Distance** | 5.5km |
| **Total ascent/descent** | 550m |
| **Grade** | 4 |
| **Time** | 4–4½hrs |
| **Maps** | 1:25,000 Bovec-Trenta, 1:25,000 Triglav, 1:30,000 Kranjska Gora |
| **Access** | Follow Walk 40 up to the hut |

These two fine peaks dominate the skyline to the north-west of the Pogačnikov dom. Razor (2601m) stands on the ridge between the Trenta and Vršič valleys; its pyramidal profile is also striking from Kranjska Gora. From the hut the two mountains can be climbed in a short day, which you will remember for its stunning views. If you have walked up from Trenta in the morning (see Walk 40), then this is a full mountain day. This is a true mountaineering route requiring via ferrata kit and helmet.

▸ The path heads north from Pogačnikov dom, with views down to your right of Srednje Kriško jezero, the middle lake of Kriški podi. In less than 5mins reach a sign – Sedlo Planja 1hr, Planja 1hr 30, Razor 2hrs – where you turn left. After a level traverse across the rocky hillside for about 10mins, the path begins to climb over scree at the foot of crags, ascending up and to the left. Soon afterwards, in rather less than 10mins, the path turns sharp right towards the rocks, and you are immediately confronted with the first steel cable.

See the route map in Walk 40.

The route is waymarked and signed 1 for the Slovene high-level route. The cable section is not long or difficult, and the path then traverses the crags, with occasional steel pegs to assist. Although it is without major difficulty, loose rock and a short traverse over some convex slabs require concentration and care. After another short section of cable reach more scree which is also traversed diagonally up and left.

A large rockfall near the summit of Razor in 2013 caused damage to this lower section of path, and the route now traverses further left than the original path and crosses more scree and protected rock sections, which bring you closer to Planja's eastern crags before heading up right up towards the **Sedlo Planja** (Planja saddle). A few metres below the saddle, after a last section of cable, come to a junction, signed Planja and Utrujeni stolp (the 'Tired Pillar') to the left and Razor to the right. Turn left, and after a few more paces a view opens up to the right of the Krnica valley. ◂

Prisank, Jalovec and Mangart are all visible.

The climb up to the summit of Planja starts with a scramble up rocky steps. There are steel pegs for security, as the route is exposed in places, although not too difficult. Pass **Utrujeni stolp**, a massive double pillar of rock, still attached to the main crag by an arch, with a large cave at the base of it. Soon after that the route follows

*Just below Pogačnikov dom, with Planja and Razor in the background*

a broad, stony shoulder, with alpine flowers and mosses growing in the cracks, and continues easily to the summit of **Planja** (2453m), about 20mins from the junction by the saddle.

Return to the saddle the same way, and head right towards Razor, signed 1hr. The path climbs quite steeply, traversing across scree and sloping rock, keeping to the right-hand side of the ridge. At one point pass the mouth of a small cave. The traverse leads to an unpleasant steep gully, filled with scree. The path avoids entering it at first by turning left up more rocky ground, but soon turns right again and heads back into the gully, keeping to the left-hand side – the centre line is badly eroded. A couple of metres before the top of the gully the path swings left, but it is worth walking up those last few metres for a good view from the small col of Triglav, Stenar, Škrlatica and Špik.

Turn left and in a few metres reach a warning sign where loose fallen rocks have covered the way ahead – note that the former path made a longer traverse from here but was obliterated by a large rockfall in 2013. The route now turns right and soon begins to ascend a very steep section of via ferrata, some of which is vertical, of almost 20m. This brings you onto the crest of the summit ridge where a final short airy walk brings you to the top of **Razor** (2601m). After all your effort, enjoy the marvellous 360° view from this mighty bastion of the Julian Alps.

The route returns the same way to the saddle and down to Pogačnikov dom for a well-earned drink!

# WALK 42

*Križ, Stenar and Bovški Gamsovec*

| | |
|---|---|
| **Start/finish** | Pogačnikov dom |
| **Distance** | 7.5km |
| **Total ascent/descent** | 450m |
| **Grade** | 4 |
| **Time** | 5½–6hrs |
| **Maps** | 1:25,000 Bovec-Trenta, 1:25,000 Triglav, 1:30,000 Kranjska Gora |
| **Access** | Follow Walk 40 up to the hut |
| **Warning** | In 2014 a rockfall here caused the first part of the descent from Križ to become even more treacherous, and some of the original waymarks have disappeared. It is hoped that by the time this guide is published, the route will be freshly waymarked and possibly even secured. |

This route makes a fine high-level circuit of three peaks to the east of the Kriški podi plateau, starting and finishing at Pogačnikov dom. These mountains are in the heart of the northern Julian Alps and offer excellent views of the pillars of Triglav's north face and the surrounding mountains. There is only this one walkers' route on Stenar (2501m), but its accessibility from Pogačnikov dom and the Vrata valley makes it one of the most visited peaks over 2500m. Križ (2410m) and Bovški Gamsovec ('chamois mountain') (2392m) round out the tour to an especially satisfying mountain day, comfortably completed from the dom, and with time over to make the descent to Trenta if you wish (3hrs). This is a true mountaineering route with via ferrata kit and helmet strongly recommended.

See the route map in Walk 40.

◄ Leave Pogačnikov dom heading north as if to Razor, but in less than 5mins, when you get to the signpost, go straight on for Križ (1hr 30mins). For the first 15mins the path climbs steadily, with occasional steel pegs for security. Then cross limestone pavement with deep fissures and karst holes for another 5mins before the route veers left and continues on a leftward-rising traverse for a few minutes, before waymarks lead you up through a notch in the rocks. Continue up for another 10–15mins, and **Zgornje Kriško jezero**, the upper Križ lake, comes into view. The path ascends quite steeply for a short while and then traverses above the lake on the slopes of Kriške rot. This brings you to a saddle on the west ridge of Križ at 2275m. There are excellent views down into the Krnica valley below the wall of Kriška Stena.

From here climb steeply towards Križ, heading immediately up the rocks via a pleasant scramble. After a few minutes' climbing the angle eases onto the broad grassy shoulder of Križ. Continue on over easy ground to reach a red sign, Križ 10mins, at **Bovška Vratica**. Ahead along the ridge you can see the rocky top of **Križ**, about 200m in distance and 40m higher. The final section involves an easy scramble with protection and a short walk along to the rocky summit and cairn with a visitors' book. ▸

The next peak, Stenar, looks enticingly close, but there is a fair amount of descent and ascent to go yet!

Continue along the summit ridge for a short distance to a waymark directing you down to the right. Descend over quite steep loose ground, looking carefully for waymarks, to reach a sign, Vrata, painted on a rock. Beyond the sign the path continues down, at first over rock ledges covered with rubble and then across more scree in a leftward descending traverse, below crags. Reach a junction, with Vrata signed down to the right and Stenar straight on.

The Stenar path begins to climb up a short scree slope and then joins a rocky rib, with views down to the col of Dovška Vrata and the peak of Bovški Gamsovec to the right. After an easy ascending traverse across the rocky rib, reach another scree slope which you cross to reach a shoulder. Ascend this steadily for about 20mins, with no difficulties, and then turn left to reach the skyline ridge. The last 20mins or so climbs steadily but easily up to the summit of **Stenar**, with its stunning views of Triglav.

Retrace your footsteps to the junction with the sign for Stenar and Vrata painted on a rock, and take the Vrata path heading down to the left (south), following waymarks. This takes you down onto the plateau between Stenar and Bovški Gamsovec. Cross the plateau for

*The north ridge of Bovški Gamsovec seen from Stenar*

15mins or so, passing a sign to the Vrata valley down to the left at the Dovška vrata saddle (2176m). Continue straight on, up a little rise to another sign – Pogačnikov dom to the right 30mins, and Bovški Gamsovec 45mins, straight ahead. The route ascends the easy rocky ridge for about 20mins before it starts traversing on the right-hand side, with considerable drops into the corrie on the right. The path feels exposed but there are steel handrails for security along its length.

The route does a short zigzag and then continues up, with more steel cables and handrails, to pass between a narrow cleft in the rock. This brings you onto a sloping ramp, again quite exposed, which the route follows to its top, where it joins the crest of the ridge. It is now an easy scramble of 5mins or so to the top of **Bovški Gamsovec** (2392m).

**Triglav** is the next peak to the south-east, and the huge bulk of its north face rears up before you. The Plemenice ridge (Walk 19), the most difficult of Triglav's waymarked paths, can be traced from just above the Luknja col right to the summit. The peak close by to the south is Pihavec.

Carefully retrace your steps from the summit to the sign for Pogačnikov dom. The path heads due west, and the hut is visible from here in clear weather. The path skirts pleasantly around rocky hollows in the high mountain karst of the **Krški Podi** plateau. The many crevices and holes of the limestone pavement require careful footwork in places, so beware of losing sight of the waymarks while choosing the best line. ▸ The path joins the main route from Trenta just below Pogačnikov dom – bear right here to return to the hut, or left to walk down to Trenta.

Lovely alpine flowers brighten the cracks and there is a good chance you will see ibex and chamois.

# WALK 43

*Krn*

| | |
|---|---|
| **Start/finish** | Dom dr. Klementa Juga at the head of the Lepena valley |
| **Distance** | 18km |
| **Total ascent/descent** | 1550m |
| **Grade** | 3 |
| **Time** | 9–10hrs |
| **Maps** | 1:25,000 Bovec-Trenta, 1:25,000 Bohinj |
| **Access** | By car: parking areas at the dom and near the lower cableway station (but please keep access to the station clear); on foot: take the bus from Bovec to the Lepena valley and walk up the valley to the hut (1½hrs). |
| **Accommodation** | Dom dr. Klementa Juga or Dom pri Krnskih jezerih; Kiln campsite at Lepena at the foot of the valley, near the main road |

The distinctive profile of the summit of Krn (2244m) can be seen from many viewpoints in the Julian Alps, and it is one of the stalwarts of the range in spite of its comparatively modest altitude. Krn is not so much a single mountain as a great massif, thrusting ridges and shoulders in all directions. There are three main walking routes on it; the western approach is the most difficult and the southern the shortest (with transport). The northern approach described here goes past the largest high-mountain lake in Slovenia, and is the most practical approach for those dependent on public transport. It is a long walk, but you can stay overnight at either Dom dr. Klementa Juga or Dom pri Krnskih jezerih (1385m), a further 2hrs along the route.

A sign just past the Dom dr. Klementa Juga says Dom pri Krnskih jezerih 2hrs. From the parking area the route heads into the forest on a well-marked stony track. After just 50m pass another sign for Dom pri Krnskih jezerih as the track turns left and ascends gently through spruce and beech trees.

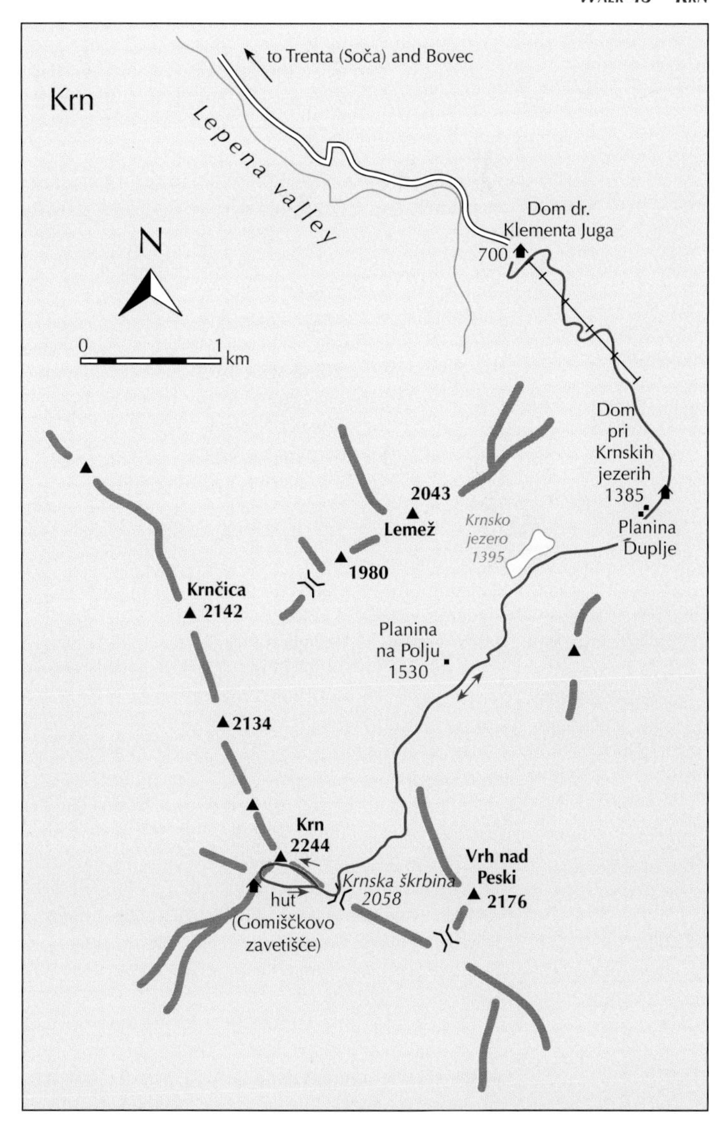
Krn
to Trenta (Soča) and Bovec
Lepena valley
N
0
1
km
Dom dr. Klementa Juga
700
Dom pri Krnskih jezerih
1385
Planina Duplje
Krnsko jezero
1395
2043
Lemež
1980
Krnčica
2142
Planina na Polju
1530
2134
Krn
2244
hut
(Gomiščkovo zavetišče)
Krnska škrbina
2058
Vrh nad Peski
2176

In about 10mins notice a narrower path that leads up into the woods on the left; this waymarked path used to be the preferred route, but the park authorities are trying to discourage its use in a bid to curb erosion, and also to keep walkers away from the hut supply cableway. So, continue up the broad main track as it makes a series of zigzags up through the wood, passing under the cableway line. In about 20mins it bears right below a line of crags and soon after this the terrain of the hillside changes somewhat – still forested, but with small outcrops of limestone with random boulders and rocks.

The route continues steadily up, passing under the cableway supply line another three times. Eventually it levels as it passes between the top cableway station and another small stone building. Continue along the level track for about 100m, with a crag to the right, before beginning to gently ascend again.

At the brow of the rise is a sign marking annual snow depths and temperatures. After a further 150m the track starts to descend a little and passes a narrow path heading left, signed Veliki Baba. Soon reach another junction where you turn left, signed Pl. dom pri Krnskih jezerih 10mins, and follow the stony path through the woods, passing through small open glades to reach **Planinski dom pri Krnskih jezerih** in its shady glade ◂

It's worth going inside the hut to see, above the bar, lots of First World War artefacts from the Soča front.

Leave the dom on a broad waymarked track, following a sign for Krn jezero 15mins, and in 100m arrive at a junction close to the pasture buildings of **Planina Duplje**. Continue straight ahead, passing to the left of the buildings, to reach a signpost; Dom na Komni is signed to the left, but continue straight on for Krn 2hrs 30. The path continues across open level ground for another 300m to arrive at the lake, **Krnsko jezero**, in its idyllic alpine setting, with the attractive peak of Velika Lemež towering above its western side. ◂

Bathing is forbidden in the interests of conservation.

The level path continues just above the shore on the left-hand side of the lake, with Krn directly ahead on the skyline. Another path (not waymarked) traverses the loose rock and hillside above the lake, but is not

The path along the lake below Krn

*Planina na polju on the ascent of Krn*

recommended. At the end of the lake the path bears left and begins to ascend gently, then steepens as it climbs to the left of a rocky outcrop. The terrain has become more alpine and rocky, with just a few sparse trees.

After a more level section the path crosses a dry watercourse and reaches the open grassy **Planina na polju**, surrounded by wild and rocky slopes. There are two small buildings over to the right, one of which is used as a hunting lodge. Cross the planina and on the other side the path begins to climb again. After about 10mins notice 'voda' painted on a rock to the left, indicating a spring about 100m away. The terrain becomes increasingly rocky and barren, although there are still many flowers to catch the eye.

After ascending between boulders and rocks reach a fork, with the left path heading to Vrh nad Peski. The path to Krn bears right and continues, waymarked and signed on a boulder a few metres ahead. Begin to zigzag up the hillside, with views to the north opening up as you climb. Pass another small spring at a level area and continue to ascend the last rocky grassy slopes to the col **Krnska škrbina** (2058m). There are signs, left to Komna and Vrh nad Peski, and right to the koča below the summit of Krn. ▸

At the col is a 149mm shell case from the First World War, mounted on a pole, and a partisan memorial plaque.

Turn right at the col, passing lots of rusted barbed wire and twisted metal, a sad reminder of terrible times. A sign says 'koča 20min'. After about 10mins or so the path forks, and a waymark and sign on a rock says 'vrh (summit)', pointing right. Follow these waymarks, and ascend a grassy path which is a little indistinct at first. This leads up to the crest of the (east) ridge and continues on the left-hand side for another 15mins or so to the summit of **Krn** (2244m).

On the top there is an **orientation plate** and more obvious signs of defences; the front line ran directly over the summit here, as it did on Rombon to the north-west (Walk 38). Uninterrupted views of the Julian Alps to the north and east, to the Adriatic down to the south, and to the Dolomites to the west entice you to linger.

From the summit follow waymarks, dropping down to the south-west, to reach **Gomiščkovo zavetišče na Krnu**, the hut on Krn, within 5mins or so.

At the hut the **views to the south** dominate your horizon, dropping down the uniformly steep grassy slope to the valley below, with tiny herders' buildings at Planina Zaslap and Planina Slapnik. The Soča river can be seen flowing along the floor of the valley, with Kobarid and Matajur to the west and, beyond them, the Adriatic Sea.

From the hut head east, following signs for the lake (1hr 30mins), and continue traversing along the hillside to reach the junction just above the col. Then retrace the outward route back to the Dom dr. Klementa Juga.

## WALK 44

*Mangart*

| | |
|---|---|
| **Start/finish** | Top of the Mangart road at Mangartsko sedlo |
| **Distance** | 4km |
| **Total ascent/descent** | 620m |
| **Grade** | 4 |
| **Time** | 3½–4hrs |
| **Maps** | 1:25,000 Bovec-Trenta |
| **Access** | By car to the top of the Mangart road (toll) |
| **Note** | It's very difficult to climb Mangart without your own transport. On foot it is a slog of 1000m of ascent (on the waymarked path) to the start of the route and there is at present no bus service over the Predel or even to the village of Strmec, 1.5km below the road junction. |

At 2679m Mangart (also known as Mangrt) is the third highest peak in Slovenia, and its mighty bulk dominates the skyline of the northern Julian Alps. A former Italian military road climbs from the Predel pass and is open for public use. This means that it is possible to drive to the Mangartsko sedlo at just over 2000m. It is worth the trip up just to witness the incredible engineering of the road, which has been damaged and repaired several times because of earthquakes and landslides, and for the excellent views from the saddle. In 2017 the upper part of the road before the sadlle was marked as closed due to recurring rockfall, but it is driveable with care and at your own risk.

The route described here takes the Slovene side in ascent and descends the easier Italian route; however, note that snow can lie very late on the Italian, northern, slopes. The difficult steep and exposed parts of the route are well protected; in fact the most danger is on the easier angled unprotected sections which cross loose scree over rock, a combination requiring great caution. An easier option would be to take the Italian route in ascent and descent.

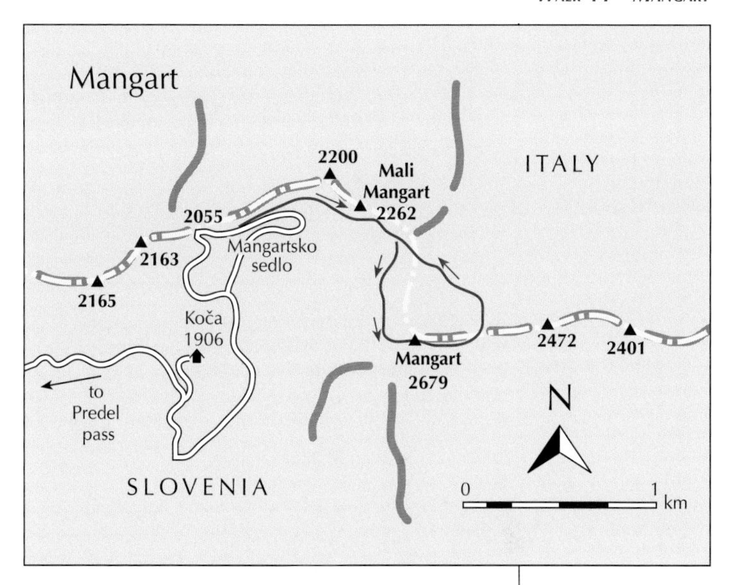


Leave the parking area at Mangartsko sedlo and head east over short grass towards the rocky top of **Mali Mangart** (2262m). The route traverses its foot, eventually bearing left and up easy rocks to reach a small saddle between Mali Mangart and Mangart itself. There are precipitous drops on the north side and views to the two small lakes lying in Mangartska dolina (the Mangart valley) at the foot of the mountain.

Just beyond the col the easier Italian route, signed Ital.smer – here used for the descent – continues straight on, while the Slovene route – signed Slov.smer with an exclamation mark that warns that this is a difficult route, now heads right. Its destination is obvious – a huge gash ascending from left to right across the west face. The path leads across boulders and scree, and then descends slightly to the foot of the route (about 40mins from Mangartsko sedlo).

Begin to ascend, scrambling steeply up on good rock (steel cables). On closer inspection the line of the route immediately begins to show the varied rock architecture within the enormous cleft in the mountain. After 150m, the cleft has become a steep gully and the route continues up its left side for about 50m before traversing right and ascending a ramp of good clean rock to reach an easier-angled rock spur.

The way ahead continues for another 40mins or so with a mixture of easier ground, albeit topped with loose stones and scree, interspersed with steeper equipped sections, to eventually arrive at an exposed little crest where a steep spur of rock abuts the west face. More cables lead steeply up from here, but the angle quickly relents and easier ground leads to a boulder-choked gully that is climbed until waymarks direct you again to the right. Like the previous gully, this one is also part of the structure of the great cleft. In another 100m arrive at a level area from where a short detour of 30m leads to a narrow grassy promontory, with a good view down into the Koritnica valley.

From the level area the route turns left and climbs over a jumble of rocky steps and boulders as it heads up into a cleft. Climb easily through the cleft and find a steep rock wall in front of you, waymarked with an arrow pointing left. Step down through a notch in the rocks and turn right. A few more paces bring you to more steel cables, but the real difficulties of the route are over. Continue to ascend over rock steps and ledges covered with loose stones for another 20mins or so before the angle finally relents at the summit of **Mangart**.

**The summit** is marked by a large wooden cross on top. There are superb views of nearby Jalovec and Ponca, as well as Triglav, Bavški Grintovec, Rombon, the Kanin group, the Jof Fuart range in Italy, and on into Austria. Mangart is also an area of great interest to botanists – due to its geographical position, plants from both the Julian Alps and the Central Alps are found here.

*High on the Slovene route up Mangart*

*Descending towards the grassy ridge where the route turns left*

From the summit turn east, and begin to descend to the right just below the ridge. The path soon drops down more steeply to a point about 100m below the summit ridge before levelling out and starting to traverse. Within a short distance the path bears left, heading down towards a grassy ridge line that leads east, signed Kotovo sedlo. Before this grassy ridge is reached the path soon turns left again, crossing the border into Italy, and in a few more minutes begins a surprisingly easy traverse that cuts across the upper section of Mangart's steep northern side. ◄ The traverse is quite level and steel cable handrail along the way gives confidence should the rock be wet.

Straight ahead down below, you can see the two lakes in the Italian corrie far below.

After about 15mins the route makes a slight rise then drops down more steeply with cables, occasional pegs and even steps cut into the rock. The path has no real difficulties, and continues over easy-angled water-worn slabs and grooves, but it is a little polished in places. It steepens a little more in the final section and then reaches the scree and boulders at the junction with the Slovene route. From here follow the ascent route the short distance back to the parking area at Mangartsko sedlo.

# 4 BLED

*Lake Bled and its island from the viewpoint on Osojnica, with the Karavanke range behind*

# INTRODUCTION

*Walkers enjoying a drink before the ascent of the ski slope on Walk 53*

Bled (475m) is arguably Slovenia's best known tourist resort, both within and outside the country, and has probably the most developed tourist infrastructure of any of the bases described in this book. The fairy-tale combination of church, island, castle and lake against the mountain backdrop has brought people to Bled for hundreds of years (Bled celebrated its 1000-year anniversary in 2004), and it has still somehow managed to retain its charm in spite of thousands of visitors each year. Buildings line the eastern shore competing for the view, but there are places to go where the hotels and casinos do not intrude, and where you can be almost alone with the scenery; some of the walks described in this section aim to reveal this 'other side' of Bled.

Bled is a mere 10mins or so from the motorway from Ljubljana to the north-west of the country. It has train connections to Ljubljana and to Jesenice, where there are international links to Austria and north-west Europe, as well as south to Nova Gorica with its links to Italy. Brnik, Ljubljana's international airport, is about 30mins by car. Bus links are also excellent.

The main street rises from the lake shore at the eastern end. On the right as you walk up from the lake there is a pedestrian area with shops and cafés, the tourist information centre and a supermarket. There are other hotels and shops on the roads leading off from the main street. The bus station is within the town, close to the Hotel Jelovica, while Bled Jezero train station is above the north-west side of the lake, on the Munich–Trieste railway line, which links Jesenice with Nova Gorica. The other train station, Lesce-Bled, has train links to Ljubljana and is found on the Radovljica road 4km to the south-east. Camping Bled is at the western end of the lake, while another large campsite, Šobec, is to the south-east, a couple of kilometres away by the Sava river.

The name Bled refers to the lake, the town and to the surrounding area, and is pronounced by the locals more like 'Blid'. There are a number of interesting places to visit, including the castle (which dates from the 11th century and is now a museum) and the ninth-century church on Slovenia's only true island, reached by the unique *pletna* boats from various places around the shore.

## THE ROUTES

Walks 45 and 46 explore the lake and its immediate vicinity. Slightly further afield is the river-carved Vintgar gorge (Walk 50) and various attractive villages and small peaks with wonderful views (Walks 47–49). Galetovec (Walk 51) is a stunning viewpoint well worth the rather greater effort needed to get there. The main Julian Alps are not within easy walking distance of Bled, with the exception of the delightful Debela peč (Walk 52) and Viševnik (Walk 53); however, it is possible to stay in the Bled area and use a car or (limited) public transport to reach the big mountains.

## MAPS

The 1:30,000 Bled map covers all the routes in this section.

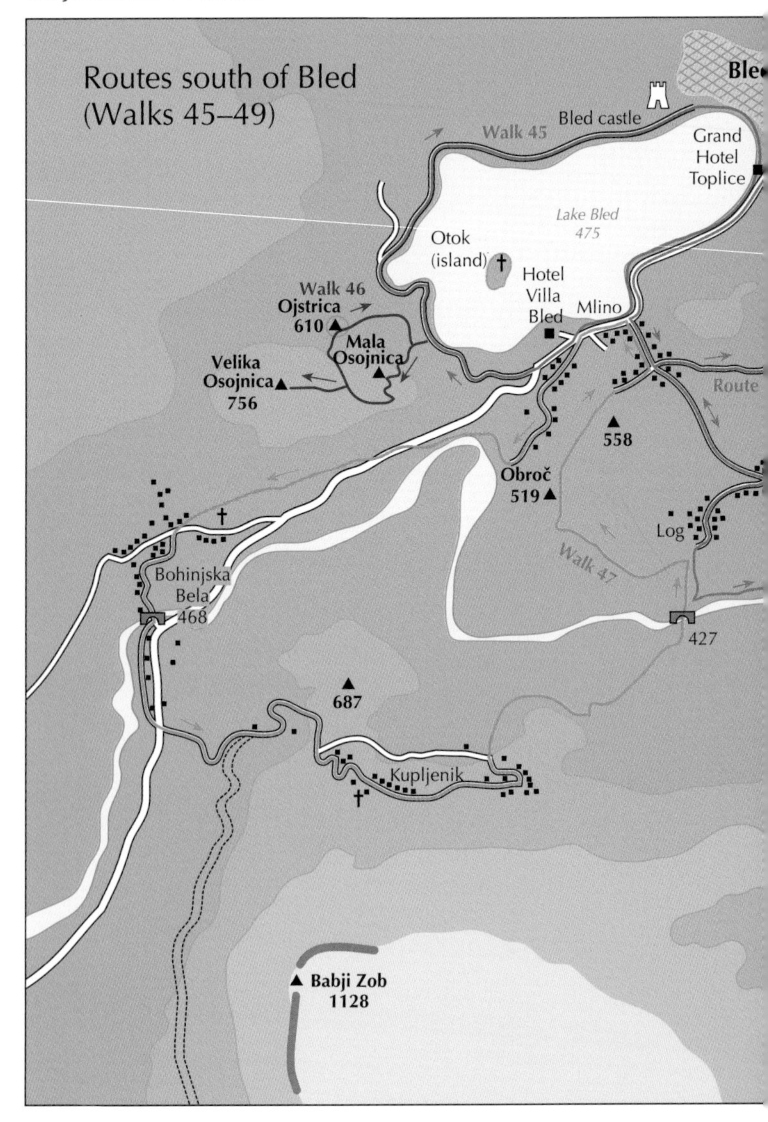
Routes south of Bled
(Walks 45–49)
Ble
Bled castle
Walk 45
Grand
Hotel
Toplice
Lake Bled
475
Otok
(island)
Hotel
Villa
Bled
Mlino
Walk 46
Ojstrica
610
Mala
Osojnica
Velika
Osojnica
756
Route
558
Obroč
519
Log
Walk 47
Bohinjska
Bela
468
427
687
Kupljenik
Babji Zob
1128

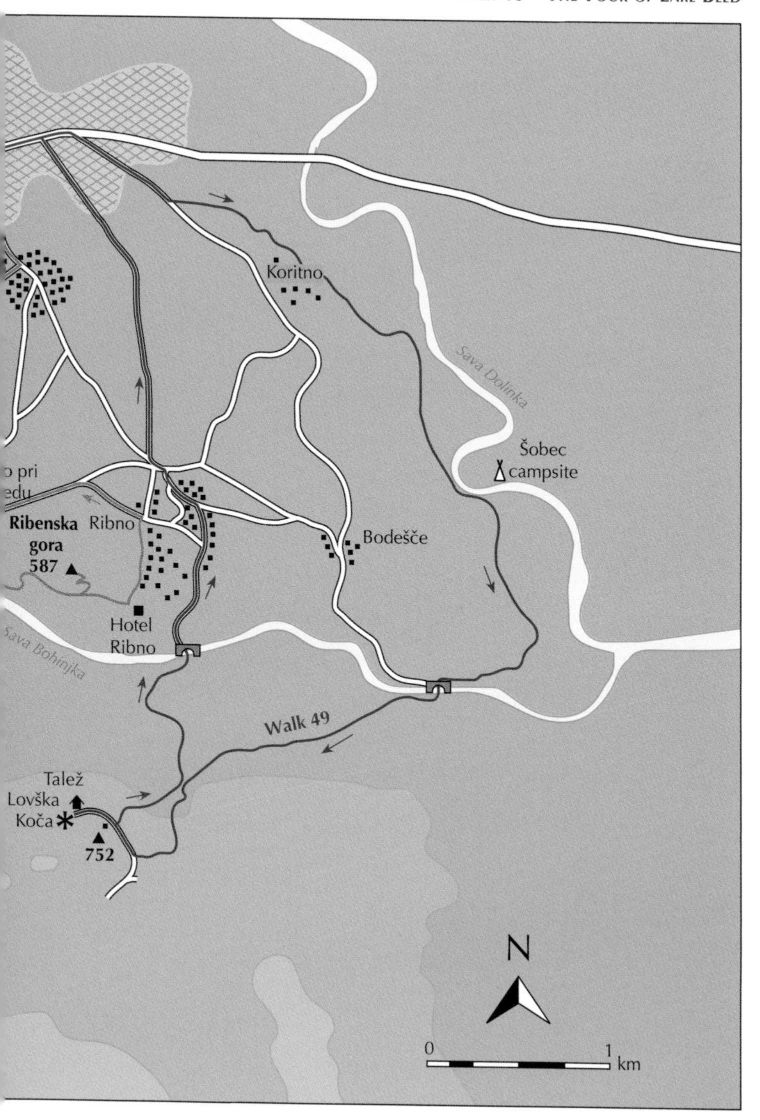
Koritno
Sava Dolinka
Šobec
campsite
o pri
edu
Ribenska
gora
587
Ribno
Bodešče
Hotel
Ribno
Sava Bohinjka
Walk 49
Talež
Lovška
Koča
752
N
0
1
km

# WALK 45

*The Tour of Lake Bled*

| | |
|---|---|
| **Start/finish** | Grand Hotel Toplice by the lake shore, Bled |
| **Distance** | 6km |
| **Total ascent/descent** | Negligible |
| **Grade** | 1 |
| **Time** | 1½–2hrs |
| **Maps** | 1:30,000 Bled |

It is a universal law that people want to walk around a body of water if it is practical to do so, and Lake Bled is no exception. The tour of the lake is an easy stroll and is a good introduction to the area. It is described here in a clockwise direction from the town end of the lake, but can be walked in either direction and started from any point – there is no navigational difficulty here!

Keeping the lake on your right, walk past the Grand Hotel Toplice along the shore path. The main road to Bohinj is on the left, and a little further on it passes through a short tunnel cut in the rock, while the shore path continues along the edge of the lake.

Continuing round, the path comes to the little hamlet of **Mlino**, a popular place for swimming.

> Pletna boats, unique to Bled, can be taken from here and other points on the lake shore to the **island**. There has been a church on the island since the ninth century. It is traditional to ring the church bell and make a wish: visitors to the island ensure that the 'wishing bell' tolls almost constantly during the high season!

This is where President Tito used to stay when he visited Bled.

At Mlino the road moves away from the lake and the path passes the grounds of **Villa Bled**, now a top-class hotel. ◄ The route here is pleasantly shady and it is often possible to see fish close by the shore, seeking shelter from the summer heat under the overhanging willows and beech. Look out for local artists who sell watercolours of the lake at very reasonable prices.

After passing below some crags, the route comes out of the woods and continues across a small grassy area to run close to the road again. Curving round the south-west corner, there follows a boardwalk section, again a good place for fish-spotting and probably the best viewpoint on the circuit. The peak of Stol (2236m), highest in the Karavanke range, makes a perfect backdrop to the combination of island, church and castle. After the boardwalk, continue on a path by the side of the road towards the western end of the lake, another popular place for swimming, close to the campsite.

The concrete stands were erected for rowing spectators and the lanes of **Slovenia's oldest rowing club** are marked with buoys.

Cross the swimming 'beach' and continue round to the right on a pedestrian-only road, in and out of trees,

*A pletna boat on idyllic Lake Bled*

past a gostilna and the rowing clubhouse. In the next section there are a number of springs close to the lake shore; Lake Bled is fed by the springs at 23°C. ◀ The path continues beneath the crags of **Bled castle**, before returning to the grassy park area below the town.

From this side of the lake the stern face of Babji zob ('old woman's tooth') makes a dramatic backdrop to the island.

## WALK 46

*Osojnica*

| | |
|---|---|
| **Start/finish** | Road bend at the south-west corner of Lake Bled |
| **Distance** | 3km |
| **Total ascent/descent** | 280m |
| **Grade** | 2 |
| **Time** | 2hrs |
| **Maps** | 1:30,000 Bled |

This highly recommended walk climbs three small tops to the south-west of the lake. Each has a different character and each offers a different view, including the best lake viewpoint of all, from Mala Osojnica (756m), which gives a bird's-eye view of the island and the church with the massif of Stol behind. The route is mostly well waymarked on a good path, although it is steep at times. It can be combined with the lake circuit (Walk 45) to make a longer walk – its position in relation to the town means you will probably have to walk around a good portion of the lake circumference anyway.

See the route map in Walk 45.

◀ The walk starts on a bend of the road at the south-west corner of the lake, about 50m before the boardwalk section (on a clockwise circuit). On the outside of the bend is a sign (local) route 6, Velika and Mala Osojnica. The path climbs steeply up from the road on a rough track with some wooden steps. Continue around the back of a chalet and begin to climb steeply up through attractive beech forest.

The path winds up through the woodland in a series of swinging hairpins which brings you to the foot of some steep crags. At one point a section of steel cable provides a handrail as the path follows a narrow ledge. After a couple more hairpins the path arrives at the bottom of a steel staircase which climbs about 20m up a narrow cleft in the crag. The 88 steps are steep but not difficult, and there is a handrail if required. You emerge at the top of the steps at a viewpoint with a bench, and from here can look directly down on to the lake, with the island, the castle and the Karavanke range.

The path continues up behind the bench, turns left and traverses above the cliffs. It then descends a little before climbing again to reach, after about 5mins, an even better viewpoint on the flat top of **Mala Osojnica**, which is clear of trees. The path then turns away from the view, back into the wood. Around 100m from the viewpoint a side path turns away on the left (arrow and waymark on a tree) which within a few metres brings you to a bench with a view down into the valley of the Sava Bohinjska river, with the road heading towards Bohinj.

Returning to the main path, continue on through the forest for about 5mins to a junction with a more obvious track where there are signs and a bench. Velika Osojnica is signed to the left and Bled and Ojstrica to the right, all numbered (local) route 6.

Turn left, ascending again, and in less than 100m reach a fork. The left track goes down to the village of Bohinjska Bela, while (local) route 6 is signposted straight on. Continue for around 300m to the summit of **Velika Osojnica** (756m). This is completely covered in trees, but if you follow the path to the left (west) from the top for about 30m there is a pleasant bench and viewpoint looking over forested hills and ridges towards the north and the Karavanke range. The prominent peak in the distance is Kepa (2139m), on the border between Slovenia and Austria.

To continue, retrace your steps back to the junction with the bench. Take the route towards Bled, descending on a broad track that is very water-eroded near the top. Arrive at a signpost that points left to **Ojstrica**; you can see its craggy top close by through the trees. A few minutes' climb brings you to yet another summit, quite different in character from the other two, but with one more wonderful view of the lake, and yes – there is another bench!

Return to the main path and continue down towards Bled. Come to a small open pasture and follow the track down along the edge of the pasture to the road and the lakeside near the starting point.

## SOUTH OF BLED

The next three walks explore the area to the south of Bled, giving an insight into the local landscape that you just don't experience if you stay by Lake Bled. In many ways this is typical Slovene scenery that can be seen all over the country – attractive compact villages, each with a church; farmland, with vegetable plots and orchards; and forested hills. However, look up to the skyline of the Karavanke and the Julian Alps and this is uniquely Bled! The three walks are described separately, but it is easy to 'mix and match' them to make a longer or shorter day out.

### WALK 47

*Bohinjska Bela and Kupljenik*

| | |
|---|---|
| **Start/finish** | Mlino village |
| **Distance** | 11.5km |
| **Total ascent/descent** | 175m |
| **Grade** | 1/2 |
| **Time** | 3½–4hrs |
| **Maps** | 1:30,000 Bled |
| **Refreshments** | Gostilna in Bohinjska Bela |
| **Access** | Follow the edge of the lake to the Penzion Mlino |

This walk is described from Mlino, the little village on the south side of Lake Bled. The route visits the attractive village of Bohinjska Bela before climbing up to Kupljenik with its views out towards the north and the Karavanke. It then descends to cross the Sava Bohinjka before returning to Mlino.

See the route map in Walk 45.

▸ From the Penzion Mlino, walk up the main road, which begins to move away from the lake (there is a pedestrian walkway on the right-hand side). Cross the road at the entrance to **Villa Bled** and walk down the lane opposite, Savska cesta, between attractive houses. At a fork bear left, signed Bohinjska Bela, (local) route 7. Continue down the hill and at a second fork stay right, and walk down this unmade road, past a sawmill on the left, to reach a T-junction where you turn right, signed Bohinjska Bela. This is a broad vehicle track which heads down towards the river and then climbs up to meet the main road to Bohinj.

Turn left and walk down the road for about 100m, and just past a big wooden sign extolling the virtues of Bohinjska Bela, cross the road to a track on the right-hand side which skirts some fields. The village of Bohinjska Bela and the church of Sveta Marjeta can be seen ahead, looking very picturesque against the backdrop of hills and crags that form the eastern edge of the Pokljuka plateau, with Galetovec (Walk 51) behind.

The path passes attractive meadows and cultivated plots with *kozolec* (hayracks). Continue along the path for about 1km to join the village road just past the church. Turn right, cross the little river Belica and walk into the centre of **Bohinjska Bela**, where there is a square with a small supermarket, and a gostilna at a crossroads. Turn left, following a sign for Babji zob, (local) route 11.

Walk down this lane, past pretty houses and gardens, to a bridge crossing the **Sava Bohinjka**, where there is an information board and some picnic tables. Over the bridge continue up the lane to meet the busy main road again; cross it and follow signs for Kupljenik on a minor road up the hill, on the other side of the valley from Bohinjska Bela. As you climb look back to see the terraced pastures of the village and the cliffs edging the plateau. The road is quiet and enjoyable, weaving up through meadows and woodland to reach the village of **Kupljenik**.

At the edge of the village is a big sign saying Dobrodosli ('welcome'), which gives walking times to

*The pretty hamlet of Kuplenik with Lake Bled and the Karavanke mountains in the distance*

local landmarks. Follow the road up through the pretty village and past the church before levelling out above fields, with good views towards Lake Bled, the castle and the Karavanke range. The minor road continues across the top of the fields, and then makes a sharp left turn, signed Selo, as it passes a water trough at the end of the hamlet. Continue down the road, passing beautiful old houses with their large wooden hay barns, to reach a little shrine, with another sign for Selo; turn right here on a gravel track that soon becomes grassy along the edge of very scenic pastures.

In 250m arrive at the bottom right-hand corner of the field, with a wooden shed to the left and a small, lonely partisan memorial on a stone pedestal just to the right at the edge of the woods. Continue on the broad track through the woods and soon pass to the right of another small field.

In a short distance the track forks – the right fork just leads to a shrine which is visible 25m ahead, so continue down left. Soon reach another junction where you once again keep left, and the track gently descends into the wood for almost 1km before merging with another gravel track alongside the river Sava Bohinjka. Continue in the same direction and a little further on arrive at a **bridge**. ▶

The river is a beautiful translucent green, teeming with fish.

Cross the bridge and continue straight on, signed for Selo. Just beyond the bridge, before a group of farm buildings marked on the map as the settlement Log, take the obvious track left signed Mlino and Bled, (local) route 7. Continue on the broad track and after about 250m it bears sharply right.

In another 500m, just as the track begins to steepen to reach a minor tarmac road, take a track right signed Mlino, (local) route 7, and within a few metres join the narrow tarmac road. Pass a small sewage works and within 50m the road ends and you continue on a stony track which ascends gently through the woods, passing houses, to reach a T junction at Mlino's little gasilski dom (fire station). Turn left and continue down through the village to reach the edge of **Lake Bled** and your starting point.

## WALK 48

*Ribenska Gora*

| | |
|---|---|
| **Start/finish** | Grand Hotel Toplice by the lake shore, Bled |
| **Distance** | 9km |
| **Total ascent/descent** | 110m |
| **Grade** | 2 |
| **Time** | 3½–4hrs |
| **Maps** | 1:30,000 Bled |
| **Refreshments** | Hotel Ribno |

This walk passes through the attractive villages of Mlino, Selo and Ribno, and climbs to the satisfying viewpoint of Ribenska gora (587m).

▶ From the Grand Hotel Toplice by Lake Bled, walk clockwise along the shore to the hamlet of **Mlino**. Turn

See the route map in Walk 45.

left on a minor road, signed Selo, and walk through the village, bearing left (uphill) at a fork to reach a crossroads by the fire station. Continue straight ahead, and follow this quiet road for about 1km down to **Selo**. Turn right at a crossroads, signed Sava and Kuplenik (local) route 11. Continue a gentle descent passing houses and farm buildings to reach the river (**Sava Bohinjka**). Turn left to walk along a track on the north bank.

Stroll along here for about 500m, with the river on the right and pastures on the left, with views across to the villages. You can see the wooded slopes of Ribenska gora rising up to the left. Reach a sign, Ribenska gora, and turn left up a rough gravel track that levels within 100m. Leave the track here and head right up into the wood on a vague path which soon becomes more defined, gently ascending across the hillside. ◂ The path makes a couple of hairpins, to reach a path junction with a sign on a tree, Ribno, pointing rightwards. Cross a track, following the sign, and continue bearing right up a path that soon joins another forest track. Continue ascending this upper track to reach a fork. Turn left here and in 100m turn left again at another fork.

In February 2014, a severe ice-storm caused a devastating amount of tree damage in Slovenia; at the time of writing this hillside path had not been completely cleared.

Climb steeply up the rough stony track for a few minutes until it levels, just before a tree-covered knoll. The track splits – continue straight ahead on the left side to the end of the knoll, and leave the ugly forest track to join a narrow path that bears left up the hillside through the small trees. Continue up this pleasant path as it makes a few zigzags to reach a bench just below the crested ridge of Ribenska gora.

The trees unexpectedly give way to give an excellent **view of the valley**. To the west is Babji zob, with the rooftops of Kupljenik below, and in the distance Bohinjska Bela. Due south is the koča at Talež, and down below is the green Sava Bohinjka.

Turn left to walk the short distance to the summit of **Ribenska gora**, via a surprisingly narrow, though not difficult, ridge, to get a good view north as well. Lake Bled

*The village of Ribno with the Karavanke mountains beyond, seen from Ribenska Gora*

is hidden behind Straža, but you can see Ribno directly below, the flat Radovljica plain stretching away to the north and east, the line, though not the river, of the Sava Dolinka, and, behind, the Karavanke range.

The route returns down the hairpins and turns left (east) a few metres before the rough track at the knoll. Continue down through the wood as the path makes a few more zigzags to reach a forest track. Turn left along the level track and within about 150m reach the end of the track at a wooden bench. Continue past the bench on a narrow path that forks just before the **Hotel Ribno**. The left fork continues past the hotel tennis courts then turns right on the edge of a field to reach the road. ▸ Follow the road heading away from the hotel; take the first left, Selska Ulica, which soon leaves the houses behind and continues between pastures towards a small quarry. Reach the road, and turn left, signed Selo, and follow the road for about 1.5km through Selo, retracing your steps back to Mlino.

If you need refreshments, then continue straight ahead to the hotel.

At the crossroads in Mlino, with the fire station on your left, turn right. It looks as if you are going into someone's garden, but a track leads up between the buildings, climbing quite steeply into the woods. Pass under a rocky slope with some crags on the left, just before the brow of the hill, and then continue down on a slightly narrower track. After about 200m, as the track makes a sharp bend to the left, continue on for a few metres to join another track. Turn left onto it and continue in the same direction; the tracks rejoin a little further on.

As the ground levels out emerge from the woods to see pastures and houses which are the outskirts of Bled. There are open views of the Karavanke hills and the Kamniske Alps beyond. Re-enter the woods at a metal barrier, continue for about another 100m, and then the road becomes tarmacked and begins to pass between houses. Reach a junction, turn left and see the castle on its crag up ahead. Continue along this road back to the centre of **Bled**.

## WALK 49

*Talež*

| | |
|---|---|
| **Start/finish** | Grand Hotel Toplice, by the lake shore, Bled |
| **Distance** | 14.5km |
| **Total ascent/descent** | 275m |
| **Grade** | 2 |
| **Time** | 4½–5hrs |
| **Maps** | 1:30,000 Bled |
| **Refreshments** | Lovska koča na Taležu |

This route skirts the village of Koritno and follows the line of the Sava Dolinka before crossing the Sava Bohinjka and climbing up through attractive forest to the viewpoint at Lovska Koča na Taležu. It then descends to cross the river again near the village of Ribno and follows quiet roads back to Bled.

See the route map in Walk 45.

◄ From the Grand Hotel Toplice, walk up the main road heading north-east out of Bled to a petrol station and a

*The koča on Talež*

right-hand turn signed to Koritno. Walk along the minor road until you are clear of the houses, and then, about 50m past the 'leaving Bled' sign, take a track which runs diagonally across the fields to the left, giving good views of Stol and the Karavanke. After about 400m the track swings right to meet a side road. Turn left here and follow the road as it bears right, descending slightly to meet another minor road where you turn right again and continue on through the edge of the village of **Koritno**. Turn left at a sign for Šobec campsite – the road goes quite steeply down at first and then levels out and bears right across the fields, soon becoming unmade. Pass a building on the left with a sign saying Šobec 2.5km, and about 50m afterwards turn left onto a side track, also signed Šobec.

The route descends a little and then bears round to the right and crosses a field before turning right again at the edge of some woods. A few more metres brings you to another sign indicating Šobec to the left. Take this and continue on through woods and across another field to reach a bench by a junction. Ignoring the track to Ribno heading up the hill, carry straight on, making another short descent, and begin to hear the sound of the river (Sava Dolinka).

The track now follows the river bank to a bridge which leads to the campsite; don't cross, but continue across the field to a gate, and then over a second field between fences. Cross a stream and follow the path alongside another field, before ascending gently for a few hundred metres. The route then heads easily down to meet a tarmac road by a bridge across the **Sava Bohinjka**.

Cross the bridge and, ignoring the road that runs alongside the river in both directions, take the gravel cart track almost opposite that goes diagonally right, up into the forest, signed Talež. The path climbs gently through the forest away from the river. In about 10mins reach a fork where a rutted forest track heads down to the right, but continue straight ahead, still ascending gently. In just over another 100m, where the track levels, reach another fork, but continue straight ahead following a small wooden sign for Lovska koča na Taležu (hunting lodge).

The track soon merges with another one that comes in from the left, and you continue on for another 50m before leaving this track to the left, signed Talež. Continue on the gentle ascent as yet another broad track from the right merges with the route and views are glimpsed through the trees to the right of the little village of Ribno and the flat plain and Karavanke mountains beyond.

Continue up the stony track as it makes a long rising ascent across the beechwood hillside, before passing a prow of rock to the left of the forest road where you notice a deep, wooded ravine or gully to the right. Ignore another broad track heading left and continue on as the track passes across the head of this ravine and the gradient steepens. Continue climbing steeply to reach a partisan memorial and bench to the right of the track with a religious shrine to the left.

A sign on a tree at the memorial directs you right for the koča on a narrow path between the trees, but you very soon join another forest road and continue along it in the same direction, quite level. Pass two attractive weekend cottages and in another 100m arrive at **Lovška koča na Taležu**.

There is a **fine view from the terrace** of the hut: the Karavanke dominate the northern skyline, from Kepa in the west all the way to Stol and beyond, while the Radovljica plain with its roads and villages is spread out below, and over to the left Lake Bled is visible. Directly below is Ribno and the return route to Bled.

Retrace your steps from the koča to the partisan memorial, and descend the road to reach two or three paths (all within 100m of each other) that fan out below the road through the forest. Descend one of these paths, which funnel their way together and meet in one good path about 150m below the road at a bench below a tree.

Continue down and in about 150m reach a fork where you turn left. Descend steeply down hairpins, with the path becoming rocky as it passes between small outcrops. Towards the bottom of the hill, come out into an open pasture and continue straight on at a path crossroads. After another short section of woodland emerge on flat meadows by the river and see a **bridge** – cross here towards the village of Ribno.

Follow the road up through the pretty village of **Ribno**. As you reach the northern edge of the village, the road bends round to the right to reach a T-junction. Turn left here and walk a few metres to a complicated five-way crossroads by a shrine. Turn right and follow either of two minor roads for about 2km back to Bled, with views of the Karavanke ahead and the small tops of Straža and Dobra gora to the left.

## WALK 50

*Vintgar gorge*

| | |
|---|---|
| **Start/finish** | Bled bus station |
| **Distance** | 12.5km |
| **Total ascent/descent** | 160m |
| **Grade** | 1/2 |
| **Time** | 3–4hrs |
| **Maps** | 1:30,000 Bled |
| **Refreshments** | Gostilna Vintgar, gorge café, pizzeria near Sveta Katerina |
| **Access** | Buses stop at the gorge if you do not want to walk the 4km or so from Bled. |
| **Parking** | Car park by the entrance to the gorge |

This spectacular gorge lies within easy walking distance of Bled. It was formed by the Radovna river as it flows east towards its confluence with the Sava Dolinka. The gorge is about 1200m long and is traversed by a series of wooden walkways and bridges that were originally constructed in 1893 (but of course repaired since!). There is an entrance fee. Afterwards the walk continues up to the pilgrimage church of Sveta Katerina, with its excellent views of the surrounding countryside, and there are several different possibilities for the return to Bled.

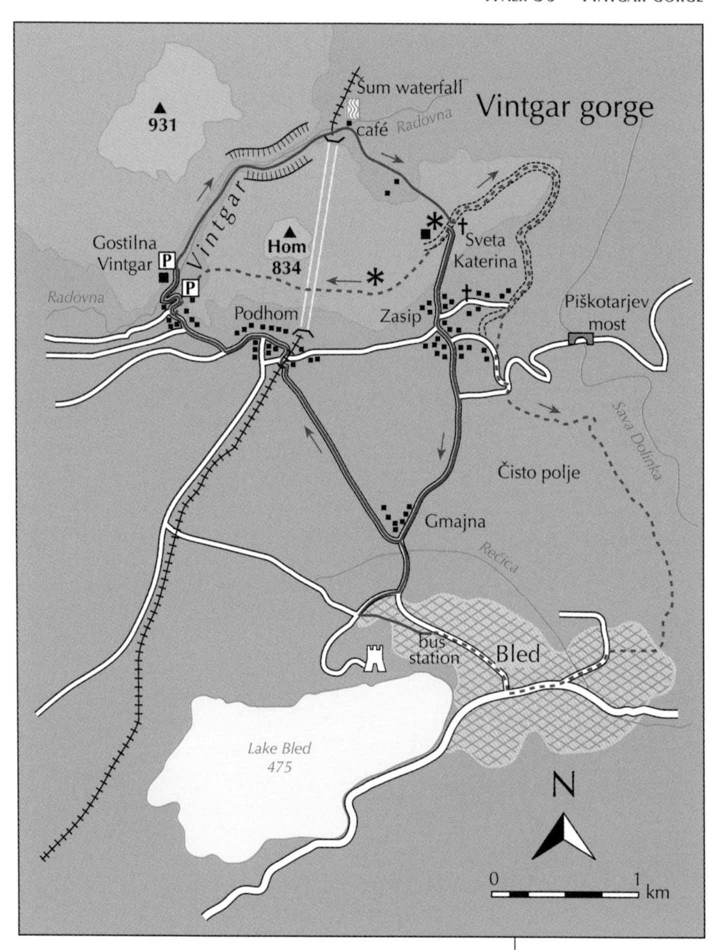


From Bled bus station, follow Grajska cesta up the hill, passing the youth hostel on the left just on the brow. The road goes downhill for a short distance to reach a T-junction. Turn right here, and continue for a few hundred metres before turning left onto a minor road, signed

Podhom, and heading towards Hom, the small hill you can see in the distance – the gorge is on the far side of this. After about 300m cross a bridge, just before the village of **Gmajna**, and turn left on a quiet side road towards Podhom. ◂

Stol, the highest peak of the Karavanke range, dominates the skyline to the right.

The road passes underneath the railway line just before **Podhom**. Continue along the narrow twisting lane following signs for Vintgar, through the delightful village, ablaze with flowers in the summer, for almost another kilometre before turning right at a bend. Notice a steep narrow road just to the right, which heads up to a small overflow car park; this is where the first alternative return path comes out. ◂

You could park here and make a shorter walk via the gorge and balcony path in about 2hrs.

Take the steep road down to the **Radovna river** around a hairpin bend, cross the river, which is beautifully clear and full of trout, and pass **Gostilna Vintgar** on the left about 250m before the gorge entrance and pay kiosk. If you have a car, the main parking area is just beyond the gostilna (but bear in mind it can be extremely crowded in the high season).

The route follows the wooden walkways and bridges for just over 1km, with impressive views of the walls of the narrow gorge and the rushing river below. Further on the gorge opens out a little and continues to reach a wooden bridge over the 13m-high **Šum waterfall**, where a small café marks the end of the gorge walk. Walk down the steps from the café to the gravel road at river level, continue on to cross a bridge over the river, then immediately turn left and walk about 50m along the river bank to gain an uninterrupted view of the falls.

Retrace your steps back up to the café and take the waymarked track signed Bled. After about 100m the track bears right, signed SV Katarina, and continues pleasantly up through the beautiful beech wood for another 300m to arrive at a fork. Either way can be taken; the right fork continues on the broader track passing through a forest plantation, while the left fork is signed Bled and continues on a narrower path that bears right to cross a grassy planina and then joins the broader track again.

*The wooden walkways of the Vintgar gorge*

Another 300m from here, reach the small medieval church of **Sveta Katarina** with its squat shingle-roofed tower. There is a pizzeria just to the right for refreshments. From here there is a magnificent view across the Radoljica plain towards the Karavanke range. You cannot see the lake, but the castle marks its position.

To return, take the narrow tarmac road leading down the hill. This passes through the pretty village of **Zasip** with its old church, and then continues through the hamlet of Gmajna where you rejoin the outward route.

## ALTERNATIVE RETURN ROUTES

From the pizzeria by Sveta Katerina there are two other routes for the return to Bled. Both add about 1hr to the time for the route.

**Along the balcony path:** In the corner of the café car park go through a small metal gate, signed Vintgar. Walk along the charming grassy balcony path with wonderful views over the plain, where you can see the line of the river Sava Dolinka and Bled castle. The path contours the hillside, passing through more gates on the way, and arrives after about 1km at a pretty viewpoint with a bench so you can admire the panorama in comfort. The view has opened out to the right giving a vista of the Julian Alps and mighty Triglav himself. The path bears right and continues to traverse the hillside before eventually passing through a larger gate to join a broader track. In another 200m the path makes a slight descent to arrive at a small field where cattle graze, and continues along its left edge. At the end of the field reach the small overflow parking area mentioned earlier. Turn left and retrace your outward route back to Bled.

**Above the Sava Dolinka valley:** Take the forest road that runs north-east to the left of the pilgrims' church (the short-cut path marked Walk 13 on the 1:30,000 map does exist, but it is unmarked, overgrown and difficult to find). Curve round and down through the forest for about 25mins, and as the track levels out there is a good view of Zasip church across the fields. Shortly after this pass a tarmac road coming down from the right through the buildings at the edge of the village, and about 50m further on take a path on the left as the road makes a right-hand turn. The path meets a tarmac road between some houses; turn left and continue on the road in the same direction until you meet another road from the right (which crosses the river at Piškotarjev most). From here there is a good view of Bled castle across the fields, with the stern nose (or tooth!) of Babji zob on the left behind it, and the viewpoint of Galetovec (Walk 51) on the right.

Directly opposite is a shady track which you follow for about 100m to a fork; take the left-hand trail and continue pleasantly, with fields to the right and the drop down to the river valley on the left. Pass a wooden weekend cottage on the left, continuing along the track which hugs the edge of the fields. Eventually the route begins to draw away from the edge across the fields; in another 200m meet a substantial cart track and turn left, following it round to the right. At an obvious worn path turn right up the bank (if you miss this, no matter – the cart track joins the road a bit further on) and at the top you can see the houses on the edge of Bled ahead and to the right. Bear left alongside the trees, and continue along the track to reach a T-junction and turn right onto a road heading directly towards the castle. At the end of the road turn left and follow this back to the main road into Bled. Turn right and walk down the road towards the lake, and turn right at the traffic lights onto Prešernova cesta. After about 600m take a left fork onto Cesta svobode to reach the bus station.

# WALK 51

*Galetovec*

| | |
|---|---|
| **Start/finish** | Square in Bohinjska Bela |
| **Distance** | 14.5km |
| **Total ascent/descent** | 800m |
| **Grade** | 3 |
| **Time** | 5–6hrs |
| **Maps** | 1:30,000 Bled |
| **Refreshments** | Take refreshments with you as there is no mountain hut on this walk. |
| **Access** | Buses run regularly from Bled; check at the Tourist Information Office or at the bus station for times. |
| **Note** | The ladders are steep and can be slippery. If you prefer to avoid them, you can use an alternative start and join the route beyond the waterfall. |

This route leads through forest and alp to the wonderful viewpoint of Galetovec (1259m), high above Bohinjska Bela. The 180° panorama from the Karavanke in the north, across the Radoljica plain and south to the Vogel hills is nothing short of stupendous. This walk is not as well frequented as others in the Julian Alps and is therefore less well signed and rather overgrown in places; take special care to cross-reference the route description, sketch map and local map (which does not always match the ground). Long trousers are recommended for protection against the encroaching vegetation.

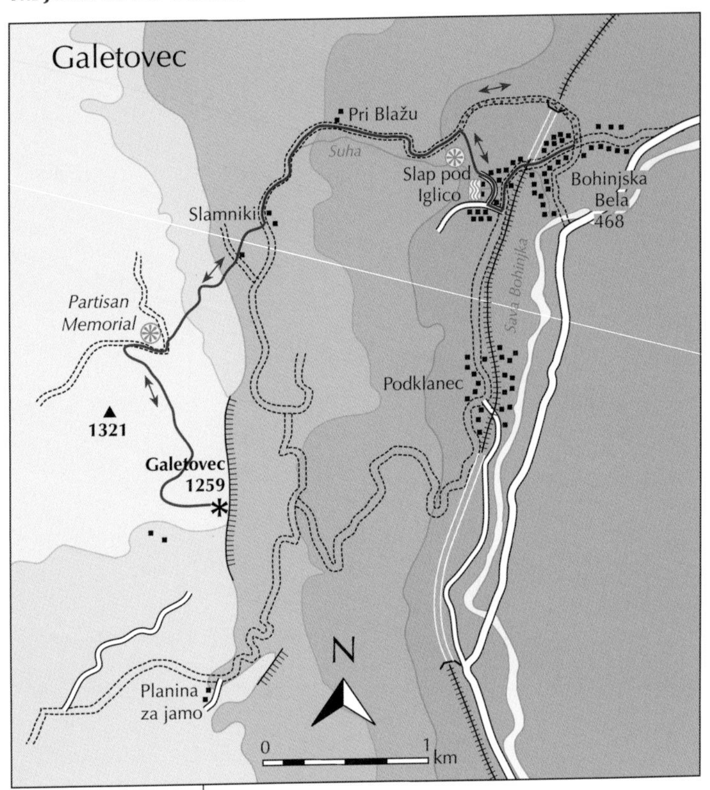


The walk starts in the main square in Bohinjska Bela, at the car park outside the small Mercator supermarket. From the square you can see the summit of Galetovec above its steep eastern crags, looking down on the village.

Ignore the sign to Galetovec, and turn left and walk along the main road through the village, passing a school and a large partisan memorial, to a railway bridge. Go under the bridge and follow a track on the right signed for pedestrians and cyclists, which immediately passes in front of a house and continues up a minor road. In

*Climbing the wooden ladders on the crag at Slap pod Iglico*

*Looking down on Bohinjska Bela from the top of the crags*

50m bear right up another minor road as it climbs steeply between the attractive houses to reach its end at house No. 95. From here continue up the now grassy track, heading right to reach the foot of the crags. Walk past a waterfall (**Slap pod Iglico**) which is seen at the back of a dark gash in the cliffs.

This is a popular rock-climbing area and there are a number of bolted routes on the crags. Tucked in a corner to the right of the waterfall, two sections of wooden steps and ladders lead up a cleft in the cliffs to give access to the top and are used as an easy descent route by rock climbers. The ladders are steep and can be a bit slippery, but metal pegs and steel cables offer an extra handhold. Climb the ladders and steps in the rock cleft to reach the top of the crag and walk a few metres to the left to an excellent **viewpoint** above Bohinjska Bela. ◄

There's a fine view of Babji Zob opposite, with the river, railway line, terraced pastures and the road up to Kupljenik laid out as if on a map.

### Alternative start avoiding ladders

If you want to avoid the steep ladders by the waterfall you can use an alternative start and join the route beyond the waterfall. Follow the Galetovec sign from the square and

bear right past a water trough. Cross a stream and walk up the tarmac road for about 1km, under the railway line and up to the planina to meet the main route at the toplar at the edge of the small meadow close to the top of the crags.
The path continues on, away from the viewpoint, into a flower meadow. Skirt the left edge of the meadow for about 50m and take a grassy track which heads right towards some houses and a small apple orchard, where you reach a tarmac road by a wooden toplar (the alternative start joins the main route here) and a sign indicating Galetovec and Slamniki (local route 5). Admire the attractive planina with its hay meadows, buildings, and good view of Stol in the Karavanke chain before taking the road, which soon becomes unmade and heads off into the forest.

Ascend gently through the forest to reach a T-junction about 10mins after leaving the meadow and houses. Take the left-hand turn, signed Galetovec, as it crosses the little **Suha stream** (the map doesn't match the ground here) that forms the waterfall lower down. Within 100m, notice a narrow waymarked path that leads right, ascending into the wood – this just cuts off a bend in the road which it soon joins again.

Continue up the road, ignoring another gravel road that heads right, as it winds its way past more small meadows with hayracks and occasional buildings. ▸ Arrive at a small attractive farm called Kmetija Pr' Vazniku with its old wooden toplar. As you pass between the farm and its holiday apartments the road swings sharply right, but take the rougher track that leads left from the bend. In another 100m arrive at a fork and take a rough stony track that leads steeply uphill to the right, signed Galetovec.

Already, good views are beginning to open up to the north and east, with the Karavanke mountains rising above the flat Radovljca plain.

In less than 10mins this track forks; take the right and continue steeply up. In another 150m, leave this stony track following waymarks on a tree for a narrower path that leads off to the right, still ascending steeply into the wood. Another 10mins or so brings you to a forest road where you turn left. Within a short distance, reach a junction with another gravel road and continue on in the same direction of travel, signed Galetovec. More wooden planina buildings are soon seen to the left of this road which has now become a grassy cart track, and a meadow opens out to the left – this is **Planina Slamniki**.

Just past the last of the buildings is an overgrown path going up into trees on the right, with a sign to Galetovec and a waymark painted on a boulder. Walk into this green tunnel and almost immediately reach a fork; the right path is signed to Rčitno, and the other (unsigned but waymarked) goes to Galetovec. Within another 50m the path passes to the left of an attractive old alpine wooden building. Climb steeply up this path through the trees, and in another 150m climb past a waymarked tree stump to the right and continue up this very overgrown section of path, fortunately only for a relatively short distance.

Soon the way clears somewhat, and in another 100m reach a rutted broad track and cross it, following waymarks, on a path that bears left as it crosses a small wooden footbridge across a tiny stream flowing from a spring and water pipe a few metres away, where a sign for 'voda' (water) indicates it is drinkable.

Pass another sign for Galetovec just before another pasture (Rižišče), seen to the left with its wooden 'week-end' cottages. About 30m further on cross a forest road and continue up on the waymarked path that becomes more distinct and open as height is gained. Another rough logging track is crossed after about 5mins and the path continues straight up, signed Galetovec.

The path now winds its way steeply up through the mature beech wood – at one sharp left-hand bend signed Galetovec, note the old logging trail that continues to the right, as that track could easily be taken by mistake during the descent if you're not careful. After about 45mins of steady climbing from Slamniki, the angle finally eases and after a few more minutes you emerge onto an unmade vehicle road, where you turn left and within a few paces reach a **partisan memorial** which lies just to the left.

Continue past the memorial, due west, for 250m, then turn sharply left onto another gravel track heading south, signed Galetovec. Stay on this track, running fairly level, as it passes on the right-hand side of a meadow which has a small water-catchment area for the cattle that graze here in the summer months.

After about 15mins as you round a bend, ignore a track going uphill on the right. Pass through a cattle gate and descend a little and in about 300m, as you arrive at the lower end of another open meadow, notice a small sign pointing left to Galetovec. The path dips to cross the lower end of the pasture close to the edge of the trees, then re-enters woods by a waymark. Climb easily through the woods following waymarks to reach a fence line and go through a 'dog-leg' gate to arrive at the **Galetovec** summit viewpoint, 20–25mins from the partisan memorial.

Picnic tables and benches, as well as an information board with its panoramic picture, **mark the summit**. The view is sensational: straight across are the crags of Babji zob, and on the plain the towns of Radovljica and Lesce, Lake Bled like a blue jewel with the castle standing guard above it, mighty Stol and the Karavanke, and the Kamnik-Savinja Alps in the distance. Bohinjska Bela lies below, huddled against the cliffs.

Return by the same route as your ascent.

## WALK 52

*Debela peč, Brda and Lipanski vrh*

| | |
|---|---|
| **Start/finish** | Šport Hotel on the Pokljuka plateau |
| **Distance** | 18.5km |
| **Total ascent/descent** | 750m |
| **Grade** | 3 |
| **Time** | 6hrs |
| **Maps** | 1:30,000 Bled, 1:25,000 Bohinj |
| **Access** | Drive to Pokljuka and park by the road (very limited space) about 250m past the turning for the Šport Hotel – there is also parking near the Šport Hotel. |
| **Accommodation** | Blejska koča if required |

This superb walk is a 'must-do' from Bled. The route runs through some of the most beautiful forest on the Pokljuka plateau to a mountain hut on a little alp and then sets off through wonderful natural gardens to Debela peč, the highest summit on the Lipanca ridge, at 2014m. The views are thrilling, with dizzying drops to the Krma valley before the vista of the northern Julian Alps, and equally panoramic views to the south. The path then runs along the ridge to Brda (2009m) and Lipanski vrh (1975m) before dropping easily back down to Blejska koča.

There are no difficulties except for one short steep descent in a narrow gully, but the route can be cut short a little to avoid this if necessary. It is a perfect introduction to alpine walking, with the sense of being in the high mountains but without any technical difficulties or extreme exposure.

From the Šport Hotel walk to the main road, turn left and after 250m take the forest road on the right, signed Lipanca and Beljska koča 1hr 30mins. After 2km of walking on an excellent forest road through beautiful woodland with tall straight spruce, arrive at the delightful open pasture of **Planina Javornik** with its wooden buildings. Here the first view of the ridge is laid out before you; Debela peč is the summit to the right, with Brda and Lipanski vrh straight ahead.

Cross the alp on a broad grassy track towards the buildings to reach the forest road at the northern edge of the planina, and continue straight ahead in the same direction. After 100m or so cross a cattle grid, rather unusual in Slovenia, and re-enter the forest. In a short distance come to a crossroads with another forest road, where cars are often parked. Cross it and follow the sign for Blejska koča and Lipanca, taking a rougher but still broad track continuing north.

The track is generally good but some sections can be very boggy after rain. After about 20mins cross another forest road and begin to climb a little more steadily. In another 10mins reach a junction; turn right, signed Blejska Koča. Continue on the good track which ascends steadily as it traverses up through the forest, and soon make a sharp left turn as you pass a log bench where

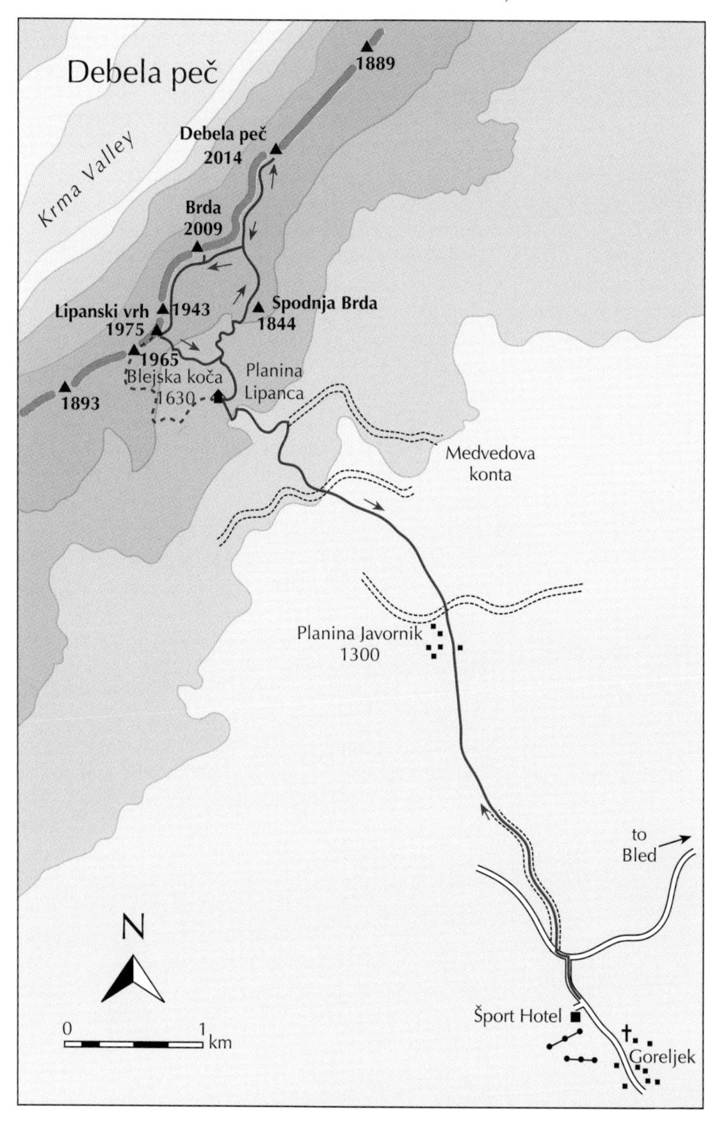
Debela peč
1889
Krma Valley
Debela peč
2014
Brda
2009
Lipanski vrh
1975
1943
Spodnja Brda
1844
1965
Blejska koča
1630
Planina
Lipanca
1893
Medvedova
konta
Planina Javornik
1300
to
Bled
N
0
1
km
Šport Hotel
Goreljek

another track heads right, signed Medvedova konta. In another 5mins or so the path bears right at a sign saying **Planina Lipanca** and asking that dogs are kept on leads as this is a grazed pasture. Rounding a right-hand corner gives a view up the planina and the roofs of the koča buildings can be seen with the ridge towering above.

The path turns left again, crossing the planina which is dotted with starry flowers, and passes a partisan memorial plaque to take a final right turn up to **Blejska koča**. There are three or four buildings on the alp and the hut is to the left, at 1633m.

Beside the koča is an elaborate signpost giving numerous directions, including Debela peč 1hr 30. Take this path, heading across the planina. From the first little rise on the right-hand side there is a good view back to Planina Javornik. About 20m past the viewpoint the path divides; take the left fork to Debela peč and Brda. The path climbs pleasantly away from the alp through sparser stands of larches and dwarf pine. About 10mins from the hut pass a sign on a tree pointing left to Lipanski vrh – this is the main descent route.

Continue straight on, zigzagging up through the rocks and the trees to emerge above the alp at a signpost. Continue straight on for Debela peč, with a waymarked rock a few paces ahead. Some 25m further on the path forks, and the Debela peč path bears round to the left and ascends again to reach a level section of grassy hillside with clumps of dwarf pine and small larch; to the right is the low rounded top of Spodnja Brda. ◂ Watch out for waymarks and signs painted on the rocks directing you left, up onto the steeper hillside again, and continue ascending, with views to the right of the Karavanke range.

This area is like walking through a carefully designed rockery, with flowers in every crevice.

About 1hr from the hut you reach the summit ridge, with the first magnificent views to the north. Turn right passing a signed boulder to Debela peč, and notice after a few paces another sign painted on a rock to the left to Brdo and Lipanska vrh. This path will be taken on the return from Debela peč.

Walk across a balcony section on the easy path with wonderfully precipitous drops to the north into the Krma

*Blejska koča on Debela Peč*

valley, and watch Triglav come into view to the left. The northern view disappears behind the ridge for a while as you cross an area of karst hollows and rocks, among dwarf pine and clusters of flowers, that leads you onto the right-hand side of the ridge. Another 10mins of delightful walking brings you to the final steep pull up to the summit of **Debela peč** (2014m).

The **panorama** from the top starts at Triglav, very obviously the biggest of them all. Looking right from Triglav you can see the whole of the northern Julian Alps, the Krma valley almost vertically below, and to the right the flat valley floor of Zgornja Radovna, with the village of Mojstrana in the upper Sava valley behind. Beyond is Kepa on the Karavanke range, with the hills of Austria behind. The Karavanke continue to Stol, their highest summit, and further right are the high peaks of the Kamnik-Savinja Alps. Lake Bled can be seen on the edge of the Radovljica plain, the whole of the Pokljuka plateau, including the massive forested karst sinkhole of Medvedova konta, is visible to the left of Planina Javornik, and on the southern skyline are the Lower Bohinj mountains, with Črna prst to the left and Vogel to the right.

Retrace your steps from the summit to where you joined the ridge, and the sign for Brdo and Lipanska vrh. Take this path that passes close to two karst hollows or sinkholes before climbing more steeply over the rocky terrain. The path then bears right following waymarks and a sign for Brdo painted on a rock. At this point, notice the path descending straight ahead. This path will be joined a little further along the ridge on the descent. In another 5mins arrive at the summit of **Brda** (2009m), where the flowers surpass even those on Debela peč!

If you are continuing to Lipanska vrh, leave the summit of Brda, still heading south-west along the ridge – in just a few metres the grassy path begins to descend, passing a direction marker on a rock. The route bears left and descends more steeply, but within 10mins it levels as it merges with the path mentioned earlier that traverses below the summit of Brda.

Continue along easily and within 150m pass a path that descends left, signed Blejska koča.

**There is a steep section of rock on the path ahead to Lipanski vrh. If you want to avoid it, you must take this path back to the koča.** Within another 50m reach another junction – a route to the right leads to a steep descent to the Krma valley, so continue straight on, signed Lipanski vrh. The dwarf pine encroaches on the path as the way traverses below left of the ridge.

Begin to climb again, and soon afterwards enter a short easy-angled rocky gully which you exit on the left just before the top. The route then picks its way through the limestone, following waymarks and paint slashes, to reach a subsidiary top at 1943m.

There is a particularly good view from here to **Triglav** – the metal stolp (tower) on the summit is visible, glinting in the sun, and two of the huts can be seen; to the left is Dom Planika and you can just make out the Kredarica hut directly below the summit.

From here the path immediately descends an unexpectedly steep gully for about 30m, which is protected with steel cable and pegs – it's an easy scramble but you might like to put your walking poles away so you can use both hands. At the bottom turn right and traverse some quite steep ground on a good path for a little longer before continuing more easily. In another 100m, and just before reaching the col below Lipanski vrh, a path goes down to the left – this is the main descent route. Continue to the right and ascend the last 25m up to the col and turn left. It is not far to the top of **Lipanski vrh**, where the vegetation is surprisingly lush.

Retrace your steps to the path descending from the col. Follow the path down towards Blejska koča, visible directly below. Soon it divides, with the right-hand fork traversing the hillside and the left continuing down, at first quite steeply and then less so, through the woods to rejoin the main path from the hut, where you turn right to follow the outward route back to the Šport Hotel.

### Alternative descent route

It is possible to continue from here along the ridge to lengthen the tour – the route is waymarked but has some difficult sections with steel cables and pegs for protection. From the summit of Lipanski vrh, continue along the ridge and soon begin to descend to reach a section of steel cable and rungs that are used to descend about 25m to a rocky niche. From the niche descend a few more pegs to the left before making a short ascent to arrive at the satellite top of Mrežce (1965m). A metal stamp on a low-lying signed and waymarked rock marks the summit. ▶

In 2014 a wooden post stood a few metres from the summit and it is hoped by the time this book is printed that it will support direction signs.

From the summit, head south south-west across what is a high grassy alp used for grazing cattle, soon passing another post. The path bears left as it passes karst hollows, the route being confirmed with waymarks. Begin to descend through dwarf pine and stands of larch that become taller as height is lost.

In another 30mins or so, arrive at a level grassy area with a small watering hole for cattle. Continue across it to a junction and take the eroded shale path that leads straight on to the **koča**, which soon becomes visible through the trees below. Within another 10mins, and just as you appear to be passing to the right of the koča, the path swings sharply left to arrive at the rear of the building. Then follow the outward route back to the Šport Hotel.

## WALK 53

*Viševnik*

| | |
|---|---|
| **Start/finish** | Rudno polje |
| **Distance** | 6.5km |
| **Total ascent/descent** | 630m |
| **Grade** | 3 |
| **Time** | 4hrs |
| **Maps** | 1:30,000 Bled, 1:25,000 Bohinj, 1:25,000 Triglav |
| **Access** | Drive to Pokljuka and park at the end of the road, at Rudno polje. |

This shapely mountain is justifiably popular, due to its ease of access from the road head at Rudno polje, which means it can be completed in a half day. At 2050m the views from the summit of the Triglav massif are spectacular. It is one of the easier 2000m peaks to do in winter, as the road to Rudno polje is kept open for the excellent cross-country skiing on Pokljuka – one of the biathlon World Cup events is held there each year.

Just past the large military building at the end of the tarmac road at Rudno polje, turn right onto a forest road. Walk up here for about 10mins and reach a junction near the foot of a ski lift. An old wooden sign on a tree at the junction reads Viševnik – 1hr 30mins and directs

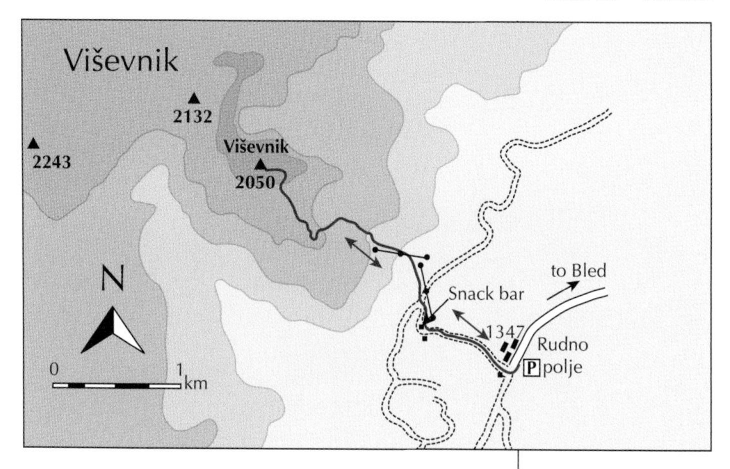


you right, up the ski slope. However, stay left and walk towards a small refreshment hut (open all year – weekends only) where another sign, saying Viševnik 2hrs, directs you onto a path just to the left of the ski slope and lift towers along the edge of the wood. The ski slope is grassy and grazed by cattle in the summer months, so keep to the waymarked path near the forest edge to avoid disturbing the livestock and trampling the alpine flowers.

In a few minutes, meet and cross the forest road again, and continue up the steep path following waymarks painted on trees. Cross a stile when passing ski tower No. 8, and soon after the path passes under the ski lift cable as it nears the top of the piste. Continue climbing steeply as the path runs through small trees and shrubs, lined with an abundance of flowers including thistles, cow parsley, red campion and even Triglav rose.

The route follows a broad gully that forms a natural grassy break in the trees, and as more height is gained views begin to open up behind of the vast tree-covered Pokljuka plateau and beyond. In another 10mins arrive at a level area where a sign on a tree directs you on to Viševnik. Bear left and continue level for almost 100m before climbing steeply again, passing a signed junction

*Looking towards Triglav from the summit of Viševnik*

– right for Blejska koča na Lipanci 2hrs and left for Viševnik 1hr.

Eventually reach a small grassy col on a tree-covered shoulder, where a wonderful panorama of the whole of the Lower Bohinj mountains can be seen on the horizon straight ahead. Turn right and continue up, initially through larch, then through dense thickets of dwarf pine. Finally the dwarf pine relents and the path emerges onto open slopes, with the summit seen up ahead to the left. Bear left along the grassy edge of a rocky escarpment to reach the summit of **Viševnik** (2050m).

Triglav dominates **the view**, with both the Planika and Kredarica huts clearly visible. To the right of Triglav, Rž and the long alpine ridge of Rjavina leads the eye all the way down to the distant Sava valley, where the village of Dojve can be seen below Kepa. Directly below to the south you can see the wooden huts of Planina Uskovnica.

Return by reversing the route.

# 5 KOBARID

*It's worth a short detour to the idyllic Planina Zaprikraj on Walk 56*

# INTRODUCTION

*The enchanting woodland en route to Matajur (Walk 58)*

Compared to the other bases in this book Kobarid is tiny, with a population of only 1500, and its Italian feel provides a stark contrast to the alpine atmosphere of the others. The village lies in the Soča valley, and although it is surrounded by peaks of around 2000m, its own more modest altitude of 234m gives it a Mediterranean climate and atmosphere, accentuated by the white houses and terracotta-tiled roofs. The little backstreets and courtyards are choked with flowerpots in the summer, not only the inevitable geranium window-boxes but also huge pots of oleanders in bright pinks and purples. Kobarid has a timeless sleepiness that not even all the visitors of July can dispel. Ernest Hemingway immortalised the village in his novel about the Isonzo (Soča) front, *A Farewell to Arms*, and it is easy to imagine that he is about to walk around the corner.

The area is of significant historical interest, as the Soča river was at the centre of the greatest mountain battle in history, when the fighting of the Isonzo front between the Italians and the Austrians raged between 1915 and 1917. In October 1917 the 12th offensive, by the weaker Austrian army, surprised the Italians and pushed the fighting back towards Italy, with massive loss of life on both sides. It is impossible to walk any distance here without seeing evidence of those turbulent times, whether it be fortifications or rusting shell cartridges. Walk 54, The Historical Walk, visits many trenches and other excavations of the First World War.

In terms of access, Kobarid lies to the west of the main Julian Alps, only 9km from the Italian border. It is 21km from Bovec by road, although only around 10km south of it as the crow flies, as the road must travel round the great ridge of Polovnik. Buses run between the two bases, going on to Tolmin and Nova Gorica. The nearest train station is at Most na Soči, on the Jesenice–Nova Gorica line. There is no taxi service in the village. The limited public transport means that some routes to the high mountains are out of reach to those without their own transport.

There is limited accommodation in Kobarid, but there is one hotel and a number of houses offering private rooms. There are two excellent campsites in the Soča valley, reflecting the fact that many visitors come here to canoe and kayak the river. There is a supermarket and a number of eating places. The helpful Tourist Information Centre is situated in the Kobarid Museum, and the fascinating WWI exhibits, which have won several awards, are well worth a visit.

The high alpine valley of Drežniški kot offers rooms, apartments and tourist farms in its several villages. Surrounded by high peaks, it has a stunning setting and would be a wonderful place to stay for a few days. The valley has its own website, www.dreznica.si, and a nice leaflet which also has a good map of the area, covering Walks 55 and 56.

## THE ROUTES

Apart from the Historical Walk mentioned above, Walk 55 visits the high valley of Drežniški kot, surrounded by wonderful mountain scenery, and Walks 56–58 climb local peaks that offer stunning views of the Julian Alps to the north and all the way to the Adriatic Sea to the south.

## MAPS

The Krn 1:25,000 map covers Walks 54, 55 and 56, as well as the starts of Walks 57 and 58, while the full length of Walks 57 and 58 is on the 1:50,000 Julijske Alpe.

# WALK 54

*The Historical Walk*

| | |
|---|---|
| **Start/finish** | Square in Kobarid |
| **Distance** | 5km |
| **Total ascent/descent** | 200m |
| **Grade** | 1/2 |
| **Time** | 3hrs |
| **Maps** | Krn 1:25,000; an excellent leaflet in English from the Tourist Office in the Kobarid Museum includes a large-scale map of the walk and information about points of interest |
| **Refreshments** | Bar at campsite |

The Historical Walk was laid out by the Kobarid Tourist Society in the mid-1990s, and it visits various historical and natural monuments. Like Walk 35 it is part of Pot miru, the Walk of Peace. A visit to the Kobarid Museum beforehand will give you an understanding of the military impasse on the Isonzo front and of the great mountain battle that ended it, which puts the fortifications into context. Most of the sites on the walk are to do with the First World War, but the route also visits an ancient fort and one of the most beautiful waterfalls in Slovenia (Slap Kozjak).

The walk starts in the square (Trg Svobode) in Kobarid. From the church, walk across the square to a minor road heading north, with an information board about the route on the left. The road starts between two large pillars, one with a star on the top and the other with a cross. Walk up the road, around several hairpins and past the stations of the cross, for about 10mins to the octagonal Italian Charnel House, completed in 1938 (there are no obvious signs of the Roman settlement – No. 2 in the Tourist Office leaflet).

There is an excellent **view from the church**, which dates back to 1649, looking down on the red roofs

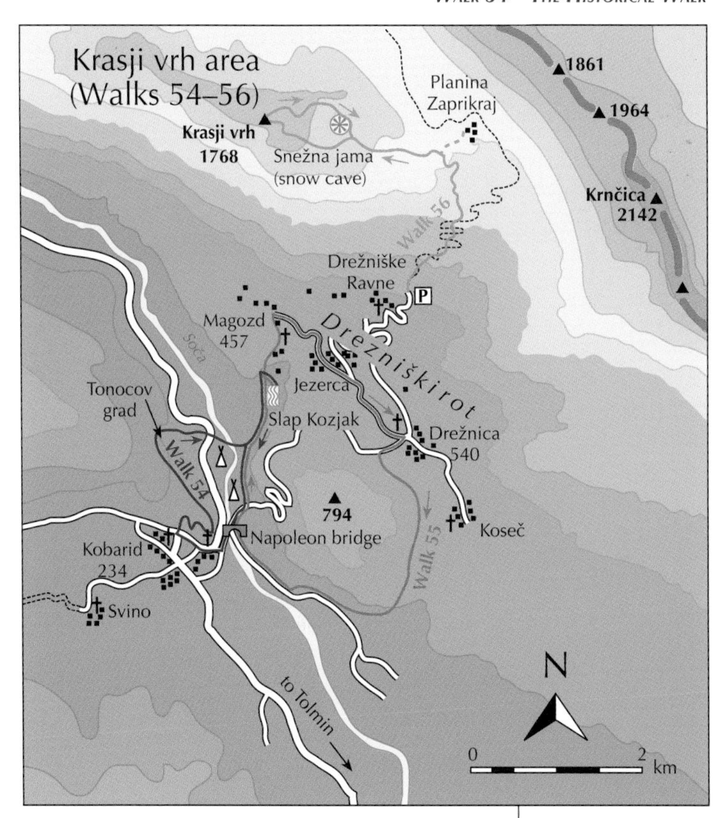


of Kobarid and, beyond, on the flat-floored valley towards the village of Staro Selo and Italy. The long ridge of Stol is to the right. To the south-east is the Soča valley and to the north the Polovnik ridge, with its high point Krasji Vrh.

The path continues along the left-hand side of the Charnel House on an unmade track which quickly becomes a path, entering the forest by a signpost for Tonocov Grad (castle). About 30m into the forest take

*The magical Slap Kozjak*

the left-hand path at a junction, signed Tonocov Grad. Continue for about 15mins through the forest to a point where the trees have been cut back for electricity cables, where there is a glimpse of the summit of Krn. Just after this pass a First World War defence position tunnelled into the rock of a small outcrop. In another 10mins come to signs directing you down and right to a rough bridge and stepping stones across a watercourse.

Cross the bridge and turn right, now heading east towards the castle. In 100m come to a junction and turn right. The path begins to climb a little and becomes rockier. A couple of minutes further on reach another junction, where the onward route goes straight on, but you follow a short diversion for **Tonocov Grad**, a Stone Age fort under archaeological investigation. Fork right, under an aerial cableway used for bringing materials up to the dig, and walk up rough stone and wooden steps to an information board.

The site at **Tonocov Grad** has been investigated systematically since 1993 and restoration is still going on. In front of a small modern building, there are some benches with good views down the Soča gorge. To the left is Krn, its steep ramparts showing clearly that the western approach to this mountain is the most difficult.

After exploring the excavations return down towards the cableway and turn right just before it to rejoin the main path. This traverses round the shoulder of the hill, descending gently at first and then more steeply, following signs. Down through the trees you can see the luminous green of the Soča beneath the suspension bridge. Just below is the first of the defence positions, and you descend steep steps through the trench, protected by a handrail. ▶ The steps continue beyond the trench, through a natural split in the bedrock, down to the main Kobarid–Bovec road.

The steps can be slippy after rain; a path bypasses them and rejoins the route below the trench.

On the other side of the road there is a pillbox gun emplacement just to the right, but the route heads left for a few paces before descending more steep steps. At the bottom of the wooden steps continue level for a short way straight on, and then continue down to another trench with walls partly natural and partly reinforced with concrete. The path continues on to enter yet another trench system and then heads down to the right to skirt a small meadow.

Re-enter the woods, where a sign directs you round to the left. Continue a little further and descend more steps which come down onto a broad track where arrows direct you to the right. About 50m along the track come to an information board at another fortification, where the path branches left down to the suspension bridge. ◂

On a hot day you may like to make the short detour, straight on, to the campsite bar.

Cross the bridge, with the amazing colour of the river Soča contrasting with the dark trees and the surrounding mountain tops. On the far side turn left onto a broad path and continue a short distance to another good view of the river, before turning away from it and continuing with the smaller Kozjak river on your left. After 3–4mins cross a stone bridge over the lower Kozjak waterfall, but don't turn back yet as better is to come! Follow a sign for Slap Kozjak, branching right at a fork, and continue on the forest path with the pretty river now on your right. After 300m cross the river on a plank bridge and walk a short distance on the far bank, then cross back again on another plank bridge as the walls of the gorge begin to close in. Rocks lead down to the water's edge, where you continue round a corner to reach a wooden walkway leading to the **Slap Kozjak** viewpoint. ◂

The water flows 15m into a cavern, and as the sun shines through the narrow cleft at the top onto the pool below, the light is reflected back onto the side walls, creating an enchanting fairy grotto.

Retrace your steps back past the first waterfall and after 200m or so take a track up to the left, signed Huljeva pot. The path climbs to a broad shoulder with more fortifications; to the right is a viewpoint of the Soča. The main path continues over the shoulder and down, but the area is worth exploring as there are several defences to see. ◂ The path continues down a couple of hairpins and rejoins the riverside track, past steep crags on the left and the river on the right. The track rises a little before crossing some open pastures. Reach a tarmac road and turn right, past Kamp Koren, and continue to a T-junction

You are directly above the suspension bridge, which was built at the exact location of a bridge that existed during the First World War.

and the **Napoleon Bridge**. Cross the bridge, with superb views of the Soča gorge. Just past the bridge look back for a photogenic view of the bridge itself, with Krasji vrh reflected in the water, and notice on the right-hand side of the road a shrine to St Anthony with a little spring beneath. Follow the road back up into Kobarid.

## WALK 55

*Drežniški kot*

| | |
|---|---|
| **Start/finish** | Square in Kobarid |
| **Distance** | 13km |
| **Total ascent/descent** | 320m |
| **Grade** | 2 |
| **Time** | 3½–4hrs |
| **Maps** | Krn 1:25,000 |
| **Refreshments** | Gostilna and a small shop at Drežnica |

This easy walk explores the beautiful valley of Drežniški kot, which opens out high above the valley of the Soča. The scenery is spectacular, with the villages and churches set against a backdrop of towering crags, dominated by the distinctive summit profile of Krn (Walk 43). The route climbs on a good track to the hamlet of Magozd, and then wanders along a quiet road to visit the larger village of Drežnica before heading back down a forest path above the gorge of the river Ročica to the Soča valley.

See the route map in Walk 54.

▸ From the square in Kobarid, take the Bovec road and walk through the village. About 100m past the museum the main road bears left; keep straight ahead on a side road signed Drežnica. Follow the road down to the **Napoleon Bridge**, cross the river and turn left on the other side. Continue up this road, and about 100m past Kamp Koren turn left onto a track signed Slap Kozjak. The craggy ridge of Krasji vrh is straight ahead. Follow the track for about 15mins, crossing fields at first with the Soča to your left. Pass a suspension bridge and shortly afterwards the track turns right and after 300m reaches the bridge above the lower Kozjak waterfall. ◂

If you haven't already been to the upper fall (see Walk 54), don't miss it now – take the 15min detour to the right just after the bridge.

After the bridge keep straight ahead on the track above the river Kozjak and emerge in a meadow with an old stone building. The route crosses the meadow before curving round to the left behind the building and beginning to climb gently into the forest. Continue up the good path, rising steadily round several hairpins to skirt the knoll to your left. After about 15mins come out into an open meadow to a stunning view of Krn to the right.

Cross the pasture and follow the track round to the left beneath some crags. Pass through a belt of trees with crags on both sides to reach a junction. Turn right, past a building on the right, and then bear left, and as you come round the corner you can see the red roofs of the village of **Magozd** about 200m away, beneath the steep slopes of Krasji vrh. Walk along the track for about another 5mins to enter the village on a tarmac road where you turn right (1hr 15mins from Kobarid).

Walk through the pretty village with grapevines covering many of the houses, and continue on the quiet road between pasture and woodland. After about 1200m reach the turning for the village of **Jezerca**. Shortly after the junction cross the river Kozjak. ◂ Come to a junction (about 2km from Magozd) and turn left into Drežnica; the gravel track almost immediately on the left leads up into the village.

The view now is dominated by the big church of the Sacred Heart of Jesus at Drežnica on its small knoll, with stunning views of Krn behind.

**Drežnica** is a large village with a gostilna and a small shop. The huge Italianesque church with its 52m-high church tower is the most striking feature. Amazingly it wasn't damaged during the First World War. Walk up to the knoll by the church for superb views of the whole of Drežniški kot, with the villages of Magozd and Jezerca below the long ridge of Krasji vrh to the north-west, while in the distance are the rocky peaks of Kanin. To the west is the enormously long ridge of Stol, and to the east the craggy face of Krn, which was greatly changed by

*The village and church of Drežnica below Krn*

the devastating earthquake of 1998. From Drežnica it is only a short walk to Sveti Just chapel.

If you are interested in church architecture, make a visit to **Sveti Just**. Follow the sign from Drežnica to Koseč, and walk about 1km south-east to the hamlet. Just after the tarmac ends cross a bridge and see a sign to the right, Sveti Just. Walk 200m down the side path to this tiny chapel which was built in the second half of the 14th century. Frescos cover the walls, and although they are now quite worn, you can still sense the vibrant colours they must once have had.

The route continues down the road from Drežnica to Kobarid, heading west out of the village, with more lovely views of the valley. About 50m past the 'Nasvidenje' (goodbye) sign take an old stone-laid track on the left, signed by an arrow, and cross a field for about 100m to a T-junction. Take the left-hand trail which goes slightly downhill, ignoring side tracks giving access to fields – if in doubt head downhill. Pass a little waterfall and continue down with the stream on your right. Reach a short level section at a fork and bear left. Pass an old building on the right, and reach a more open area, overgrown in summer; in a few paces see a track coming down from the left and bear right in its direction on a narrow path.

As you re-enter the forest the path becomes more distinct again, with the sound of the river Ročica to the left. About 100m further on cross a stream and continue on the path, which is now obvious all the way (but without waymarks). At first it traverses close above the gorge, gaining height above the water, and then bears away from the river a little, although you can still hear the rushing water to the left. Cross a small stream and continue on, traversing steep ground on the level track, which has been broadened for logging activity – this means that you get gratuitous views of Krn through the gaps in the trees! Descend a little and then traverse again before beginning a gradual descent.

Pass an open field on the left with a building, and a grassy track leading from it merges with the route, with a marker signed Pot miru, the Peace Walk. The river gorge is on the left, a good 100m below, appearing almost bottomless as you peer over the edge. Shortly afterwards make a right-hand bend, again signed Pot miru, with a good view of the village of Smast on the floor of the Soča valley at the corner. Head down on the broad rocky track in the direction of Kobarid. ◄

As you descend, the atmosphere seems to change quite suddenly to a Mediterranean feeling, with clouds of butterflies in the warm dry air.

After about 1km bear left by a small quarry to emerge on a tarmac road, where you turn right; you can walk along here for about 1km to the Napoleon bridge. However, a nicer route is to take the tractor track on the right a few metres further on; follow this between the fields for about 500m, then bear right, slightly uphill, and left again to reach a house. Take a track on the right between stone walls and then leave it to bear left on a narrow path following the outside edge of the left-hand field. Begin to descend and pass another house, and then join the concrete road which serves the house, leading down to rejoin the main road about 250m short of the Napoleon Bridge. Cross the bridge and walk back up the road into Kobarid.

# WALK 56

*Krasji vrh*

| | |
|---|---|
| **Start/finish** | Spring above Drežniške Ravne |
| **Distance** | 9km |
| **Total ascent/descent** | 950m |
| **Grade** | 3 |
| **Time** | 4–5hrs |
| **Maps** | 1:25,000 Bovec-Trenta |
| **Refreshments** | Take refreshments with you as there is no mountain hut on this walk. |
| **Access** | Drive through Drežnica and continue for another kilometre or so to cross the river Kozjak on a bend. Follow the road around to the left, and at the top of the slope turn right at a 90° bend by a house. Take the first right, which comes almost immediately, and drive up for about 500m to a right turn signed 'Planina Zapleč and Planina Zaprikraj'. Continue up here for about 1km, and just past the end of the tarmac is a parking area with a water trough and spring signed Krasji vrh. |

If you have your own transport, then Krasji vrh is a lovely half-day walk from the spring above Drežniške Ravne. Krasji vrh (1773m) is the highest point on the Polovnik ridge, which leads roughly east from the massif of Krn, forcing the Soča river into a wide curve between Bovec and Kobarid. Its position allows for spectacular views of the Julian Alps to the north and east, and of Italy and the Adriatic Sea to the south and west.

▸ Continue along the gravel road ignoring a path to the right signed for Krn after about 100m. In another 40m, leave the road on a narrow path heading right, signed and waymarked Krasji vrh and Pot miru – this is another stage of the Peace Walk. Soon join the road again and continue up it for almost 200m before turning left onto another waymarked path.

See the route map in Walk 54.

The path meets and crosses the road several more times before emerging at a hairpin bend where a track immediately heads right, signed Slap Curk; don't take this but stay on the road for a few more metres to see waymarks and the continuation of the path heading steeply up right. Reach and cross the road again following waymarks, and within 10mins pass a sign for Krasji vrh and Planina Zaprikraj – the road can be seen through the trees close by to the right at this point. Carry on for another few minutes to where the track swings sharply right, but continue straight on where direction waymarks on rocks soon confirm the way. The path climbs pleasantly in the shade of the trees, with the floor of the forest littered with limestone boulders.

After 20mins or so reach a junction where a rough broad stony track heads up to the right and a waymarked tree can be seen about 30m away. Although direction arrows indicate a track that continues straight on, turn right here and then left onto a narrower marked path just beyond the waymarked tree. Within another 10mins arrive at a broader track where Krasji vrh is signed left along it and Planina Zaprikraj is signed straight ahead.

*Looking towards Krn from the summit of Krasji vrh*

For a pleasant detour of about 30mins to **Planina Zaprikraj**, follow the narrow path up through the wood for about 5mins and cross a fence by a stile. Head across a somewhat more open area on an indistinct narrow path with occasional waymarks. Soon the trail drops down a little to reach the working planina with its numerous buildings, some quite run down but others still used for cattle. It is set in a pretty valley below the Krnica ridge, with many paths leading off onto the surrounding hills. Retrace your steps to the stile and now follow the path that heads right along the fence line. The path passes close to a *lovška koča* (hunting lodge) before bearing left to reach the signed junction in the description below.

Turn left along the broad track and in another 7 or 8mins arrive at a junction where a sign for Krasji vrh points left on a good broad track, with Planina Zaprikraj signed to the right. Continue on for Krasji vrh, where after 10mins the path forks; an older track goes off left, but continue following the waymarked route that climbs up to the right. In just over another 5mins the track narrows briefly as it crosses a small grassy glade, then re-enters the woods by a waymark on a tree, immediately becoming broader again.

Soon the path begins to zigzag steeply up through the woods to arrive at a T-junction at 1450m. Krasji vrh is signed both left and right – the path to the right is also signed Snežna jama (snow cave), and this will be the descent route. Turn left and begin to traverse the wooded hillside where in another 10mins the trees abruptly cease and wonderful views open to the south. The Soča winds along the floor of the valley as it passes Kobarid, while in the distance is the Adriatic Sea.

The path curves round onto the open hillside, becoming narrow and grassy. Continue, rising gently on the left-hand side of the hill, with the grassy summit visible up to the right – it looks deceptively close but is still over 30mins away. Soon the path turns sharply right and in another 10mins you arrive at a junction. Straight ahead is signed to a viewpoint called Koluji, but turn right, signed Krasji vrh. The way continues up the hillside in a series of zigzags over the tussocky grass to the crest of the summit ridge. Turn left to reach the summit of **Krasji vrh** (1768m) in about 100m (2–2hrs 30mins from the start point).

On the grassy top there is a visitors' book, and you can take a moment to linger over the **wonderful view**. Clockwise from Krn, you can see the villages of Drežniški kot below, then Kobarid with Matajur behind and beyond that the sea. Further round is the long ridge of Stol leading into Italy with the Dolomites sometimes visible in the distance. Next is the Kanin ridge, and the view continues uninterrupted taking in all the giants of the Julian Alps including Triglav.

Either retrace your steps for the descent or continue; from the summit cairn take the waymarked path on the north side that almost immediately bears right and drops down steeply over fissured limestone rocks to reach the dwarf pine. As height is lost the path levels and becomes more distinct as you pass the entrance to a WW1 bunker built into the rock. Large sinkholes and other karst rock formations make up the wild terrain and soon more ruined buildings are passed – one with an ornate stone pillar. ◂

These were Italian defences used as anti-aircraft gun emplacements to deter Austrian surveillance missions during the battles on the Izonso front.

About 25mins after leaving the summit of Krasji vrh, reach a junction where a narrow path heads right signed **Snežna jama**.

The **snow cave** is an interesting geological feature. To visit it, follow the vague path, which within a short distance descends past a sinkhole and then rises a few metres to a small level area. The snow-filled shaft of the cave can be seen below and the path drops down closer to it – but the last few metres of path leading to it are extremely steep and slippery, and it is not really recommended to go too close.

From the junction follow the path through dwarf pine and conifers and soon notice a WW1 mule track over to the left. Continue straight on down the path which soon broadens as it reaches beech woods once again. In a few more minutes arrive back at the T-junction passed on the ascent and retrace your steps to the start of the route.

## WALK 57

*Stol*

| | |
|---|---|
| **Start/finish** | Square in Kobarid |
| **Distance** | 22.5km |
| **Total ascent/descent** | 1450m |
| **Grade** | 3 |
| **Time** | 7–8hrs |
| **Maps** | 1:50,000 Julijske Alpe |
| **Refreshments** | Take refreshments with you as there is no mountain hut on this walk. |

This long, long whaleback is only part of an even longer ridge which continues into Italy, and Stol (the chair) (1673m) is its highest point within Slovenia. The ridge can be seen to the south of Bovec as a high wall marking the southern extent of the Julian Alps. Its sub-alpine feel gives an excellent day out, with the initial steep ascent through the forest giving way to a gently rising ridge. The views to both sides are superb, and the vista of the Kanin range above Bovec is particularly spectacular.

A sign in the northern corner of the square in Kobarid, opposite the church, says Stol 4hrs, pointing up a narrow road. Fork right within a few paces and follow the pretty cobbled street, lined with flowers, up the hill. Once you pass the last house the route enters trees and becomes a

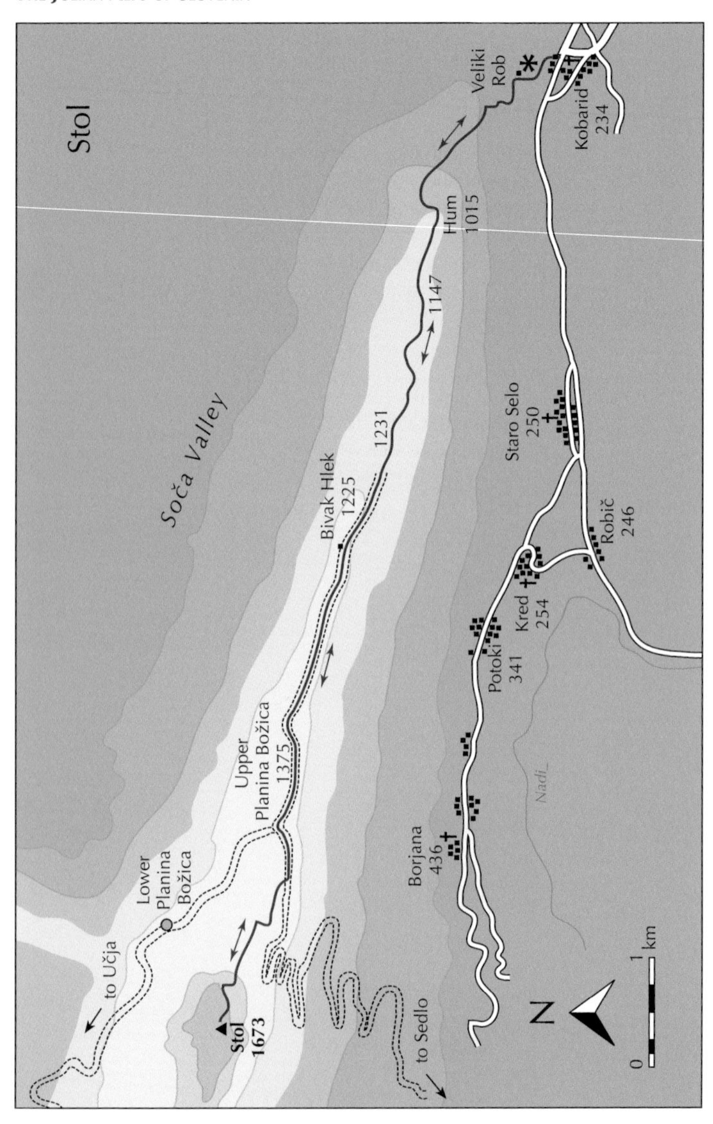
Stol
Soča Valley
Veliki Rob
Kobarid 234
Hum 1015
1147
Staro Selo 250
1231
Bivak Hlek 1225
Robič 246
Kred 254
Potoki 341
Upper Planina Božica 1375
Nadi_
Borjana 436
Lower Planina Božica
to Učja
Stol 1673
to Sedlo
N
0
1 km

broad stony track up through the forest, well waymarked and signed. After 10–15mins there is a path signed right to Veliki rob.

It is worth making the 15min detour to **Veliki rob** for a good aerial view of Kobarid. Follow the sign off the main route and in less than 100m another one directs you right ('Veliki rob 5mins'). Waymarks lead you to a little glade in the woods before you drop down 20m or so in height to the viewpoint, atop a rocky outcrop. Retrace your steps back to the main path.

The excellent mule track continues winding up through the trees for about 40mins and then traverses the hillside on the left of the ridge. After another 10mins come to a small clearing, with views to the left of Matajur, where the track narrows a little and becomes

*The long ridge of Stol (centre) seen from Matajur*

grassy. In about 50m reach another sign – Stol, 3hrs. Pass a weekend cottage on your left and then continue up through the woods, now on the right-hand side of the hill. Join a broad track at a bend and continue, passing another sign for Stol. The going is easy, although in parts the trees encroach a little on the track.

About 20mins from the weekend cottage, waymarks direct you onto a path heading left, leaving the broader track. This narrower path ascends a little more steeply and soon bears more to the left. In another 100m skirt a small clearing in the trees, bearing right. Re-enter the wood and continue ascending steadily, quickly joining the crest of the ridge, which is still forested, although with smaller trees. This section is surprisingly narrow, with steep wooded slopes on both sides, although the path is easy. In another 20mins the path levels out at an open grassy area, with the first good views to the right. ◂

The TV mast on top of Stol can be seen ahead, still looking a long way away!

The path continues along the broad grassy ridge, and then begins to descend slightly. The walking now is really pleasant among beautiful flowers. Reach a junction of paths at a saddle, where a broad track comes up from the left. A sign says Stol 2hrs straight on, to the left Staro Selo 6km, and to the right Trnovo 10km. Go straight ahead on the now broad track and up some zigzags before continuing on the left of the ridge. The track now continues on a fairly level route, passing through several cattle gates.

There are good views down to the valley on the left, with the curve of the **river Nadiža** clearly visible at the foot of Matajur; it rises in Italy and enters Slovenia for only about 11km before crossing the border again. Out in the distance you can see the Adriatic Sea.

Pass a lovška koča (hunting lodge) and further on reach **Bivak Hlek** (1225m), an unmanned hut with tables outside and running water for picnics. The broad track continues almost level for about 3km past the *bivak*, until it meets the driveable track which comes up from Sedlo to the south and Učja from the north just above **Planina Božica**. Again there is a picnic table with views south. From here it is about 1hr to the top.

The track divides 200m further on; take the right-hand fork and continue up for about 500m before following waymarks through a gap in the fence to the right and crossing the hillside for about 150m to a small marker post. The path now heads quite steeply to the left up the ridge, following waymarks, then levels out and continues for about 20mins more to the summit of **Stol**.

From Stol there are excellent views north and back along the broad crest, but it is to the right, and the **Julian Alps**, that the eye is constantly drawn. At the summit you can see the continuation of the ridge, with its steep bare slopes to the south and the trees reaching to the crest on the north side.

Return the same way.

## WALK 58

*Matajur*

| | |
|---|---|
| **Start/finish** | Avsa village, above Livek, south of Kobarid |
| **Distance** | 14km |
| **Total ascent/descent** | 750m |
| **Grade** | 3 |
| **Time** | 5hrs |
| **Maps** | 1:50,000 Julijske Alpe |
| **Access** | By car: leave Kobarid on the Tolmin road, and turn right in the village of Idrsko, following a sign to Livek. From Livek, again turn right and follow the steep twisting minor road for another 2km to reach the little hamlet of Avsa. As you approach the houses the road forks – take the right fork signed Matajur and parking 300m. |

Matajur (1642m) is the forested mountain to the south of Kobarid, and its bare summit, right on the Italian border, gives particularly extensive views, from Austria down to Venice and the Adriatic Sea. The mountain can be climbed from Kobarid, but the route can be overgrown in places and difficult to follow. The walk described here starts from the village of Avsa at 860m and mostly follows the 'stara pot' (old way) then ascends the broad eastern ridge of Matajur for the final section.

At the small parking area there is a large panoramic picture sign of Matajur and the waymarked path heads into the woods to the right of the road. The path bears right and within 50m joins a broad stony track. Turn left onto it; the track soon forks, but keep left and in just 40m leave the track for a narrower path on the right following liberally painted waymarks on the trees.

The path continues up through the wood, soon passing a small grassy planina on its right side. At the top of the planina a good view opens out to the right, of Krn across the valley. Carry on straight ahead, going steeply up with tangled knots of exposed tree roots covering the path. The path enters a section of beautiful mature beech wood and passes directly between the moss-covered walls of two small ruined crofts that are being reclaimed by nature. ◄

The woodland scene is enchanting; boulders and small outcrops lie draped in lush green moss while an almost mystical silence pervades the air.

After walking through this enchanted wood, go through a gate and turn right up a broad rough track. In another 100m, as the track levels, follow waymarks to the left through the edge of the wood to emerge onto open pasture where cattle graze. Continue up the meadow and bear left at the top between stands of trees, where straight ahead the summit of Matajur can be seen on the skyline, marked by a small chapel.

Continue straight ahead across the open grassy hillside, noting a forest road close by, below and to your left. In another 100m the path merges with the road opposite a small cottage, where a sign outside reads Matajur 1hr 30mins. Walk up this gravel road, soon rounding a hairpin bend. Beyond the bend, the road reaches a rise

*Mountain bikers on the descent*

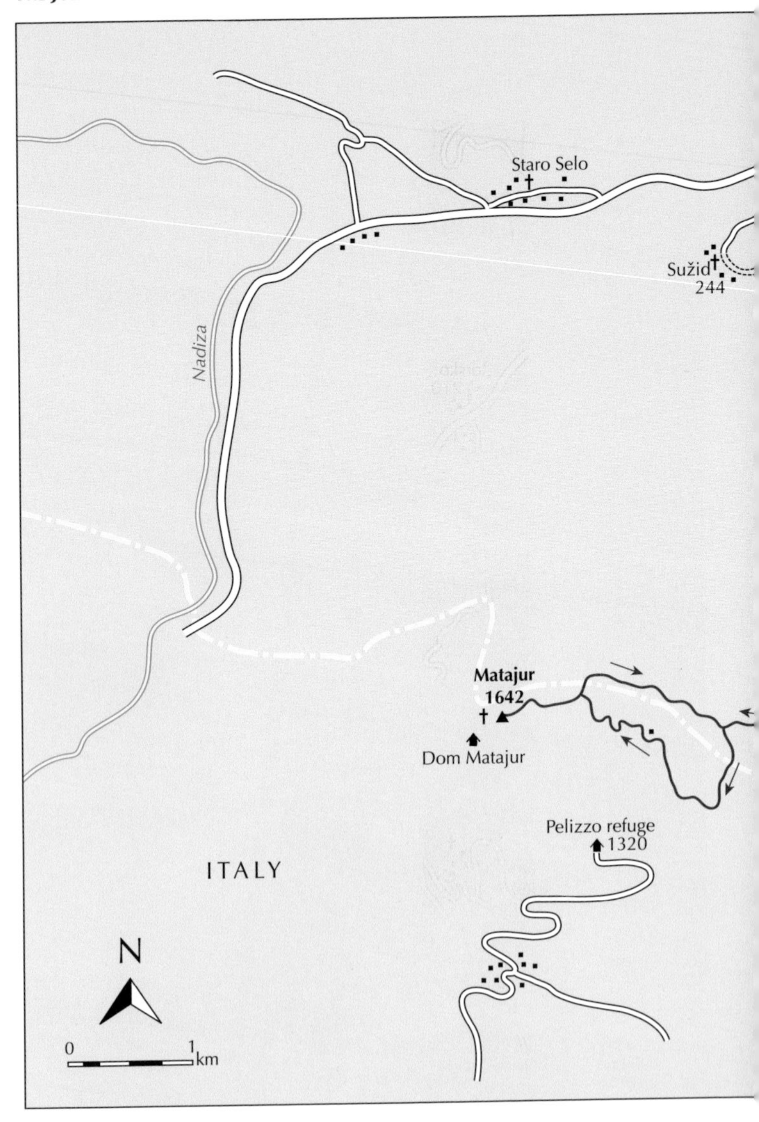
Staro Selo
Sužid
244
Nadiza
Matajur
1642
Dom Matajur
Pelizzo refuge
1320
ITALY
N
0
1
km

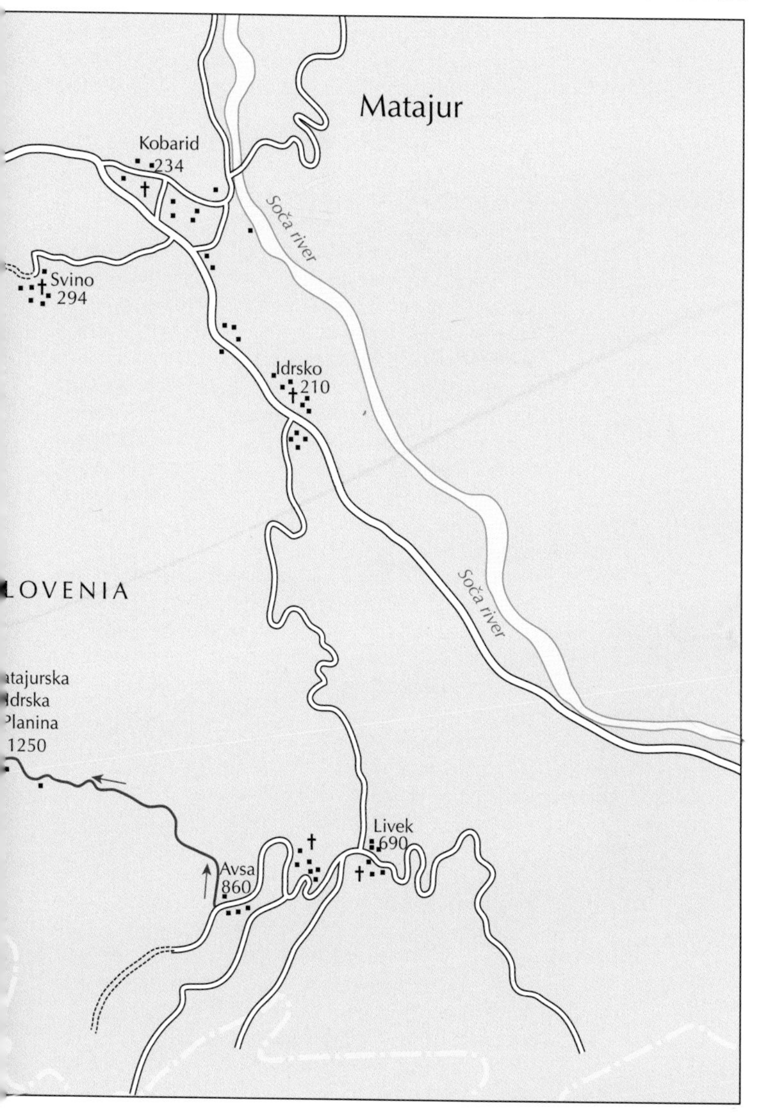
Matajur
Kobarid
234
Soča river
Svino
294
Idrsko
210
LOVENIA
atajurska
Idrska
Planina
1250
Soča river
Livek
690
Avsa
860

then begins a gentle descent to reach a fork. The right fork leads a short distance to the open ground of the Matajur planina with its farm buildings (marked as **Idrska planina** on the map).

This path stays inside Slovene territory until the final summit section and is slightly more direct. It will be used for the descent.

Take the left fork and continue down the road, passing through a gate after a further 100m. In another 250m or so reach a junction where a narrower path leads off the main track to the right, signed Matajur. ◂ Stay on the broad track, bearing left and signed for Dom na Matajure.

The track gently ascends and a wonderful view, of Krn and some of the Lower Bohinj mountains further to the right, opens out briefly to the north-west. Arrive at another junction at a gate where the main track appears to fork right, but go through the gate, still following signs for Matajur. This track is more grassy and seemingly less frequented than the track you have just left as it begins to traverse the hillside, now on the Italian side of the mountain. Pass a path heading down to the left to Bivio Maseri – notice the Italian signs and waymarks. Matajur 50mins is signed straight ahead.

As you continue the trees begin to recede opening out more views. Tall purple willow-leaved gentians line the path in early autumn and the open south side of Matajur has quite a Mediterranean feeling.

In another 100m a view opens out to the left and the large Refugio Pelizzo (1320m) can be seen on the southern flank of Matajur, with the flat plains beyond the Friuli hills stretching all the way to the sea. Dom na Matajure (1545m) is located higher up the hillside slightly to the west. ◂

The broad grassy track is now fairly level; pass the door of a neatly-maintained cottage and make a sharp left-hand bend past its open well. In another 5mins or so reach a sign that points left along a narrow path for the Pelizzo refuge, but continue straight ahead for Matajur.

In about 100m the track swings left past rocks painted with both Italian and Slovene waymarks. Leave the track at this bend and follow the narrower path straight ahead, which soon leads to a junction of paths on the skyline ridge (150m). Here the view opens out to the north and the long mountain – Stol – lies below to the left in the mid-ground while Krn, with the Julian Alps in the background, is to the right. Note the path that leads right at this junction for Livek and the Kobarid Svino path, which will be used for the descent. Turn left along the ridge. White border stones can occasionally be seen a few metres to the right that mark the Slovene northern side of Matajur. Continue up the final section of the ridge, following waymarks, to reach the little chapel and brass orientation plate on the summit of **Matajur**. ▶

The extent of the view will depend on how hazy it is – an early morning ascent in the clear air following a previous night's storm and rain can reveal views as far afield as Austria, Venice and the Adriatic Sea.

Retrace your steps back to the junction where you joined the ridge and follow the path for Livek and Kobarid Svino. The path turns left and drops down on the northern side to reach another junction in about 100m. The path bears right here, signed Avsa and Livek, and soon crosses shale-covered slabs of rock that lie in an area of clay-like soil. Just beyond, the Kobarid Svino path descends to the left, but don't take it; instead continue straight ahead quite level, then make a short descent and cross another slab of rock before arriving at a gravel track.

Looking ahead below to your left, you may see Matajurska planina and its buildings. Continue straight ahead on the narrow path that descends over grass and yet more slabby rock lying exposed and barely covered by the thin topsoil. Ten minutes of descent brings you back to the junction on the broad track and the stara pot. Turn left and retrace your steps back to the car park at Avsa.

# APPENDIX A

*Route summary table*

| No | Name | Distance | Grade | Time | Total ascent | Total decent | Page |
|---|---|---|---|---|---|---|---|
| **1 KRANJSKA GORA** | | | | | | | |
| **1** | Zelenci | 14km | 1 | 3–3½hrs | 100m | 100m | 50 |
| **2** | Peč (Tromeja) | 7km | 2 | 3½–4hrs | 640m | 640m | 56 |
| **3** | Srednji vrh | 11km | 2 | 3½–4hrs | 300m | 300m | 59 |
| **4** | Slap Martuljek | 8km | 2 | 2½–3hrs | 400m | 400m | 63 |
| **5** | Vršič pass | 19km | 2 | 5½–6hrs | 800m | 800m | 68 |
| **6** | Visoki Mavrinc | 3km | 2 | 2hrs | 360m | 360m | 76 |
| **7** | Vitranc/Ciprnik | 15km | 2/3 | 4½–5hrs | 640m (from top of 1st chairlift) | 930m | 79 |
| **8** | Sleme | 5.5km; 13km via Slatnica saddle; 11.5km via Grlo | 2; 3 via Slatnica saddle and Grlo | 2½–3hrs; 4½–5hrs via Slatnica saddle or Grlo | 300m | 300m | 82 |
| **9** | Tamar and Planica | 20km | 1 | 4–5hrs | 300m | 300m | 86 |
| **10** | Mala and Velika Mojstrovka | 5km | 3 | 3½–4hrs | 720m | 720m | 89 |

| No | Name | Distance | Grade | Time | Total ascent | Total decent | Page |
|---|---|---|---|---|---|---|---|
| **11** | Mala Mojstrovka via Hanzova pot | 4.5km | 4 | 4–5hrs | 720m | 720m | 92 |
| **12** | The Vrata valley | 20km | 2 | 6hrs | 350m | 350m | 94 |
| **13** | Jerebikovec | 9.5km | 2/3 | 4–5hrs | 890m | 890m | 100 |
| **14** | Prisank | 9km | 4 | 5½–6hrs | 940m | 940m | 103 |
| **15** | Jalovec | 12km | 4 | 9–10hrs | 1540m | 1540m | 107 |
| **16** | Špik | 17km | 4 | 10–11hrs | 1700m | 1700m | 115 |
| **17** | Škrlatica | 15km | 4 | 10–11hrs | 1700m | negligible | 121 |
| **18** | Triglav by the Tominškova pot/ Prag Route | 15km | 4 | 2 days | 1700m | 1700m | 127 |
| **19** | Triglav by Plemenice (Bamberg) Route | 22.5km | 4 | 2 days | 2160m | 2160m | 134 |
| **20** | Kanjavec | 4km | 4 | 3–3½hrs | 420m | 420m | 139 |
| **2 BOHINJ** | | | | | | | |
| **21** | The Tour of Lake Bohinj | 11.5km | 1 | 3½–4hrs | 160m | 160m | 144 |
| **22** | Slap Savica | 7km | 1/2 | 2–2½hrs | 240m | 240m | 149 |

| No | Name | Distance | Grade | Time | Total ascent | Total decent | Page |
|---|---|---|---|---|---|---|---|
| **23** | Rudnica | 10km | 2 | 3hrs; 3½–4hrs by alternative route | 410m | 410m | 153 |
| **24** | Korita Mostnice | 11km | 2 | 3½–4hrs | 300m | 300m | 158 |
| **25** | Pršivec | 17km | 3 | 7–8hrs | 1260m | 1260m | 162 |
| **26** | Vogel | 10.5km | 3 | 4–5hrs | 600m | 600m | 168 |
| **27** | Črna prst | 12km | 3 | 6hrs | 1400m | 1400m | 173 |
| **28** | Spodnje Bohinjske Gore | 17km | 3 | 9hrs | 600m | 1300m | 179 |
| **29** | Bogatin and Mahavšček | 21km | 3 | 8½–9½hrs | 1400m | 1400m | 185 |
| **30** | The Triglav Lakes valley | 23km | 4 | 2 days | 1750m | 1750m | 189 |
| **31** | Triglav – the southern approach | 34km | 4 | 2 days | 2500m | 2500m | 196 |
| **3 BOVEC** | | | | | | | |
| **32** | The Bovec Basin | 9km | 1 | 2½–3hrs | 160m | 160m | 208 |
| **33** | Kluže | 13km | 2 | 3–4hrs | 440m | 440m | 212 |
| **34** | Svinjak | 8km | 3 | 5hrs | 1200m | 1200m | 216 |
| **35** | Čelo | 2km | 2 | 1½hrs | 190m | 190m | 220 |

| No | Name | Distance | Grade | Time | Total ascent | Total decent | Page |
|---|---|---|---|---|---|---|---|
| **36** | Izvir Glijuna and Slap Virje | 6.5km | 1 | 2–2½hrs | 190m | 190m | 223 |
| **37** | Visoki Kanin and Prestreljenik | 7km to Visoki Kanin; 2.5km to Prestreljenik | 4 | 3½–4hrs to Visoki Kanin; 1½hrs to Prestreljenik | 385m (Visoki Kanin); 300m (Prestreljenik) | 385m (Visoki Kanin); 300m (Prestreljenik) | 227 |
| **38** | Rombon | 15.5km | 3/4 | 8–9hrs | c400m | 1750m | 232 |
| **39** | The Soča Trail | 11km | 2 | 3½–4hrs | negligible | 1000m | 237 |
| **40** | Pogačnikov dom and Kriški podi | 16km | 3 | 7½–8hrs | 1450m | 1450m | 243 |
| **41** | Planja and Razor | 5.5km | 4 | 4–4½hrs | 550m | 550m | 247 |
| **42** | Križ, Stenar and Bovški Gamsovec | 7.5km | 4 | 5½–6hrs | 450m | 450m | 250 |
| **43** | Krn | 18km | 3 | 9–10hrs | 1550m | 1550m | 254 |
| **44** | Mangart | 4km | 4 | 3½–4hrs | 620m | 620m | 260 |
| **4 BLED** | | | | | | | |
| **45** | The Tour of Lake Bled | 6km | 1 | 1½–2hrs | negligible | negligible | 270 |
| **46** | Osojnica | 3km | 2 | 2hrs | 280m | 280m | 272 |

| No | Name | Distance | Grade | Time | Total ascent | Total decent | Page |
|---|---|---|---|---|---|---|---|
| **47** | Bohinjska Bela and Kupljenik | 11.5km | 1/2 | 3½–4hrs | 175m | 175m | 274 |
| **48** | Ribenska Gora | 9km | 2 | 3½–4hrs | 110m | 110m | 277 |
| **49** | Talež | 14.5km | 2 | 4½–5hrs | 275m | 275m | 280 |
| **50** | Vintgar gorge | 12.5km | 1/2 | 3–4hrs | 160m | 160m | 284 |
| **51** | Galetovec | 14.5km | 3 | 5–6hrs | 800m | 800m | 289 |
| **52** | Debela peč, Brda and Lipanski vrh | 18.5km | 3 | 6hrs | 750m | 750m | 295 |
| **53** | Viševnik | 6.5km | 3 | 4hrs | 630m | 630m | 302 |
| **5 KOBARID** | | | | | | | |
| **54** | The Historical Walk | 5km | 1/2 | 3hrs | 200m | 200m | 308 |
| **55** | Drežniški kot | 13km | 2 | 3½–4hrs | 320m | 320m | 313 |
| **56** | Krasji vrh | 9km | 3 | 4–5hrs | 950m | 950m | 317 |
| **57** | Stol | 22.5km | 3 | 7–8hrs | 1450m | 1450m | 321 |
| **58** | Matajur | 14km | 3 | 5hrs | 750m | 750m | 325 |

# APPENDIX B

*Useful contacts*

If ringing from overseas to Slovenia, use the dialling code +386, then dial the Slovene number as listed here omitting the initial 0.

**Tourist Information Offices**
For in-depth information about Slovenia:
www.slovenia-tourism.si

Kranjska Gora
Tičarjeva 2
SI-4280 Kranjska Gora
Tel 04 588 17 68
www.kranjska-gora.si

Bohinj
Ribčev Laz 48
SI-4265 Bohinjsko jezero
Tel 04 574 60 10
www.bohinj.si

Bovec
Trg golobarskih žrtev 8
SI-5230 Bovec
Tel 05 384 19 19
www.bovec.si

Bled
Cesta svobode 10
SI-4260 Bled
Tel 04 574 11 22
www.bled.si

Kobarid
LTO Sotočje
Gregorčičeva 8
SI-5222 Kobarid
Tel 05 380 04 90
www.dolina-soce.com

**Mountain huts**
Dom v Tamarju (Tamar dom)
Tel 04 587 6055
(Walks 9 and 15)

Erjačeva koča
Tel 050 610 031
(Walk 5)

Poštarski dom
Tel 041 610 029
(Walks 5, 14)

Tičarjev domTel 050 634 571
(Walks 5, 14, 39)

Koča v Krnici
Tel 041654339
(Walks 16 and 17)

Aljažev dom
Tel 04 589 1030
(Walks 12, and 17–19)

Triglavski dom na Kredarici
Tel 04 202 3181
(Walk 18)

Tržaška koča na Doliču (Dolič hut)
Tel 050 614 780
(Walk 19 and 20)

Koča na Vojah
Tel 051 308 959
(Walks 24 and 31)

Dom Zorka Jelinčiča na Črni prsti
Tel 050 332 071
(Walk 27)

Kosijev Dom na Vogarju (Vogar dom)
Tel 050 613 367
(Walk 25)

Koča na Planini pri Jezeru
Tel 050 632 738
(Walk 25)

Dom na Komni
Tel 04 572 1475
(Walk 29)

Koča pod Bogatinom
Tel 050 621 943
(Walk 29)

Koča pri Savici
Tel 050 622 695
(Walks 29 and 30)

Koča pri Triglavskih jezerih
Tel 050 656 571
(Walk 30)

Zasavska koča na Prehodavcih
Tel 050 614 781
(Walk 30)

Vodnikov dom
Tel 050 615 621
(Walk 31)

Planika dom
Tel 050 614 773
(Walk 31)

Koča pri izviru Soče
Tel 041 603 190
(Walk 39)

Pogačnikov dom
Tel 051 221 319
(Walks 40–42)

Dom dr. Klementa Juga
Tel 050 622 719
(Walk 43)

Dom pri Krnskih jezerih
Tel 05 302 3030
(Walk 43)

Gomiščkovo zavetišče na Krnu
Tel 050 611 363
(Walk 43)

Koča na Mangrtskem sedlu
Tel 050 630 86
(Walk 44)

Blejska koča na Lipanci
Tel 050 633 769
(Walk 52)

**The Slovene Alpine Club**
Planinska zveza Slovenije (PZS)
Dvoržakova 9, 1000 Ljubljana
Tel 01 434 5680

Contact information for Slovene mountain guides can be obtained from Tourist Information Offices

**Transport**
Adrija Airways
www.adria-airways.com

Easyjet
www.easyjet.com

Wizzair
wizzair.com

Ryanair
www.ryanair.com

For bus timetables
www.ap-ljubljana.si

For train timetables
www.slo-zeleznice.si

**Embassies and consulates**
Consulate of Canada
Linhartova cesta 49a
1000 Ljubljana
Slovenia
Tel 01 252 44 44

Embassy of Ireland
Palača Kapitelj
Poljanski nasip 6
1000 Ljubljana
Tel 01 300 89 70
irish.embassy@siol.net

Embassy of the United Kingdom of Great Britain and Northern Ireland
Trg Republike 3
1000 Ljubljana
Tel 01 200 39 10
info@british-embassy.si
www.gov.uk/government/world/organisations/british-embassy-ljubljana

Embassy of the United States of America
Prešernova cesta 31
Ljubljana
Tel 01 200 55 00
email@usembassy.si
www.usembassy.si

**Map suppliers in the UK**

Edward Stanford Ltd
7 Mercer Walk
London WC2H 9FA
Tel 020 7836 1321
www.stanfords.co.uk

The Map Shop
15 High Street
Upton on Severn
Worcs WR8 0HJ
Tel 0800 40 80 (freephone) or 01684 593 146
www.themapshop.co.uk

Cordee
Tel: 0116 254 3579
www.cordee.co.uk

# APPENDIX C

*Language notes*

There is no doubt that Slovene is one of the harder European languages for English speakers to learn. The six cases, three genders and extra 'dual' form, used whenever there are two of something (and unique now in European languages), give a dizzying array of 54 possible word endings, and that's just the nouns! These different case endings can make references to place names confusing, as their endings depend on their relationship to other words; for example, the Slovene for 'castle' is 'grad', but 'Castle Road' becomes Grajska cesta. However, it is always pleasant to be able to manage some words and phrases in a foreign country, and while you will find that the majority of Slovenes speak English, they will be delighted if you attempt to say something in their language.

**Pronunciation**

The pronunciation of sounds does not present a big problem in Slovene; more difficult are the varied stress patterns which can completely change the sound of a word. Listed below are the sounds in Slovene – once you have mastered them, the sound always correlates to the written spelling (unlike in English).

c – always pronounced ts like zz in pizza, even at the beginning of words

č – as ch in church

j – as y in yacht

h – as ch in loch

r – always rolled as in Scottish English

š – sh as in ship

v – this sound is not pronounced at the end of words; this means for example that the final three letters in Triglav rhyme with cow

ž – the sound in the middle of the English leisure, or at the beginning of French gîte

**Glossary of useful words and phrases**

| | |
|---|---|
| goodbye | *nasvidenje* |
| goodnight | *lahko noč* |
| no | *ne* |
| yes | *ja* |

| English | Slovenian |
|---|---|
| please | *prosim* |
| thank you | *hvala* |
| I don't speak Slovene | *ne govorim slovensko* |
| tea | *čaj* |
| coffee | *kava* |
| water | *voda* |
| milk | *mleko* |
| beer | *pivo* |
| wine | *vino* |
| cheese | *sir* |
| meat | *meso* |
| sausage | *klobasa* |
| potato | *krompir* |
| soup | *juha* |
| salad | *solata* |
| ice cream | *sladoled* |
| enjoy your meal! | *dober tek!* |
| **Accommodation** | |
| mountain hut | *dom, koča* |
| log cabin | *brunarica* |
| room | *soba* |
| apartment | *apartma* |
| eating house | *gostilna, gostišče* |
| **Weather** | |
| forecast | *napoved* |
| sun | *sonce* |
| wind | *veter* |
| rain | *dež* |

| English | Slovenian |
| --- | --- |
| snow | *sneg* |
| cloudy | *oblačno* |
| thunderstorm | *nevihta* |
| hot | *vroče* |
| cold | *mrzlo* |
| good/bad weather | *lepo/slabo vreme* |
| **Landscape** | |
| mountain | *gora* |
| summit | *vrh* |
| face, wall | *stena* |
| ridge | *greben* |
| edge | *rob* |
| hill | *hrib* |
| river | *reka* |
| mountain stream | *potok* |
| source, spring | *izvir* |
| lake | *jezero* |
| forest | *gozd* |
| waterfall | *slap* |
| open pasture, alp | *planina* |
| path | *pot* |
| col, saddle | *sedlo* |
| valley | *dolina* |
| bridge | *most* |
| church | *cerkev* |
| limestone formation | *skarst* |
| double hayrack | *toplar* |

| English | Slovenian |
|---|---|
| **Miscellaneous** | |
| Help! | *na pomoč!* |
| day, today | *dan, danes* |
| night | *noč* |
| evening | *večer* |
| tomorrow | *jutri* |
| yesterday | *včeraj* |
| week | *teden* |
| month | *mesec* |
| year | *leto* |
| one hour | *ena ura* |
| Monday | *ponedeljek* |
| Tuesday | *torek* |
| Wednesday | *sreda* |
| Thursday | *četrtek* |
| Friday | *petek* |
| Saturday | *sobota* |
| Sunday | *nedelja* |
| man | *moški** |
| woman | *ženska** |
| child | *otrok* |
| *Useful in toilets, which are often labelled 'M' and 'Z' | |

# APPENDIX D

*Bibliography*

While there are many books dealing with the Alps in general, this section includes only books specifically about the Julian Alps and Slovenia. Several books on mountaineering techniques, navigation, etc, have also been included. There is little written in English about the Julian Alps; most of the books given here are translated from Slovene. This does not, of course, detract from their usefulness, but they may assume a certain cultural knowledge on the part of the reader.

*Mountaineering in Slovenia* by Tine Mihelič (Sidarta, Ljubljana 2003) – A definitive guide, not just to the Julian Alps but to the other Slovene mountain ranges as well. Useful for orientation and history, but the route descriptions are rather brief and sometimes assume you have a car.

*How to Climb Triglav* by Stanko Klinar (Planinska založba, Ljubljana 1991) – A very useful pocket guide to all the routes on Triglav, available from the Slovene Alpine Club (see Appendix B for address).

*A Guide to Walks and Scrambles in the Julian Alps* by Mike Newbury (Zlatorog Publications, Perth, Scotland 2003) – Scrambles and mountain walks in the Kranjska Gora area, often describing several different routes on a mountain.

*Triglav National Park* by Peter Skoberne (Walks in Nature Series, Cankarjeva založba, Ljubljana 1991) – Translated from Slovene, a useful pocket book briefly describing 74 interesting natural features in the National Park, many of which are visited on routes in this book.

*The Triglav National Park* edited by Ivan Fabjan (ČGP Delo, Bled 1987) – Guide to all aspects of the park, its history, biology and geology, with some suggested (brief) route descriptions to places of interest.

*Nature of Slovenia: The Alps* edited by Tomi Trilar, Andrej Gogala and Miha Jeršek (Slovenian Museum of Natural History, Ljubljana 2004) – A beautifully produced book of essays on different aspects of the natural world in the Julian Alps – geology, plants and wildlife, the mountain landscape.

*The Hillwalker's Guide to Mountaineering* by Terry Adby and Stuart Johnston (Cicerone Press, Milnthorpe 2004) – A guide to mountaineering skills for the hillwalker. Includes advanced navigation, survival, scrambling and first-aid techniques.

*Map and Compass* by Pete Hawkins (Cicerone Press, 2013) – A guide to navigation for walkers, useful for everyone from the novice to the experienced hillwalker.

*Lonely Planet Slovenia* by Mark Baker, Paul Clammer and Steve Fallon (Lonely Planet, 2013) – Full of useful information about the whole country, with details of accommodation, eating houses, places of interest and so on.

*The Rough Guide to Slovenia* by Norm Longley (Rough Guides, 2007, 2nd edition) – Similar to the Lonely Planet Guide – in-depth and well-documented.

*Questions about Slovenia* by Matjaž Chvatal (Turistika Publishing House, Kranj 2003) – Interesting guide to different aspects of Slovene history, culture and geography.

*Slovene Phrase Book* by Nika Fon Leben and Charles I Abramson (CIP, Ljubljana 2002).

# NOTES

# NOTES

# NOTES

# LISTING OF CICERONE GUIDES

**BRITISH ISLES CHALLENGES, COLLECTIONS AND ACTIVITIES**

Cycling Land's End to John o' Groats
Great Walks on the England Coast Path
The Big Rounds
The Book of the Bivvy
The Book of the Bothy
The Mountains of England and Wales: Vol 1 Wales
The Mountains of England and Wales: Vol 2 England
The National Trails
Walking the End to End Trail

**SHORT WALKS SERIES**

Short Walks Hadrian's Wall
Short Walks in Arnside and Silverdale
Short Walks in Cornwall: Falmouth and the Lizard
Short Walks in Dumfries and Galloway
Short Walks in Nidderdale
Short Walks in Pembrokeshire: Tenby and the south
Short Walks in the South Downs: Brighton, Eastbourne and Arundel
Short Walks in the Surrey Hills
Short Walks Lake District – Coniston and Langdale
Short Walks Lake District: Keswick, Borrowdale and Buttermere
Short Walks Lake District: Windermere Ambleside and Grasmere
Short Walks on the Malvern Hills
Short Walks Winchester

**SCOTLAND**

Ben Nevis and Glen Coe
Cycling in the Hebrides
Cycling the North Coast 500
Great Mountain Days in Scotland
Mountain Biking in Southern and Central Scotland
Mountain Biking in West and North West Scotland
Not the West Highland Way
Scotland
Scotland's Best Small Mountains
Scotland's Mountain Ridges
Scottish Wild Country Backpacking
Skye's Cuillin Ridge Traverse
The Borders Abbeys Way
The Great Glen Way
The Great Glen Way Map Booklet
The Hebridean Way
The Hebrides
The Isle of Mull
The Isle of Skye
The Skye Trail
The Southern Upland Way
The West Highland Way
The West Highland Way Map Booklet
Walking Ben Lawers, Rannoch and Atholl
Walking in the Cairngorms
Walking in the Pentland Hills
Walking in the Scottish Borders
Walking in the Southern Uplands
Walking in Torridon, Fisherfield, Fannichs and An Teallach
Walking Loch Lomond and the Trossachs
Walking on Arran
Walking on Harris and Lewis
Walking on Jura, Islay and Colonsay
Walking on Rum and the Small Isles
Walking on the Orkney and Shetland Isles
Walking on Uist and Barra
Walking the Cape Wrath Trail
Walking the Corbetts
Vol 1 South of the Great Glen
Vol 2 North of the Great Glen
Walking the Galloway Hills
Walking the John o' Groats Trail
Walking the Munros
Vol 1 – Southern, Central and Western Highlands
Vol 2 – Northern Highlands and the Cairngorms
Winter Climbs in the Cairngorms
Winter Climbs: Ben Nevis and Glen Coe

**NORTHERN ENGLAND ROUTES**

Cycling the Reivers Route
Cycling the Way of the Roses
Hadrian's Cycleway
Hadrian's Wall Path
Hadrian's Wall Path Map Booklet
The Coast to Coast Cycle Route
The Coast to Coast Walk
The Coast to Coast Walk Map Booklet
The Pennine Way
The Pennine Way Map Booklet
Walking the Dales Way
Walking the Dales Way Map Booklet

**NORTH-EAST ENGLAND, YORKSHIRE DALES AND PENNINES**

Cycling in the Yorkshire Dales
Great Mountain Days in the Pennines
Mountain Biking in the Yorkshire Dales
The Cleveland Way and the Yorkshire Wolds Way
The North York Moors
Trail and Fell Running in the Yorkshire Dales
Walking in County Durham
Walking in Northumberland
Walking in the North Pennines
Walking in the Yorkshire Dales:
North and East
South and West
Walking St Cuthbert's Way
Walking St Oswald's Way and Northumberland Coast Path

**NORTH-WEST ENGLAND AND THE ISLE OF MAN**

Cycling the Pennine Bridleway
Isle of Man Coastal Path
The Lancashire Cycleway
The Lune Valley and Howgills
Walking in Cumbria's Eden Valley
Walking in Lancashire
Walking in the Forest of Bowland and Pendle
Walking on the Isle of Man
Walking on the West Pennine Moors
Walking the Ribble Way
Walks in Silverdale and Arnside

**LAKE DISTRICT**

Bikepacking in the Lake District
Cycling in the Lake District
Great Mountain Days in the Lake District
Joss Naylor's Lakes, Meres and Waters of the Lake District
Lake District Winter Climbs
Lake District:
High Level and Fell Walks
Low Level and Lake Walks
Mountain Biking in the Lake District
Outdoor Adventures with Children – Lake District
Scrambles in the Lake District – North
South
Trail and Fell Running in the Lake District
Walking The Cumbria Way
Walking the Lake District Fells – Borrowdale
Buttermere
Coniston
Keswick
Langdale
Mardale and the Far East
Patterdale
Wasdale
Walking the Tour of the Lake District

**DERBYSHIRE, PEAK DISTRICT AND MIDLANDS**

Cycling in the Peak District
Dark Peak Walks
Scrambles in the Dark Peak
Walking in Derbyshire

Walking in the Peak District –
White Peak East
White Peak West

**SOUTHERN ENGLAND**

20 Classic Sportive Rides in
South East England
South West England
Cycling in the Cotswolds
Mountain Biking on the
North Downs
South Downs
Suffolk Coast and Heath Walks
The Cotswold Way
The Cotswold Way Map Booklet
The Kennet and Avon Canal
The Lea Valley Walk
The North Downs Way
The North Downs Way Map Booklet
The Peddars Way and Norfolk Coast Path
The Pilgrims' Way
The Ridgeway National Trail
The Ridgeway National Trail Map Booklet
The South Downs Way
The South Downs Way Map Booklet
The Thames Path
The Thames Path Map Booklet
The Two Moors Way
The Two Moors Way Map Booklet
Walking Hampshire's Test Way
Walking in Cornwall
Walking in Essex
Walking in Kent
Walking in London
Walking in Norfolk
Walking in the Chilterns
Walking in the Cotswolds
Walking in the Isles of Scilly
Walking in the New Forest
Walking in the North Wessex Downs
Walking on Dartmoor
Walking on Guernsey
Walking on Jersey
Walking on the Isle of Wight
Walking the Dartmoor Way
Walking the Jurassic Coast
Walking the South West Coast Path
Walking the South West Coast Path Map Booklets
– Vol 1: Minehead to St Ives
– Vol 2: St Ives to Plymouth
– Vol 3: Plymouth to Poole
Walks in the South Downs National Park

**WALES AND WELSH BORDERS**

Cycle Touring in Wales
Cycling Lon Las Cymru
Great Mountain Days in Snowdonia
Hillwalking in Shropshire
Mountain Walking in Snowdonia
Offa's Dyke Path
Offa's Dyke Path Map Booklet
Ridges of Snowdonia
Scrambles in Snowdonia
Snowdonia: 30 Low-level and Easy Walks
– North
– South
The Cambrian Way
The Pembrokeshire Coast Path
The Pembrokeshire Coast Path Map Booklet
The Snowdonia Way
Walking Glyndwr's Way
Walking in Carmarthenshire
Walking in Pembrokeshire
Walking in the Brecon Beacons
Walking in the Forest of Dean
Walking in the Wye Valley
Walking on Gower
Walking the Severn Way
Walking the Shropshire Way
Walking the Wales Coast Path

**INTERNATIONAL CHALLENGES, COLLECTIONS AND ACTIVITIES**

Europe's High Points
Walking the Via Francigena Pilgrim Route – Part 1

**AFRICA**

Kilimanjaro
Walking in the Drakensberg
Walks and Scrambles in the Moroccan Anti-Atlas

**ALPS CROSS-BORDER ROUTES**

100 Hut Walks in the Alps
Alpine Ski Mountaineering Vol 1 – Western Alps
The Karnischer Hohenweg
The Tour of the Bernina
Trail Running – Chamonix and the Mont Blanc region
Trekking Chamonix to Zermatt
Trekking in the Alps
Trekking in the Silvretta and Ratikon Alps
Trekking Munich to Venice
Trekking the Tour du Mont Blanc
Trekking the Tour du Mont Blanc Map Booklet
Walking in the Alps

**PYRENEES AND FRANCE/SPAIN CROSS-BORDER ROUTES**

Shorter Treks in the Pyrenees
The Pyrenean Haute Route
The Pyrenees
Trekking the GR11 Trail
Walks and Climbs in the Pyrenees

**AUSTRIA**

Innsbruck Mountain Adventures
Trekking Austria's Adlerweg
Trekking in Austria's Hohe Tauern
Trekking in Austria's Zillertal Alps
Trekking in the Stubai Alps
Walking in Austria
Walking in the Salzkammergut: the Austrian Lake District

**EASTERN EUROPE**

The Danube Cycleway Vol 2
The High Tatras
The Mountains of Romania
Walking in Hungary

**FRANCE, BELGIUM AND LUXEMBOURG**

Camino de Santiago – Via Podiensis
Chamonix Mountain Adventures
Cycle Touring in France
Cycling London to Paris
Cycling the Canal de la Garonne
Cycling the Canal du Midi
Cycling the Route des Grandes Alpes
Mont Blanc Walks
Mountain Adventures in the Maurienne
Short Treks on Corsica
The Elbe Cycle Route
The GR5 Trail
The GR5 Trail – Benelux and Lorraine
The GR5 Trail – Vosges and Jura
The Grand Traverse of the Massif Central
The Moselle Cycle Route
The River Loire Cycle Route
The River Rhone Cycle Route
Trekking in the Vanoise
Trekking the Cathar Way
Trekking the GR10
Trekking the GR20 Corsica
Trekking the Robert Louis Stevenson Trail
Via Ferratas of the French Alps
Walking in Provence – East
Walking in Provence – West
Walking in the Ardennes
Walking in the Auvergne
Walking in the Brianconnais
Walking in the Dordogne
Walking in the Haute Savoie: North
Walking in the Haute Savoie: South
Walking on Corsica
Walking the Brittany Coast Path

**GERMANY**

Hiking and Cycling in the Black Forest
The Danube Cycleway Vol 1
The Rhine Cycle Route
The Westweg
Walking in the Bavarian Alps

**IRELAND**

The Wild Atlantic Way and Western Ireland
Walking the Wicklow Way

**ITALY**

Alta Via – Trekking in the Dolomites – Vols 1&2
Day Walks in the Dolomites
Italy's Grande Traversata delle Alpi
Italy's Sibillini National Park
Ski Touring and Snowshoeing in the Dolomites
The Way of St Francis
Trekking in the Apennines
Trekking the Giants' Trail: Alta Via 1 through the Italian Pennine Alps
Via Ferratas of the Italian Dolomites – Vols 1&2
Walking in Abruzzo
Walking in Italy's Cinque Terre
Walking in Italy's Stelvio National Park
Walking in Sicily
Walking in the Aosta Valley
Walking in the Dolomites
Walking in Tuscany
Walking in Umbria
Walking Lake Como and Maggiore
Walking Lake Garda and Iseo
Walking on the Amalfi Coast
Walking the Via Francigena Pilgrim Route – Parts 2&3
Walks and Treks in the Maritime Alps

**MEDITERRANEAN**

The High Mountains of Crete
Trekking in Greece
Walking and Trekking in Zagori
Walking and Trekking on Corfu
Walking in Cyprus
Walking on Malta
Walking on the Greek Islands – the Cyclades

**NEW ZEALAND AND AUSTRALIA**

Hiking the Overland Track

**NORTH AMERICA**

Hiking and Cycling the California Missions Trail
The John Muir Trail
The Pacific Crest Trail

**SOUTH AMERICA**

Aconcagua and the Southern Andes
Hiking and Biking Peru's Inca Trails
Trekking in Torres del Paine

**SCANDINAVIA, ICELAND AND GREENLAND**

Hiking in Norway – South
Trekking in Greenland – The Arctic Circle Trail
Trekking the Kungsleden
Walking and Trekking in Iceland

**SLOVENIA, CROATIA, SERBIA, MONTENEGRO AND ALBANIA**

Hiking Slovenia's Juliana Trail
Mountain Biking in Slovenia
The Islands of Croatia
The Julian Alps of Slovenia
The Mountains of Montenegro
The Peaks of the Balkans Trail
The Slovene Mountain Trail
Walking in Slovenia: The Karavanke
Walks and Treks in Croatia

**SPAIN AND PORTUGAL**

Camino de Santiago: Camino Frances
Coastal Walks in Andalucia
Costa Blanca Mountain Adventures
Cycling the Camino de Santiago
Cycling the Ruta Via de la Plata
Mountain Walking in Mallorca
Mountain Walking in Southern Catalunya
Portugal's Rota Vicentina
Spain's Sendero Historico: The GR1
The Andalucian Coast to Coast Walk
The Camino del Norte and Camino Primitivo
The Camino Ingles and Ruta do Mar
The Camino Portugues
The Mountains Around Nerja
The Mountains of Ronda and Grazalema
The Sierras of Extremadura
Trekking in Mallorca
Trekking in the Canary Islands
Trekking the GR7 in Andalucia
Walking and Trekking in the Sierra Nevada
Walking in Andalucia
Walking in Catalunya – Barcelona
Walking in Catalunya – Girona Pyrenees
Walking in Portugal
Walking in the Algarve
Walking in the Picos de Europa
Walking La Via de la Plata and Camino Sanabres
Walking on Gran Canaria
Walking on La Gomera and El Hierro
Walking on La Palma
Walking on Lanzarote and Fuerteventura
Walking on Madeira
Walking on Tenerife
Walking on the Azores
Walking on the Costa Blanca
Walking the Camino dos Faros

**SWITZERLAND**

Switzerland's Jura Crest Trail
The Swiss Alps
Tour of the Jungfrau Region
Trekking the Swiss Via Alpina
Walking in the Bernese Oberland – Jungfrau region
Walking in the Engadine – Switzerland
Walking in the Valais
Walking in Ticino
Walking in Zermatt and Saas-Fee

**CHINA, JAPAN AND ASIA**

Hiking and Trekking in the Japan Alps and Mount Fuji
Hiking in Hong Kong
Japan's Kumano Kodo Pilgrimage
Trekking in Tajikistan

**HIMALAYA**

Annapurna
8000 metres
Everest: A Trekker's Guide
Trekking in Bhutan
Trekking in Ladakh
Trekking in the Himalaya
Trekking in the Karakoram

**MOUNTAIN LITERATURE**

A Walk in the Clouds
Abode of the Gods
Fifty Years of Adventure
The Pennine Way – the Path, the People, the Journey
Unjustifiable Risk?
Unjustifiable Risk?

**TECHNIQUES**

Fastpacking
Geocaching in the UK
Map and Compass
Outdoor Photography
The Mountain Hut Book

**MINI GUIDES**

Alpine Flowers
Navigation
Pocket First Aid and Wilderness Medicine
Snow